NON-TARIFF DISTORTIONS

OF AUSTRALIAN TRADE

By the same author

International Trade Problems of Small Nations (1968)
New Zealand Manufacturing Production and Trade with Australia (1971)

Non-Tariff Distortions of Australian Trade

P. J. LLOYD

AUSTRALIAN NATIONAL UNIVERSITY PRESS
CANBERRA 1973

First published in Australia 1973

Printed in Australia for the Australian National University Press, Canberra

North, South, and Central America:
International Scholarly Book Services, Inc., Portland, Oregon
Southeast Asia: Angus & Robertson (S.E. Asia) Pty Ltd, Singapore
Japan: United Publishers Services Ltd, Tokyo

© P. J. Lloyd 1973

This book is copyright. Apart from any fair dealing for the purposes of private study, research, criticism, or review, as permitted under the Copyright Act, no part may be reproduced by any process without written permission. Inquiries should be made to the publisher.

Registered in Australia for transmission by post as a book

ISBN 0 7081 0403 7
Library of Congress Catalog Card no. 73-87269

Preface

This study is one of a number of studies of non-tariff instruments affecting international trade which were done at roughly the same time in seven countries. These studies are being co-ordinated by the Trade Policy Research Centre in London. I am grateful to the Australian National University and the Trade Policy Research Centre for allowing me to travel to a conference in London of the persons engaged in these country studies and to benefit from the parallel work which is going on in other countries. This difficult area of trade policy is at last receiving more of the attention it deserves. Hitherto in Australia there have been only passing discussions of a small number of non-tariff instruments in some Tariff Board reports, in the Report of the Vernon Committee and a few other places.

This study provides a view of non-tariff instruments in Australia over a short period which has not been available before. The descriptions relate to non-tariff instruments as of mid-1972. I have tried to keep the information up to date until the time I finished the research in August 1972. Keeping up with the changes in non-tariff instruments was itself a major task. There are a few cases in which I have not attempted to keep up to date after completing the original research on these instruments. The material on quarantine describes the situation as of January 1972 and I have not looked at dumping decisions in 1972. Thus the text should be read as applying to the period before the Labor Party victory in the December 1972 elections. I have put together in the Postscript some of the initial actions and statements of the new government which concern non-tariff interventions in Australia's international trade.

The study would not have been possible without the considerable and generous assistance given to me by several Departments of the Commonwealth Government, especially the Departments of Customs and Excise and Trade and Industry. I am very grateful to the numerous officers of these departments, who tried to guide me through the intricacies of non-tariff practices. I am also very grateful to the Tariff Board and the Bureau of Agricultural Economics for providing me with the data used in Chapter 10 to make estimates of the protection implied by some non-tariff instruments restricting imports. Their help enabled me to put a little flesh on the bare bones of description. Finally I acknowledge the comments of my professional colleagues which led me to polish some of the rough edges. Richard Snape and Sir Leslie Melville read the whole manuscript. Geoff Edwards commented on Chapters 8 and 13, Bob Gregory on Chapter 13, members of the Monash University Seminar on Chapter 12 and members of the University of New England Seminar on Chapter 10.

Canberra 1973   P.J.L.

Contents

	Preface	v
	Abbreviations	ix
1	Introduction	1
2	Direct Quantitative Restrictions on Imports	10
3	Restrictions on Imports Through Customs Valuation and Assessment	28
4	Dumping and Support Value Duties	55
5	Purchasing Policies of the Commonwealth Government	68
6	Non-Tariff Barriers Through Government Regulation of Industry	79
7	Discriminatory Features of the Sales and Excise Taxes	85
8	Assistance to Producers	92
9	General Features of Non-Tariff Distortions in Australia	130
10	The Costs of Non-Tariff Distortions	135
11	Australian Participation in Multilateral Reduction in Non-Tariff Distortions	166
12	Possibilities of Unilateral Changes in Non-Tariff Distortions	178
13	The Role of Adjustment Assistance	195
14	Conclusions and Recommendations	204
	Postscript Election of a Labor Government	213
	Appendix Notes on Tables 10.2, 10.3 and 10.4	225
	References	232
	Index	237

Tables

2.1	Value of licences issued for goods subject to import licensing in 1972	15
2.2	Statistics of the developing country preference scheme	26
3.1	Landed duty-paid prices with f.o.b. and c.i.f. valuations	34
3.2	Customs clearances and duty collected, by type of duty, 1970-71	37
4.1	Dumping actions	58
5.1	Imports for Commonwealth Government, by country of origin	72
5.2	Defence procurement expenditures	73
8.1	Commonwealth Government subsidies on production, 1972	96-7
8.2	Commonwealth Government subsidies on production, 1969-72	101
8.3	Commonwealth Government subsidies based on exports	106
8.4	Devaluation compensation payments	116
8.5	Export market development rebates, 1967-70	118
10.1	Effects of by-laws on the pattern of effective protection of manufactures	147
10.2	Rates of subsidies for selected agricultural commodities, 1947-71	151
10.3	Implicit price changes to producers for selected agricultural commodities, 1947-71	153
10.4	Implicit price changes to consumers for selected agricultural commodities, 1947-71	157
11.1	Classification of non-tariff instruments in Australia	172-3
A.1	Australian imports, 1970-71	230-1

FIGURE

Figure 10.1	A non-equivalent production subsidy and tariff	162

Abbreviations

AIDA	Australian Industries Development Association
ASB	Australian Shipbuilding Board
ASP	American Selling Price
BAE	Bureau of Agricultural Economics
BTN	Brussels Tariff Nomenclature
CBCS	Commonwealth Bureau of Census and Statistics
CEDA	Committee for Economic Development of Australia
CPD	*Commonwealth Parliamentary Debates*
CPP	*Commonwealth Parliamentary Papers*
EEC	European Economic Community
EFTA	European Free Trade Association
EPIC	Export Payments Insurance Corporation
GATT	General Agreement on Tariffs and Trade
IMF	International Monetary Fund
ISIC	International Standard Industrial Classification
MFN	Most Favoured Nation
NAFTA	New Zealand-Australia Free Trade Agreement
OECD	Organisation for Economic Co-operation and Development
SAA	Special Advisory Authority
SEATO	South East Asia Treaty Organisation
UNCTAD	United Nations Conference on Trade and Development

1 Introduction

One of the principles underlying the General Agreement on Tariffs and Trade (GATT) when it was drawn up after World War War II was that countries should rely exclusively on the tariff for control of imports. Articles of the Agreement outlawed measures such as quantitative restrictions and, on the side of export trade, export subsidies, and laid down the permissible scope and operation of such measures as value for duty and the use of dumping and countervailing duties. Exceptions were made for the use of quantitative restrictions for balance of payments reasons and for trade in agricultural commodities but these were intended to be used infrequently. Unfortunately, the GATT has not prevented the rapid growth in recent years of the use of non-tariff trade-distorting measures by its signatory members. This failure has been due partly to the 'grandfather clause' (Protocol of Provisional Application) which permitted countries acceding to the Agreement to continue all pre-existing practices, partly to the absence of GATT regulation of some non-tariff measures,[1] and partly to the absence of any effective enforcement procedures in the Agreement.[2]

The growing use of non-tariff measures has led to an increasing concern that they may be used to thwart the lower level of intervention in world trade which the GATT has achieved in six post-war rounds of tariff negotiations. An increase in the use of non-tariff interventions could even reverse the strong downward trend in the levels of protection.

---

[1] Government purchasing, standards, and private restrictive practices such as territorial market sharing and price fixing are examples of non-tariff measures which are not discussed specifically in the GATT Articles.

[2] GATT's enforcement procedures are mostly limited o discussing a notification or complaint without a ruling against or in favour of it. Article XXIII of the Agreement authorises the withdrawal of concessions which were granted in return for others which have subsequently been nullified or impaired by the action of another Contracting Party. This has seldom been used.

A brief review of the GATT and non-tariff distortions is given by Gerard and Victoria Curzon, *Global Assault on Non-Tariff Trade Barriers* (Trade Policy Research Centre, London, 1972), chapter 1.

This trend has lost momentum since the conclusion of the Kennedy Round of GATT negotiations in 1967. Moreover, non-tariff interventions could become important in the increasing division of the world into trading blocs and the dangers of trade wars between blocs.[3] During 1972 there was concern in the EEC in particular with the new US tax deferments to exporting corporations and the pending regulations prepared by the US Treasury for enforcement of the 1921 Anti-Dumping Act. The US Congress has refused since 1967 to ratify the GATT Anti-Dumping Code. Moreover, the Hartke-Burke Bill threatens the use of import quotas. At the same time the Americans, Japanese and others became more concerned with the European Economic Community after the British decision to accede. On the other hand the US in February 1972 agreed with the EEC and Japan to begin the seventh round of GATT negotiations in 1973. These discussions are to include non-tariff measures (see pp. 166-9).

The GATT survey of 800 non-tariff barriers in 1968 and recent studies of the nature and the extent of non-tariff interventions have indicated that they are widespread and important.[4]

In the light of these developments a group of economists in the major industrial countries decided in 1970 to bring about separate studies of the non-tariff barriers to imports in the major trading countries of the world. These studies were begun in 1970. Australia was added to the list of countries in 1971[5] and I was asked in early 1971 by Sir John Crawford of the Australian National University if I would undertake the Australian study. Each study addressed itself only to the non-tariff measures affecting the trade of the respective country. There are different emphases in these studies but it is hoped that together they will give a more precise indication of the extent of non-tariff interventions than existed beforehand. The emphasis of this international program of studies was on the domestic constraints on governments in negotiating the elimination or reduction of non-tariff barriers to international trade. A conference of the persons preparing the national studies was held in London in January 1971 out of which will emerge an international volume containing summaries of the national studies, and discussions of the nature of constraints on the negotiations of non-tariff barriers

---

[3] See H. B. Malmgren, *Trade Wars or Trade Negotiations? Non-tariff Barriers and Economic Peacekeeping* (Atlantic Council of the United States, Washington, D.C., 1970).

[4] Two other general studies of non-tariff distortions in world trade were published in 1970; R. E. Baldwin, *Nontariff Distortions in International Trade* (The Brookings Institution, Washington, D.C., 1970) and Gerard and Victoria Curzon, *Hidden Barriers to International Trade* (Trade Policy Research Centre, London, 1970).

[5] The other countries in the program are Canada, Japan, the United States, Federal Republic of Germany, Italy, Benelux countries, the United Kingdom. There is an additional study of the EEC.

and the various options for multilateral negotiation of these trade-distorting measures.[6] For brevity, I shall refer to this program of studies as the London Program.

The Selection of Non-Tariff Distortions

The definition of non-tariff distortions is slightly troublesome. Readers will note that the term is defined in a broad and seemingly arbitrary way. The terms 'non-tariff barriers' or 'non-tariff distortions' have come to be a shorthand for all those measures or *instruments* other than tariffs imposed by governments which restrain or distort free international trade by discriminating between locally-produced and imported goods.[7] This definition calls for a little amplification. There are some measures which do not discriminate between locally-produced and imported goods but which indirectly distort trade; for example, differential consumption taxes or subsidies. These are excluded from the definition. We also follow a convention in excluding exchange rate changes and other monetary and fiscal policies which affect all export and import-competing commodities and are designed to maintain external balance. The term 'non-tariff' distortions is an omnibus term for the remaining set of instruments and practices which may be used as alternatives to tariffs to restrain particular imports or which distort export trade.

The term 'non-tariff distortion' is preferred as a general description to the term 'non-tariff barrier' because some of the practices and programs listed result in a lowering of duty or protection for particular commodities and lead to over-importing rather than under-importing, or on the export side, to over-exporting rather than under-exporting. For example, the system of by-law imports and tariff quotas increases the imports of some commodities, and high levels of export subsidies increase the level of exports beyond the level that would prevail if the Australian economy were distortion-free. Fundamentally, the use of the term 'distortion' reminds us that the practices with which we shall be concerned distort the relative prices of commodities to producers or consumers. Unless there is some sound argument on the basis of pollution or defence or some other kind of externality or public good, these distortions reduce the value of national production and economic welfare. The nature of these distortions is considered more fully below.

Non-tariff instruments include many practices which are usually regarded, in Australia and in other countries, as tariff instruments; for

---

[6] H. G. Johnson and S. D. Metzger (eds.), *International Negotiations on Non-Tariff Barriers* (Allen and Unwin, London), to be published in 1973.
[7] For similar definitions, see Baldwin, *Nontariff Distortions*, chapter 1 and Kiyoshi Kojima, 'Nontariff Barriers to Japan's Trade', *Hitotsubashi Journal of Economics*, 13 June 1972, pp. 2-7.

example, dumping and countervailing duties or value for duty. The definition is, nevertheless, consistent. In the Australian context non-tariff instruments which distort import trade can be regarded as including all tariffs, restrictions, subsidies and other practices other than the fixed rates of normal substantive duty on individual tariff items which are clearly set out in the schedules of the Customs Tariff. In many cases non-tariff barriers to imports overlap the protection given by the normal tariffs but this definition does bring together several areas of restriction and administrative discretion which may be used as alternatives to higher normal tariffs.

All of the instruments which come within this definition can be classified in several ways. We shall sometimes draw a distinction on the import side between para-tariff 'non-tariff' distortions and other non-tariff distortions of imports. Para-tariff distortions are those administered as a part of the Customs Tariff or Customs Act and include value for duty, by-laws and administrative methods of determining tariff rates. These are more important in Australia as a form of non-tariff distortion than in most countries. The distinction between para-tariff and other distortions of imports is a simple case of classification according to the nature of the instrument which causes the distortion. A classification according to six different types of instruments was used in the London Program. One alternative criterion is to classify distortions according to the intent, that is, the policy objective they are designed to foster; for example, the protection of the industries concerned, improvement of the balance of payments, protection of national health, etc. While this classification is less helpful for the analysis of the effects of non-tariff distortions it is important in chapters 11 and 12 in discussing the possibilities of multilateral and unilateral changes to non-tariff trade-distorting instruments.

The scope of this book was largely determined by the list of non-tariff distortions which were agreed to by all of those in the various countries participating in the London Program. Because the number of non-tariff distortions is so large it was necessary to concentrate on those which appeared to be more important in world trade. These studies were restricted to distortions of import trade alone. The common list for the countries participating in the London Program is as follows:

(a) Quantitative restrictions, including 'voluntary' restraints affecting other countries' exports;
(b) Customs valuation methods and procedures, including such devices as the American Selling Price;
(c) Anti-dumping and countervailing duties;
(d) Public procurement policies and practices;

(e) Government aids to industry, such as regional policies and 'adjustment assistance' to import competition; and

(f) Industrial standards, including technical, health and safety standards.

I have adhered to this grouping of non-tariff distortions of imports. Some of the groups are rather loosely defined and some discretion had to be used as to what particular practices used in Australia should be included in the study. Where there was any doubt I have included the practice.

There are four instances where the practices included in this book go beyond the scope of counterpart restrictions in the other country studies. On the import side the first is the area of administrative discretion in deciding on the rate of duty levied on particular imports. These have been regarded as a part of the group of general customs valuation methods and procedures listed under (b) above. Moreover, the most important area of administrative tariff-making in Australia, namely the system of concessional entry under by-law, has a pervasive influence on imports in all divisions of the Customs Tariff and is more important than any other non-tariff distortion of imports entering Australia. Any study of protection in Australia which did not include by-law entry would be seriously deficient. The second group of inclusions concerns agricultural products. It was agreed by the institutions participating in the London Program that restrictions on agricultural trade should be excluded because of the special difficulties of liberalising world trade in these products. However, in the case of Australia at least, this is clearly unsatisfactory since potential import and export trade in agricultural products is important and there are many distortions of this trade both overseas and in Australia by means of export sudsidies, restrictions on imports of agricultural products, dual price schemes and other ways. Moreover, the official concern in Australia over non-tariff distortions has centred on non-tariff barriers to Australian exports of agricultural products. The third inclusion on the import side is the additional group of discriminatory provisions of the Australian sales taxes. Thus, there are seven categories of distortions which are studied here.

The last area of study which has been included but was omitted from most of the other country studies is those distortions of export trade which parallel those of import trade within the general groups. The most important of these are subsidies to export producers and exporters.

Within the boundaries of the seven groups of non-tariff distortions I endeavoured to give a census of all instruments which significantly influence Australian trade. The list of these instruments in Australia is short compared to that of some other developed countries and this made it barely possible to describe them all. However, the list is considerably longer than I believed it to be when I set out on the study. Indeed, it includes a few practices which restrict trade of which I was completely ignorant at that time. Discriminatory provisions of sales taxes, by-laws for exports and manufacturing in licensed warehouses are three practices I did not know of and which I suspect are not widely known, even among economists and Commonwealth officials familiar with most tariff practices.

The distortions studied here do not exhaust the total number in use in Australia. First, there are some distortions of Australian trade which fall outside the seven groups; for example, rules of origin and those resulting from international commodity agreements, such as sugar. Most of these appear minor in Australia. Others such as the content plans for the automobile and petroleum industries, which some would consider non-tariff instruments, are very important. Second, the study is confined to non-tariff distortions imposed or controlled by the Commonwealth Government. Under the federal structure of government in Australia the State Governments do not regulate imports directly but they have considerable ability to influence imports indirectly, most particularly by granting subsidies or preferential treatment in regard to taxes or zoning or sale of land or State Government purchases. As these subsidies are selective and often go principally to producers in particular industries they may distort trade patterns. These subsidies appear to be important for mining industries as well as manufacturing. None of these State instruments are examined in this study because they affect international trade only indirectly. Mention is made of State quotas on the production of margarine and of State Government purchasing procedures. Similarly, practices by private producers or organisations which distort trade have generally been omitted. The best known of these are the distortions of both import and export trade which are alleged to take place because of agreements between Australian-registered companies and their overseas parents or associates. Further, the discussion of distortions of export trade is incomplete and cursory, with the exception of direct subsidies on production and exports. In particular, nothing is said about the many regulations and policies affecting exports of minerals. Many of these are imposed or controlled by State Governments. Policies affecting mineral exports and State Government policies which significantly affect exports and imports both deserve separate studies. Finally, there is no discussion of distortions created by some of the instruments studied here when they discriminate among *domestic* producers. As examples, some Commonwealth and State Government purchases appear to discriminate among domestic suppliers as well as import suppliers, and the shipbuilding subsidy was confined until 1972 to Recognised Yards.

Method of Analysis Employed in this Study

This study proceeds in two stages. First, in chapters 2 to 8, the various non-tariff instruments in each of the seven groups are identified and described. Later in chapters 9 to 14 various strands of description and analysis are pulled together. Readers concerned with general features of non-tariff instruments rather than individual instruments should skip immediately to chapter 9.

The discussion of each non-tariff instrument in chapters 2 to 8 begins with an outline of the way it affects trade. In most cases a general qualitative assessment of the distortion due to each instrument is made but no attempt is made in these chapters dealing with each group to estimate quantitatively the rates of protection which are implied by these instruments or other effects on Australian trade. Where it is relevant, the ways and the extent to which a non-tariff instrument departs from some international agreement or convention which encompasses this instrument are noted. For example, the Australian anti-dumping procedures are compared to those set out in the GATT Anti-Dumping Code. The origin of and the economic arguments used to justify the use of each instrument are also set out. Sometimes a brief history of important developments is recorded. All of this information provides essential background to the main purpose of the Australian study as one of eight co-ordinated studies of non-tariff barriers to imports in the respective countries. This is to determine the domestic constraints on governments in negotiating the reduction and elimination of non-tariff barriers to international trade and the most appropriate strategies that might be employed to this end.

For most instruments, comparisons are made between some features of Australian practice and that of other countries. This gives some perspective to the minutiae of Australian practice and further background to the discussions later of multilateral negotiation or unilateral change.

There are certain economic arguments that have been advanced by the government to justify some non-tariff instruments which are not considered at the time of describing the non-tariff instruments in chapters 2 to 8. These arguments relate particularly to by-law imports, subsidies to producers and customs drawback. They are considered together in chapter 12 because they raise the same complex general equilibrium issues. These arguments illustrate the necessity of employing general equilibrium methods to analyse particular policies when these policies have significant indirect effects on other commodities. This method of discussing them in chapter 12 does mean that the critical comments on the value of some non-tariff instruments follow conveniently the descriptions of these instruments whereas some criticisms of other non-tariff instruments are separated from the earlier discussion of these instruments.

Following the chapters discussing the individual non-tariff instruments, chapter 9 summarises the general features of all of these instruments. Chapter 10 discusses the nature and cost of distortions. These chapters are a prelude to chapters 11 and 12 in which I discuss the possibilities of multilateral and unilateral change in these trade-distorting instruments. The focus of the London Program was on multilateral negotiation and reduction of these instruments. Nevertheless, I have come to the conclusion that their significance and their inseparable relationship with the protection given Australian manufacturing industries through tariffs make unilateral reconsideration of these instruments more important for Australia than multilateral negotiation. Chapter 12 considers some of the complex issues of piecemeal changes to particular policy instruments. This issue has not received much attention in Australia and this chapter is probably the most important for anyone considering how we should reduce the serious distortions in the Australian economy that are due to non-tariff instruments. Chapter 13 deals with the advantages of introducing adjustment assistance to expedite the reallocation of resources that must accompany any substantial reduction of distortions. My recommendations are made in chapter 14.

The little space devoted in this study to the quantitative estimation of the effects of these non-tariff instruments requires more comment. There are several reasons for this emphasis. The London Program expressly requested authors to concentrate on the negotiability of these instruments. More important, there are several reasons why it is more difficult to make quantitative estimates of the effects of non-tariff instruments than of tariffs. First, there is the inherent complexity of these instruments. Many commodities are subject to multiple instruments. Many of the instruments have a large element of administrative discretion and hence the rules which are being applied are far from clear. This last feature is aggravated by the secrecy which surrounds many of these practices in Australia. This secrecy hides the rules which are being practised from the scrutiny of economists and others but, even worse from the point of view of the quantitatively-oriented economist, it also means that there are no data of imports, duty remitted, etc. for many of the instruments. For example, I was not able to obtain any statistics of the imports or import prices affected by voluntary agreements, manufacturing in bond, discriminatory sales taxes, individual government purchases, and imports which may be affected by standards and related regulations. Moreover, one needs more data than just the series for imports. For example, to evaluate the protective effect of government purchases one would need to inspect the prices of goods offered to the government in the unsuccessful tenders and to make adjustments for differences in quality and other characteristics of the alternative supplies. In some cases, such as the commodities subject to discriminatory sales tax exemptions or to manufacturing in bond, no statistics are kept of the imports of the particular commodities affected. In other cases the data are compiled but are not available to the public.

Another factor making the study of non-tariff instruments difficult is the continual change in these instruments. This distinguishes non-tariff instruments from most substantive tariffs which remain fixed for many years. (This was one of the reasons for the Tariff Board's Tariff Review.) The administrative discretion involved in many non-tariff instruments means that there must be many decisions and changes made every year; this applies, for example, to by-laws and dumping duties. But the problem is much greater than this. In the 18 months over which the research in this book was spread there were significant changes made to the commodity coverage or the rules applied for the non-tariff instruments in all of chapters 2 to 8.

In the light of these difficulties I, who had to work with only my own resources and the co-operation of several government departments, decided to limit the quantitative estimates in chapter 10 to two areas, by-laws, and certain agricultural commodities subject to non-tariff instruments. These illustrate most features of non-tariff distortions.

Despite the lack of quantitative estimates, it seemed to me that much of the information which had been made available from several government departments and other sources should be published. Most of the descriptive information is either not available from any published source or is to be found only in *Government Gazettes*, Regulations, occasional ministerial statements or other sources which are difficult to locate. In presenting the largely descriptive material of chapters 2 to 8, I have emphasised the aspects of the non-tariff instruments which are important from the point of view of their economic effects and I have tried to isolate qualitatively the nature of the distortions.

Much work remains to be done on non-tariff instruments in Australia. The purpose of this book is to set out the nature of some non-tariff instruments whose importance is not widely appreciated in Australia and to point the way for future research. The seriousness of the distortions created by some non-tariff instruments is obvious and not disputable. The importance of non-tariff distortions is likely to increase as the Tariff Board continues its Tariff Review and hopefully results in a lowering of protection by means of tariffs. We can begin to reconsider non-tariff instruments without waiting for precise estimates of the effects of these instruments as they are currently applied.

2   Direct Quantitative Restrictions on Imports

After the abandonment of import licensing as a method of regulating total import payments in 1960, the government has on many occasions repeated that the tariff is the normal instrument for the protection of Australian production from import competition. Although some advocates of protection have continued to press for the use of quantitative restrictions as the preferred instrument, especially for temporary protection, the basic reliance on the Customs Tariff[1] has not been seriously challenged in the government or outside, though other non-tariff trade-distorting instruments are more important than is generally believed.

There are, however, three areas in which private imports are presently regulated, in whole or part, by direct quantitative restrictions. These are import licensing restrictions on a very limited number of items and, second, the regulations prohibiting imports, or imports from a particular origin, of certain goods and third, the tariff quotas. We also consider in this chapter voluntary quota agreements which involve the Commonwealth Government. Although the other three areas are each much more important today in Australia than import licensing, we shall consider import licensing first because it is the simplest and classic type of non-tariff barrier to imports. Moreover, it was in relation to the relaxation of import licensing in the late 1950s and early 1960s that the Commonwealth Government gave its most explicit statement that Australia would rely on tariffs to protect domestic industries.

Import Licensing

Import licensing was introduced in Australia as a wartime measure in 1939 and used extensively during World War II. After 1945 the

---

[1] The Customs Tariff is an Act that specifies rates of duty on individual items. It also makes provisions for certain types of duty such as by-laws, support value duties and tariff quotas which are discussed in this book as para-tariff instruments within the total set of non-tariff instruments. It is administered in conjunction with the Customs Act which lays down the rules for entry, valuation and so on.

proportion of imports subject to licensing was steadily reduced. It was not until 1952 that import licensing was applied to most Australian imports during peacetime. On 8 March 1952 all but 2 per cent in value of Australian imports became subject to import licensing.[2] The reintroduction of import licensing was prompted by the extraordinary decline in international reserves resulting from the high level of imports in 1951-52, and by the sudden increase in unemployment in 1952. These events followed the 1950-51 Korean War boom. The controls were intended as a temporary measure to restrain total import payments and the Australian Government never changed its policy of abolishing the licensing as soon as the balance of payments difficulties had eased. There were separate discriminatory quotas on imports from the hard currency areas of the Dollar Area and Japan.

After an abortive attempt to remove import licensing in 1954, almost 90 per cent of imports were freed from quantitative control on 22 February 1960. The discriminatory quotas on imports from the Dollar Area were abolished at this time, with the exception of those relating to motor vehicles, which were abolished on 1 October 1960. The remaining 10 per cent of imports related mainly to licensed imports from Japan. Under the 1957 trade agreement with Japan Australia accorded Most Favoured Nation (MFN) treatment to Japan for the first time and abolished most discrimination but the Agreement included an escape clause (Article V) which permitted Australia to continue to discriminate against imports from Japan if these imports caused or threatened serious injury to Australian producers. The potential licensing restrictions on Japanese imports under this Article were removed in November 1962 and the Article was omitted when the Trade Agreement was renegotiated in 1963. This left only a few items which 'must remain under [import licensing] control until special problems associated with them are resolved'.[3]

Since 1960 Australia has not employed import licensing as an instrument to control the balance of payments, although after their removal in 1960 the reimposition of licensing was avoided only by the severe deflationary measures introduced in November 1960 and an increase in the net capital inflow and a loan of $156 million from the International Monetary Fund. The recession of 1961 was the severest in recent Australian history and almost resulted in the defeat of the

---

[2] For a detailed discussion of import licensing during this period, see Department of Trade, *History of Australia's Import Licensing Measures from December, 1939* (Canberra, 1959), pp. 1-21 and G. G. Moffat, *Import Control and Industrialisation* (Melbourne University Press, Melbourne, 1970). Some of the important documents relating to this period are reproduced in J. G. Crawford, *Australian Trade Policy 1942-1966* (Australian National University Press, Canberra, 1968), pp. 500-25.

[3] From a statement by the Minister for Trade on 22 February 1960, reprinted in Crawford, *Australian Trade Policy*, p. 523.

Liberal Party-Country Party coalition which was in office then and has been ever since. The Australian balance of payments has not been a major concern since 1960 except in the last two years when the steady accumulation of reserves has led to pressure for appreciation of the Australian dollar. For these reasons there has been no discussion in recent years of the possibility of import licensing as a balance of payments instrument.

Since 1960 the use of import licences for protective purposes has been very limited and decreasing. When the Tariff Board Act was amended in 1962 to have a Special Advisory Authority rather than a Deputy Chairman of the Tariff Board consider applications for temporary protection, provision was also made for temporary protection by means of quantitative restrictions. In supporting this legislation in the House of Representatives a spokesman for the government gave reasons for the provisions relating to quantitative restrictions:[4]

> Where an inflow of imports has reduced the Australian industry's share of the market so as to make an otherwise stable economy unprofitable and even, perhaps, uneconomic, it may be more appropriate to apply a quantitative limitation of imports, rather than a temporary duty.
>
> Another circumstance which may warrant temporary protection through import restrictions may be that substantial reduction of domestic demand resulting from general economic circumstances operating in Australia may reduce an Australian industry to a serious situation unless the volume of imports is temporarily diminished . . . I must make it clear that the special advisory authority, where he finds grounds for a recommendation for temporary protection, will consider the use of temporary quantitative restrictions only *after* . . . he has considered a temporary duty. This will be the firm approach to our temporary protection machinery—the tariff first; quantitative restrictions where the tariff is not appropriate . . . when temporary protection is accorded an industry it is in the nature of emergency first-aid. It is essentially a holding action pending a full inquiry by the Tariff Board . . .

These restrictions, like temporary tariffs, expire if still in effect three months from the date on which the minister receives the report of the Tariff Board upon this reference, unless the Board recommended their continuation (see pp. 53-4).

At the same time the government extended to the Tariff Board the authority to recommend quantitative restrictions for the long-term protection of an industry. Section 15 (1A) of the Tariff Board Act:

[4] This statement is reprinted in Crawford, *Australian Trade Policy*, pp. 485-6.

Where the Minister has referred to the Board for an inquiry and
report the matter of the necessity for new or increased duties on
any goods, the Board may, in its report, recommend the restriction
of the importation of those goods (either in addition to or in lieu
of new or increased duties on those goods) for such period as is
specified in the report.

The government had the power to apply quantitative restrictions on
imports under the Customs Act for many years but it had not previously
recognised that import restrictions could be applied in any industry for
protective purposes. The reasons given for long-term restrictions were
similar to those for the temporary restrictions:[5]

It is the Government's intention that protection shall be effective ...
Generally speaking it has proved to be effective, but there have
been occasions when that has not been so. We have had experience
of our intention of giving tariff protection being systematically
countered, and not always by means which could be regarded as
being entirely ethical. There are circumstances in which tariff
protection can be undermined to an extent which can make it an
inadequate medium for protection.

Similarly, modern industrial developments have created industries
which must have an assured volume of output to maintain production efficiency and a reasonable cost level. Endeavours to avoid
serious injury to such an industry by use of the tariff may not be
effective where overseas competitors with tremendous advantages
of scale can adopt pricing policies aimed at undermining protection ...

It could, of course, be claimed that in any of these circumstances
a tariff could be set sufficiently high to be effective. What this would
mean in many if not most cases would be a prohibitively high
tariff. That would not be in keeping with our principles of tariff
making, and moreover would offer difficulties where part of the
demand must be met by imports. It is clear that there are occasions
when the use of quantitative restrictions will avoid unnecessary
cost increases.

The Government stated clearly that 'the need to use quantitative restrictions would arise on very few occasions ... as a last resort'.[6] However,
the only limitation on the Board in making its recommendation is that
it is required to specify the period for which the restrictions will operate
in each case. While the government envisaged that 'the Tariff Board
should recommend the use of such restrictions only under conditions in
which the consumers would be adequately safeguarded'[7] there is no such

[5] Ibid., pp. 476-7.
[6] Ibid., p. 477.
[7] Ibid.

safeguard required in the Act, though there is provision for an inquiry by the Board at any time under Section 15 (1) (h) of the Act where 'a manufacturer is taking undue advantage of the protection afforded against him by the Tariff or by the restrictions of the importation of any goods' which result in 'unnecessarily high prices for his goods or . . . restraint of trade to the detriment of the public'.[8]

The potentiality for restricting imports severely through the use of quantitative restrictions under the Tariff Board Act has not been realised to any significant degree because both the provisions for temporary and long-term protection have been used very sparingly.

None of the forty reports on references to the Deputy Chairman of the Tariff Board from 1960 to April 1962 recommended quantitative restrictions. When the Special Advisory Authority took over in 1962 he continued to rely on tariffs for temporary protection. However, at this time quantitative restrictions were provided for explicitly in the Act, and the SAA did recommend quantitative restrictions, pending the Tariff Board reports on long-term measures, on timber and on penicillin and streptomycin, and in 1964 on aluminium and aluminium alloy waste and scrap.[9] In considering long-term protection for these commodities the Tariff Board recommended that protection be afforded by increased tariffs rather than quantitative restrictions and the import licensing was ended when the government accepted the Board's recommendations.[10] Polyethylene twine rope, cordage and cable were subject to import licensing for the three years January 1966 to December 1968, after an inquiry by the Special Advisory Authority. The Tariff Board again recommended that the import restrictions on these products and on polypropylene, a new substitute on which the Board also recommended interim quantitative restrictions, be replaced after December 1968 by duties that were to be reduced over time.[11]

Table 2.1 gives a brief description of the only three sets of commodities that were subject to import licensing in Australia in 1972, and the value of licences issued in recent periods. These will be considered briefly.

[8] Explicit reference to the Board of goods under this sub-Section has been made only once, in November 1967. It is normal practice for references to the Board to be made under Section 15 as a whole. The Board could, therefore, consider whether prices are unnecessarily high or trade is restrained.
[9] See reports of the Special Advisory Authority on *Timber*, 27 June 1962, on *Penicillin and Streptomycin*, 27 July 1962 and on *Aluminium and Aluminium Alloy Waste and Scrap*, 13 November 1963 (Commonwealth of Australia, Canberra).
[10] Tariff Board reports on *Timber*, 6 September 1963, on *Penicillin and Streptomycin*, 29 March 1963 and on *Aluminium Ingots* etc., 3 April 1964 and *Alumina, Unwrought Aluminium and Aluminium Products*, 10 March 1967. In the case of aluminium and aluminium alloy the import licensing was retained until December 1971 on the Board's advice.
[11] The relevant reports are the *Report of the Special Advisory Authority on Polyethylene Monofil and Rope*, 24 December 1965, and the Tariff Board *Concluding Interim Report on the General Textile Reference*, 21 September 1967.

Direct Quantitative Restrictions 15

Table 2.1 Value of licences issued for goods subject to import licensing in 1972

Goods	Period	Value of licences issued ($)
Knitted coats, jumpers, cardigans, sweaters and the like	19.12.67–30.6.68 1.7.68 –30.6.69 1.7.69 –30.6.70	5,057,538 5,246,317 5,665,347
Men's and boy's knitted shirts	1.7.69 –30.6.70	1,700,072
Used, second-hand and disposal machinery and equipment*	18.3.68 –31.12.68 1.7.69 –31.12.69 1.1.70 –31.12.70 1.1.71 –30.6.71	283,148† 221,334† 2,061,856‡ 3,299,008‡

* These refer to the following classes:
  (a) Earthmoving or excavating vehicles, machinery or equipment (e.g. rock buggies, dumpers, mechanical shovels, excavators, scrapers, bulldozers) and parts thereof.
  (b) Tractors, roadrollers and parts.
  (c) Materials handling equipment (e.g. cranes, forklift trucks) and parts thereof.
  (d) Other vehicles being four-wheel drive commercial road transport vehicles and other four-wheel drive vehicles, excluding omnibuses.
† These figures include licences only for classes (a) and (b).
‡ These include only classes (a), (b) and (c).

Sources: Government *Gazettes* and Department of Trade and Industry.

In its 1967 report on a reference to consider the assistance to producers of earthmoving, excavating and materials handling machinery and equipment, the Tariff Board recommended the continuation in the long-term of import licensing. Licensing had initially been brought in to provide protection against the disposal of surplus US armed forces stock.[12] It was confirmed that, in many instances, prices of second-hand or disposal machinery and equipment were less than 30 per cent of the prices of comparable new equipment in Australia. Protection by duty would have required substantially higher duties than those recommended for new goods under this reference, even if an arbitrary valuation of the equivalent 'new' price of the second-hand or disposal goods were used. Hence, the Board recommended import licensing that would allow only imports of goods not available from Australian production.

Knitted goods illustrates another factor behind import licensing, namely, the difficulties associated with a sudden increase in imports. The first inquiry by the Special Advisory Authority in 1967 was held against a background of a rate of increase of imports over the two years 1965-66 and 1966-67 of more than 100 per cent per annum, almost

[12] *Report on Earthmoving, Excavating and Materials Handling Machinery and Equipment*, 16 October 1967, pp. 25-6.

all of the increase coming from Japan, Hong Kong, Taiwan and Mainland China. The Special Advisory Authority reported:[13]

> I have given consideration to the question of whether the necessary protection can be appropriately provided by means of temporary additional duties. The circumstances of the case are that, if temporary duties were imposed, they would need to be in the form of sliding scale duties, or, in the form of a duty subject to a reduction equal to the amount by which the f.o.b. price of the imported garment exceeds a specified figure. However, because of the variety of styles, qualities, weights, etc., in which these types of knitted outerwear could be imported it would be extremely difficult to provide suitable base prices for each type of garment, and the difficulties of administration would be considerable. In the circumstances I consider that the necessary protection can be appropriately provided only by means of temporary restriction of the importation of these goods.

The circumstances and the reasons given for the further application of import licensing to knitted shirts on 1 July 1969 were very similar to the earlier reference.[14] These two cases are also of interest in that emergency protection was granted because of a threat of injury rather than any actual injury.

In its report on the knitted goods the Tariff Board recommended the removal of the temporary protection by import licensing and lower levels of duty than existed before the temporary protection was imposed.[15] In order to give the industry time to adjust to the recommended long-term duty of 45 per cent (General) the Board recommended interim assistance until December 1973 in the form of an alternative duty of $1.30 per ℔ (General) and a by-law concession which would allow man-made fibre shirting to be admitted duty-free. In the view of the Board there is a need for rationalisation in the industry and a reduced level of production.

The government accepted the need for rationalisation of the industry but decided that import licensing should be retained for a further period of 18 months from September 1971, instead of the alternative assistance proposed by the Board. During this time the government intended to initiate negotiations for voluntary restraint arrangements with the principal low-cost Asian suppliers, similar to those other developed countries have negotiated to protect their established textile industries.[16]

[13] Report of the Special Advisory Authority on *Knitted Coats, Jumpers, Sweaters and the Like*, 8 December 1967, p. 5.
[14] Report of the Special Advisory Authority on *Knitted Shirts*, 14 May 1969.
[15] Tariff Board, *Report on Knitted Shirts and Outergarments*, 29 April 1971.
[16] These proposals were outlined by the Minister for Trade and Industry in the House of Representatives on 7 September 1971; *CPD*, H. of R., 1971, pp. 813-14.

No reason was given for rejecting the Board's specific proposals for interim protection though reference was made to the fact that 'these are substantial industries involving significant employment and activity in many areas throughout the country' which were depressed because of sharp falls in price for dairy products and wool in 1970 and 1971 (see pp. 124-6). These negotiations apparently failed and in August 1972 the government announced the introduction of tariff quotas on knitted goods (see p. 27) to supplement the import licensing restrictions.

While these import licensing restrictions have been reserved for situations in which there are special complications, they have severely restricted imports of the items affected. Table 2.1 gives the statistics of the value of licenses issued of these items over the period. In the cases of second-hand and disposal machinery and equipment, it has been government policy to grant import licences only when 'suitably equivalent goods are not reasonably available from local producers'.[17] Import licences are not granted even when there is a delivery lag on locally-manufactured goods.[18] These restrictions have eliminated almost all potential imports of these goods.

Import licensing is certainly a breach of the spirit and the intention of GATT. A basic feature of GATT is that quantitative restrictions are not permitted except in a few prescribed circumstances. The only article of GATT which can be invoked to justify new quantitative restrictions on non-agricultural trade is the market disruption clause, Article 19, which permits member countries to use temporary quotas in the presence of 'serious injury' or threatened injury to domestic producers. Other countries have used this clause in recent years to attempt to slow down the growth of imports, particularly of textiles from developing countries.

Insufficient thought has been given by the Australian Government to the basic question of whether these goods should continue to be supplied mainly by Australian producers. In the case of textile imports considerably cheaper supplies of comparable goods are available from overseas suppliers and this is likely to continue. In the case of knitted shirts, duties of $57\frac{1}{2}$ per cent or $1.57 whichever is the higher plus 5 per cent primage, being the General rate applied to imports from the Asian countries of Taiwan, Hong Kong, Korea and Japan which supplied most of the increased imports, did not deter the very rapid increase in the imports.[19] We should certainly not extend import licensing to any

---

[17] With the exception of class (d) in the note to Table 2.1. One such vehicle is allowed to each local fire fighting authority, or each immigrant and each other case is considered on its merits.
[18] *Report on Earthmoving, Excavating*, p. 53. This is similar to the interpretation of 'reasonably available' for by-law admission (see pp. 45-6).
[19] Knitted outerwear exported from Hong Kong, Macao and Mainland China was also subject to dumping duty from 23 November 1967 and outerwear from

more commodities. In 1972 the Cotton and Manmade Fibres Federation called on the government, during a Tariff Board Hearing, to introduce some form of quantitative restriction on textile imports which would ensure the Australian producers 70 per cent of the domestic market. In protecting permanently these goods Australia is forgoing substantial benefits from buying them from the cheapest sources. The special factors of sudden change in market conditions do not reduce the long-term costs of these protective policies. However, there should be adequate protection against genuine predatory dumping. (This is distinguished from marginal cost pricing in the section on dumping.) There should also be adjustment assistance to facilitate the adjustment of the affected domestic suppliers (chapter 13).

The case of second-hand and disposal machinery and equipment is similar. At the Tariff Board hearing a brokerage firm dealing in second-hand and disposal equipment claimed most items of equipment were freely available from second-hand or disposal sources throughout the world.[20] If these goods are likely to remain freely available overseas at very cheap prices, as is the case at least for second-hand four-wheel drive vehicles which are included in the current licensing, there is no more reason to forgo these cheap supplies from other countries than with new goods.

Import licensing is maintained under the provisions of the Customs (Import Licensing) Regulations. While the Minister for Customs and Excise or his delegate has discretion in determining which products are subject to licensing, such decisions are normally made by the government, largely upon the advice of the Department of Trade and Industry. The licensing of imports of goods may be abolished by the government without legislative approval.

Prohibited and Restricted Imports

The Customs Act provides that the Governor-General may, by regulation, prohibit the importation of goods into Australia. This power may be exercised by

(i) prohibiting the importation of goods absolutely;
(ii) prohibiting the importation of goods unless permission in writing is granted by the Minister for Customs and Excise;
(iii) prohibiting the importation of goods unless specified conditions or restrictions are complied with;
(iv) prohibiting the importation of goods from a specified place.

(Provision exists in the Act for the Governor-General to prohibit the

---

Poland was subject to dumping duty from 8 July 1968. Tentative dumping duties had been imposed on 18 April 1966. See Tariff Board *Report on Knitted Shirts (Dumping and Subsidies Act)*, 16 June 1967.

[20] *Earthmoving, Excavating*, p. 25.

exportation of goods from Australia under the same conditions as apply to prohibited imports. This provision is used to control the export of arms and military stores, preserve Australian native fauna and mineral resources, to control the quality of Australian goods for export and to enforce commitments under primary products marketing agreements. However, the quantitative regulation of exports is not examined.) The prohibition of imports of various goods is intended broadly to protect community welfare. This rubric includes a number of disparate categories of goods. The current list of goods whose importation is prohibited absolutely or subject to written permission or specified conditions is published in the schedules attached to the Customs (Prohibited Imports) Regulations, comprising Statutory Rules 1956, No. 90 as amended.

The first and most important category in terms of the number of items prohibited or restricted are goods whose importation is considered (by the Minister) to be injurious to national health, morality or security. These include goods commonly restricted in many countries; for example, films, pictures and written material which is judged to be 'blasphemous, indecent or obscene', firearms, certain pharmacological products, harmful chemical substances and seditious literature. Some of these are prohibited absolutely; for example, opium prepared for smoking and counterfeit bank notes. Other goods may be imported under specified conditions (drugs, radioactive materials or substances) or at the discretion of the Minister for each individual case (for example, daggers, flick-knives and knuckle-dusters, fireworks and cannabis). Clearly, for this category of goods the intention is to restrict the availability of these goods to potential users or consumers and not to protect domestic producers of the same or like goods. In many cases the manufacture, sale or possession of these same goods is illegal or legally restricted to specified individuals or institutions. However, in some cases there is an incidental protective effect. As an example, the role of the Commonwealth in the censorship of literature is confined to regulation of imports, the States and Federal Territories being responsible for the control of the distribution and sale of both locally-produced and imported literature within their respective geographic borders. This has allowed, in some States, the production and sale of goods which are absolutely prohibited imports. The prohibition of imports into Australia of some goods absolutely (for example, absinthe or cigars and cigarettes containing explosive substances and trick cigars), or subject to permission (perhaps daggers and aphrodisiacs), or subject to specific conditions (certain drugs of dependence)[21] may seem unusually or unnecessarily

---

[21] Licit activities in Australia, as set out in the Narcotics Drug Act, embody Australia's commitment under the ratification of the United Nation's Single Convention on Narcotics Drugs.

strict to residents of some other countries. However, judgment in all of these cases is a matter for Australia alone and is not negotiable. Prohibitions for these goods are permitted by the Articles of GATT.

A second category of prohibitions are those relating to goods of which the control of imports is a means to achieve or to help to achieve some other primary objective. The most notable example in Australia is the prohibition of imports of aircraft, airframes and aircraft engines without the permission of the Director-General of Civil Aviation. This is a part of the official 'two-airlines policy' and is intended to protect and control the operations of the two major domestic airlines in the country by regulating the number and type of aircraft each airline acquires. Australian manufacture of aircraft or aircraft engines is insignificant relative to the demands of these companies. The method of controlling the operations of domestic airlines by the Customs regulations of imports of aircraft is a rather backhand method that was used because of the uncertain powers under the Constitution of the Commonwealth Government vis-à-vis the State Governments to regulate corporations. However, the 1971 decision of the High Court in the concrete pipe manufacturers' case appears to have given the Commonwealth greatly increased powers to regulate corporations directly.

The third category contains goods whose importation is prohibited or restricted largely or substantially to protect the domestic manufacturers of these goods or their close substitutes. The notable goods are margarine and other similar butter substitutes, liquid or powdered milk with non-milk fats added, potatoes for food purposes, and ships of any description, new or second-hand.[22] Imports of margarine and other similar butter substitutes must be coloured a distinct pink colour and branded with the name of the contents to distinguish them clearly from butter.[23] Both the dairy farmers and shipyards in Australia also receive substantial protection and assistance through tariffs, direct subsidy

---

[22] All of these restrictions originated many years ago. The goods now covered by 'margarine and similar butter substitutes' were declared prohibited imports in the first Customs Act 1901, Section 52(f) Regulation 22. After the present provisions for prohibited imports were introduced in 1952, this item was transferred to the Customs (Prohibited Imports) Regulations. The restriction on potatoes dates back to 1928. The filled milk prohibition dates from 1961. Filled milk was considered by the Australian Agricultural Council to be a serious threat to the Australian dairy industry.

[23] Under the authority of the Dairying Industry Act the State Governments also impose quotas on all producers of table margarine, including polyunsaturated margarine, in each State. The national quota total is only 16,072 tons. To circumvent this restriction, the margarine industry developed a soft margarine suitable as a table spread which was not subject to production quotas because it was a cooking margarine. Sales of this margarine have increased despite the requirements that it contain no less than 90 per cent animal tallows. Two of the main butter-producing States, Victoria and Tasmania, passed legislation banning the sale of cooking margarine flavoured and coloured to resemble butter. The margarine industry has counter-attacked by developing a new spreadable cooking margarine which it believes does not contravene the State legislation.

payments and other measures. Any reconsideration of the prohibition or restriction on imports of these products would have to take place within the framework of an overall review of these combined policies. In the ships case there is the added complication that the prohibitions are partly intended to deal with imports of second-hand vessels: 'Such vessels are available for immediate delivery, and at prices against which the local industry would be unable to compete'.[24]

The desirability of protecting Australian producers against imports of second-hand goods was discussed in the previous section in connection with import licensing restrictions on imports of earthmoving, excavating and materials handling equipment. The restriction on potatoes implements a long-standing agreement between the Governments of Australia and New Zealand that neither will permit importation of potatoes except when locally grown crisping potatoes are in short supply.[25] The Minister for Customs and Excise permits imports of potatoes only after a report on any request for imports by an interdepartmental committee consisting of officers of the Department of Primary Industry, the Department of Health, the Department of Trade and Industry, the Treasury and the Department of Customs and Excise.

All goods from North Vietnam and specified goods from Southern Rhodesia are prohibited imports without the consent in writing of the Minister.

There are also some prohibited import regulations relating to technical specifications but these are considered on pp. 82-3.

Voluntary Agreements Restricting Imports

The most important of the agreements between the Australian Government and overseas exporters concerns imports of agricultural goods. In the case of lamb the Australian and New Zealand Meat Boards co-operate in marketing their produce in third-country markets, especially in the United States where the producer authorities of Australia, New Zealand and the US established jointly a Lamb Promotion Coordination Committee. New Zealand is the largest exporter and Australia is the second largest exporter to world markets of lamb. It is reasonable to believe they will not export large quantities of lamb to each other that would disturb home markets. Lamb was included in the initial free

---

[24] Tariff Board *Report on Shipbuilding*, 4 October 1963. This is still true today. The Tariff Board sent another *Report on Shipbuilding* to the government, signed on 25 June 1971, which was tabled on 15 August 1972. As well as recommending an increase in subsidy payments in the short term, which was accepted by the government, it recommended that the import prohibitions on ships be ended, which was not accepted by the government.

[25] Since 1971 quarantine restrictions on imports of potatoes from New Zealand have been further tightened because of the detection of the disease 'black wart' in the South Island of New Zealand. In future imports will be permitted only for processing under quarantine and that only for wholesale distribution.

trade list of goods included in Schedule A of the New Zealand-Australia Free Trade Agreement in 1965. Imports from New Zealand reached the highest level, a meagre 972 tons, in 1968 and since the establishment under the Agreement of an Industry Panel to review these imports there have been no imports.

Similarly, there is agreement between the Australian Dairy Produce Board and the New Zealand Dairy Board and a tacit agreement between the two governments that New Zealand butter will not be exported to Australia.[26] New Zealand and Australia are both large-scale exporters of butter but the domestic prices in both countries are divorced from the prices received for exported butter (see pp. 102-3) and the domestic wholesale prices for butter in Australia are substantially above the New Zealand export and domestic retail prices. New Zealand producers are, on average, the more efficient producers of butter. The Australian Government has instituted a reconstruction scheme to reduce the number of dairy farms and increase their average size and efficiency and the position of the Australian industry may worsen after the British entry into the EEC. In mid-1971, during a price war among retailers in Canberra, one chain of supermarkets endeavoured to import 75,000 lb of New Zealand butter which they said they could sell at 39 cents a lb including freight and customs duty, compared to the normal wholesale price of 52 cents and the retail price of 56 cents a lb. The New Zealand Dairy Board refused the sale, ostensibly because of short supplies for export after a poor season.

The butter arrangement restricts Australian imports of butter. Despite the fact that there is a duty of only 5 cents a lb on butter imported into Australia and no prohibitions or quota, no butter has been imported for many years. (Quarantine regulations also restrict butter imports; see p. 81.) Nevertheless, the effect of these import restrictions on the quantity produced is much less than the restriction of imports. Since the price the farmer receives for sales of butter on the domestic and foreign markets is equalised each season, domestic production is not directly related to the Australian export or the potential import prices. Imports from New Zealand would in the first instance increase the supply of Australian butter for export to other markets correspondingly and have little effect on export prices or supplies to other countries. It would, however, be difficult to maintain the Australian wholesale and retail prices for butter in this situation, and in the longer run domestic production would fall. (See also pp. 150-3.)

[26] In testimony by the Australian Dairy Industry Council before the Senate Standing Committee on Primary and Secondary Industry and Trade's hearings on Australia-New Zealand Trade, it was stated that representatives of the Australia and New Zealand Dairy Boards meet every 6 months, but the nature of the agreement on sales in the other member country was not given—despite a direct question from one of the Senators: *Hansard,* 21 June 1972, pp. 275-80.

Under the terms of the New Zealand-Australia Free Trade Agreement signed in 1965 there is provision for consultation. The governments have decided to use the consultation procedures rather than the suspension of tariff concessions as the means to regulate trade in items added to the free trade list of Schedule A of the Agreement in the event of actual or threatened market disruption. They have set up a Joint Consultative Council on Forest Industries and a Pea and Bean Industry Panel on which the governments and industries of the two countries are represented. These consultation provisions provide a valuable mechanism for overcoming short-term difficulties and have partially freed trade in these products between the two countries. However, they have also led to negotiated arrangements which amount to market-sharing agreements, condoned by both governments, which restrict competition and prevent specialisation along the lines of greatest advantage in the two countries. These arrangements have included voluntary export quotas, as in the case of New Zealand exports of peas and beans to Australia. In August 1971 the Australian Trade Practices Tribunal found the major pea processing companies in Australia and J. Watties Canneries Ltd of New Zealand guilty of an orderly marketing agreement which had increased the prices of these products in Australia.[27]

Under the 1963 Trade Agreement with Japan, Japan was given the right to consult with Australia before action is taken to refer requests to the Special Advisory Authority for temporary protection on items of particular interest to Japan with a view to Japan offering alternatives to temporary protection. This clause replaced the safeguard clause in the 1957 Agreement which enabled Australia to take immediate action after consultation to protect an Australian industry that was threatened with serious disruption by imports from Japan. 'Voluntary restraints' under the new clause have been a significant feature of the operation of the Agreement and have formed the basis of informal trade discussions between representatives of business in the two countries. In mid-1972 there were no government-to-government agreements on Japanese voluntary restraints in force. An earlier voluntary restraint on conveyer belting negotiated between the governments in 1966 had lapsed after the 1967 Tariff Board *Report on Metal Reinforced Rubber Belts or Belting* had recommended increases in duty from free to 25 per cent (Preferential) and $7\frac{1}{2}$ per cent to 35 per cent (General). After industry-to-industry negotiations, some Japanese trade associations have agreed to restrict exports of particular manufactured goods to Australia. In mid-

[27] Trade Practices Tribunal, *Report on Frozen Vegetables and Other Matters*, 6 August 1971. The author has discussed the NAFTA negotiations in forest products and the role of these industry panels in *New Zealand Manufacturing Production and Trade with Australia* (New Zealand Institute of Economic Research, Wellington, 1971), chapter V.

1972 agreements on ball bearings, ceramic wall tiles and unilateral restraint by the Japanese Government on PVC products were known to exist.

Two general features of voluntary agreements restricting imports stand out. The first is that there is no public investigation of any of these agreements and none of the agreements are published. It is therefore impossible to assess the restrictiveness of these agreements and their relation to the protection afforded by the Customs Tariff. The second general feature is that all relate to sensitive areas of import competition where high levels of protection by the Customs Tariff and other non-tariff restrictions exist. (See pp. 137-41.) This makes it even more important that the underhand nature of these agreements be ended. The obvious and most desirable policy is to replace these restrictions by increased tariff protection, if this higher protection is considered desirable, by sending a reference to the Tariff Board.

Tariff Quotas

Tariff quotas have been used to a very limited extent in Australia and only in recent years, though they are increasing in importance. The first tariff quotas to be introduced were those relating to cheddar cheese and pork under the New Zealand-Australia Free Trade Agreement which came into effect on 1 January 1966. This Agreement provides for duty-free entry for pork meat and cheddar cheese from New Zealand, subject to a quota of 1,000 tons per annum in the case of cheese and in the case of pork 3,000 tons in the first year of the Agreement with an increase in the second and subsequent years equal to 5 per cent of the previous year's quota. Concessional entry of these products is made by means of by-laws. For imports from other countries the present General duty on pork is $2\frac{1}{2}$ cents per lb plus 10 per cent primage and the Preferential duty is $2\frac{1}{2}$ cents per lb plus 5 per cent primage.[28] The present duty on cheddar cheese is 5·8 cents per lb General and 5 cents per lb Preferential. Under the animal quarantine regulations uncanned meat of all kinds is prohibited from all sources except New Zealand.

The intention and the effect of these tariff quotas was to give New Zealand, within the terms of the New Zealand-Australia Free Trade Agreement, preferential access to the Australian market but in the case of cheese the amount is a token amount that is not a significant threat to the Australian dairy industry. The Australian Government had made it quite clear during the negotiations for the Agreement that it would not consider free trade in dairy products that would damage the Aus-

---

[28] The Preferential rate applies to imports from the United Kingdom, Ireland, Canada and Papua New Guinea. Pork from New Zealand enters duty free but there is currently a duty of 2 cents per lb on imports of cheddar cheese from New Zealand as the initial duty has not yet been phased out.

tralian industry. In the case of pork no imports from New Zealand have occurred because of quarantine restrictions.

In the annual discussions of the Agreement in 1970, both governments agreed to use, where practicable, new measures such as tariff quotas and special conditions on free trade which would limit the degree of increased competition following the addition of new items to Schedule A of the Agreement and the subsequent freeing of trans-Tasman trade in these items over the 8-year period provided for in the Agreement. This new provision for tariff quotas has not yet been used.

A second area of tariff quotas in the Customs Tariff occurs as one part of Australia's unilateral scheme giving preferences on selected commodities to the developing countries. Imports from the developing countries under the scheme consist of two broad groups: specified manufactures and semi-manufactures admitted at preferential rates but subject to tariff quotas, and specified traditional hand-made products of cottage industries which are admitted duty-free and without quota limitation.[29] Australia obtained a waiver from the 'no new preference' provision of GATT in March 1966 and the preferences first came into effect for handicrafts on 12 April 1966 and for quota items on 1 July 1966. The scheme is highly selective with respect to commodity coverage and preference margins.[30] The commodity coverage and quotas have been progressively increased. There are at present some 450 commodity groups (tariff items or groups of tariff items) subject to quotas, of which more than one half are admitted duty-free from the developing countries.[31] Quotas have generally been set at levels equivalent to less than 10 per cent of total actual imports in the corresponding year, except for a few goods supplied predominantly by developing countries such as hand-made carpets and cricket bats. The basic statistics of imports under the scheme are given in Table 2.2.

These tariff quotas,[32] like those of the New Zealand-Australia Free Trade Agreement, are trade-expanding rather than trade-restricting, though they may also to a small extent have encouraged imports from

---

[29] The reasons for assisting the developing countries in this way were set out in a statement by the then Minister for Trade and Industry to the House of Representatives on 19 May 1965, which is reprinted in Crawford, *Australian Trade Policy*, pp. 192-8. Further description and analysis of the scheme is given in a paper by the author, 'The Value of Tariff Preferences for the Developing Countries: Australian Experience', *Economic Record*, March 1971, pp. 1-16.

[30] For 1967-68, I calculated the unweighted average of the margins of preference, defined as the difference between the general tariff plus primage and the preferential rate available to the developing countries, as over 20 per cent for the items subject to tariff quotas. It was approximately 32 per cent for the handicraft items.

[31] The tariff items, quotas and other features of the scheme are described in the Department of Trade and Industry booklet, *The Australian System of Tariff Preferences for Developing Countries*, 3rd ed. (Canberra, 1 July 1971).

[32] There are also quotas on by-law imports which enter at concessional rates for bananas from Fiji and of plywood from Papua New Guinea.

Table 2.2 Statistics of the developing country preference scheme ($m. f.o.b.)

	1966–67	1967–68	1968–69	1969–70	1970–71
Total preferential quotas available	13·3	20·4	30·1	36·2	47·0
Total imports under DC tariff quotas	1·7	5·0	7·6	9·8	11·9
Handicrafts imported under preference	0·6	1·3	2·1	2·5	4·2
Total DC preferential trade	2·3	6·3	9·7	12·3	16·1
Total Australian imports from DCs	436·9	463·4	489·4	524·2	476·6

Source: CBCS, 'Imports under the Australian System of Tariff Preferences for Developing Countries', no. 8, 23 April 1972.

these countries in substitution for imports from other countries. They were intended to increase the exports of the developing countries to Australia. Moreover, as a result of UNCTAD II in New Delhi in 1968, eighteen Western developed countries announced in October 1970 new country schemes for tariff preferences for the developing countries. The countries included EEC, the USA, United Kingdom, Japan and New Zealand but not Australia. While the Australian scheme was actually the very first country scheme to grant preferences in selected commodities to *all* developing countries, it is now much smaller in commodity coverage and importance than the preference schemes of several of the individual countries with more recent schemes.

The quotas were designed as an additional safeguard for Australian industry and to ensure that the preferences did not cause serious injury to third countries. This cautious approach was due to the uncertain effects of introducing this new kind of preference and to Australia's primary reliance on the Tariff to protect its own rapidly growing manufacturing industries.

The scheme has led to a small but useful increase in the exports of the developing countries to Australia. I estimated the net increase in Australian imports attributable to the scheme to be about $A9 million in 1968-69.[33] However, in the last few years the quotas themselves have imposed restrictive limits on many of the items, including some of the more important in the scheme in terms of the value of preferential imports such as hand-made carpets, cotton piecegoods, even though quotas for most items have been increased. In 1970-71 many of these quotas were fully used. While the imports from the developing countries at preferential tariff quota rates of all commodities in the scheme subject

[33] 'The value of Tariff Preferences', p. 11.

to quota preferences were $11·9 million in 1970-71, the total imports of these same items from the developing countries at non-preferential rates were $40·1 million for the same period.[34]

In August 1972 the government announced the introduction of new tariff quotas, which were deliberately import-*restricting*, on certain knitted textile goods.[35] These new restrictions followed the failure of negotiations with Taiwan, Hong Kong and Mainland China to establish voluntary quotas on exports from these countries. Tariff quotas on knitted shirts, woven shirts and outer garments and knitted blouses will continue until 30 June 1974. The quotas provide for a 27½ per cent and 5 per cent increase in imports of knitted goods and woven shirts respectively by 1973-74 over the value of imports during 1971-72. Imports above the quota will be subject to duties of $7 a kilogram in addition to the normal duties of 45 per cent. While the government position is still that it wishes to encourage a reorganisation in the industry and more efficient production, this action protects inefficient segments of the industry and is a movement towards the permanent quantitative restrictions on textiles which many developed countries now maintain.

Shortly after the introduction of tariff quotas on textiles the government announced the introduction of new tariff quotas for small-pitch chain and parts for up to two years. These quotas will limit imports of this commodity to 60 per cent of the value of imports of complete chains in 1971-72, any imports beyond this being subject to a prohibitive supplementary tariff of $8 a kilogram. This tariff quota was also justified by the Minister for Trade and Industry as a temporary measure to give producers time to adjust to lower duties recommended by the Tariff Board.[36] This new instrument is very import-restricting, and in both cases was against the advice of the Tariff Board in earlier reports on the areas of production.[37]

---

[34] In addition to the quotas, some of this discrepancy is accounted for by rules of origin and other preferences by the developing countries.
[35] *CPD*, H. of R., 31 August 1972, pp. 1076-7.
[36] *CPD*, H. of R., 28 September 1972, p. 2187.
[37] See Tariff Board reports on *Knitted Shirts and Outergarments*, 29 April 1971 and *Chain and Chains (Dumping and Subsidies Act)*, 26 June 1970.

3 Restrictions on Imports Through Customs Valuation and Assessment

Duty payable on imported commodities and, therefore, the level of protection of domestic producers of these commodities, depends on value for duty and the rate of duty. As the rates of duty differ among commodities it is useful to consider the three aspects of duty determination:

(a) tariff classification;
(b) value for duty;
(c) rates of duty.

Tariff Classification

The Australian tariff classification has been based on the Brussels Tariff Nomenclature (BTN) since June 1965. Like the EEC and some other countries which have adopted the BTN classification, Australia has a Tariff containing many sub-items, paragraphs, and sub-paragraphs within the roughly 1,100 items of the BTN, on which different duties are levied. Hence the classification is more complex than the BTN itself. It was hoped that the translation of the former Australian classification into the BTN would make the Tariff more easily understood and result in a decrease in the number of classification queries to the Department of Customs and Excise. The change has generally been well received but the number of inquiries has continued to increase. However, this is chiefly attributable to the continual introduction of new products, materials and parts. The number of inquiries might well have been significantly greater if the former classification had been retained.

In May 1970 the Ministers for Trade and Industry and for Customs and Excise announced that their departments were to undertake a joint review of the Tariff so that a shorter and more simple form could be adopted. The resulting Tariff Simplification went into effect on 1 July

1971.[1] The number of classifications was reduced by 25 per cent (from 4,039 to 3,014). This was accomplished by eliminating many paragraphs and sub-paragraphs within BTN items. Except where the volume of trade was not significant, the changes to existing rates of duty were no greater than $2\frac{1}{2}$ per cent. Thus the changes did not significantly increase or reduce protection available to any Australian industry. In terms of the number of items or sub-items which have different tariffs the Australian Tariff is still complex but not noticeably so by comparison with other developed countries.

Valuation for Duty

The assessment of value for duty is an important but neglected aspect of tariffs. About three-fourths of the rates of duty in the Australian Customs Tariff are *ad valorem* rates or variable rates (sliding-scale, composite, alternative or support value rates) which involve the calculation of monetary values for duty. The basis of Australian valuation is provided by Section 154 of the Customs Act:

> The value for duty of any goods shall be the sum of the following:
> (a) (i) the actual money price paid or to be paid for the goods by the Australian importer plus any special deduction, or
> (ii) the current domestic value of the goods, whichever is the higher; and
> (b) all charges payable or ordinarily payable for placing the goods free on board at the port of export.

The 'current domestic value' (c.d.v.) is defined as the 'amount for which the seller of the goods to the purchaser in Australia is selling or would be prepared to sell for cash, at the date of exportation of those goods, the same quantity of identically similar goods to any and every purchaser in the country of export for consumption in that country'. A 'special deduction' is defined as 'any discount or other deduction allowed to the Australian importer which would not ordinarily have been allowed to any and every purchaser at the date of exportation of an equal quantity of identically similar goods'.

There is supplementary provision for valuation by experts in cases when the collector doubts the accuracy of the declared value and the owner objects to the collector's assessment. The Minister may determine value for duty in cases where this is difficult because the goods are not sold for use in the country of production, or the goods are leased or have a royalty or are sold by or to agents or by subscription 'or are sold or imported in or under any other unusual or peculiar manner or conditions (of all which matters the Minister shall be the judge)'. There

---

[1] *Commonwealth Gazette*, 28 June 1971.

is an unusual clause relating to inland freight charges on goods of Canadian origin[2] as well as more standard provisions for seizure of goods, payment of cash securities, refunds, drawbacks and disputes.

Thus the principal feature of the Australian method of valuation is the use of an f.o.b. rather than a c.i.f. or landed cost basis of valuation. In this respect the Australian practice differs from that recommended in the Brussels Agreement.[3] Australia is one of only a very small number of countries that use an f.o.b. basis; the other substantial trading countries which do so are the US, Canada, New Zealand and South Africa. The United States Tariff Commission is holding hearings in 1972 on a simplification of the US tariff system including the possibility of adopting a c.i.f. basis of valuation. Because of the prevalence of *ad valorem* and variable rates in the Australian Tariff[4] the choice and administration of the system of valuation may significantly affect aggregate imports and the average level of protection as well as the imports of individual commodities.

[2] As part of the Trade Agreement with Canada the inland freight charges included in the value for duty are not greater than the freight that could have been charged if the goods had been forwarded from the point of origin to the nearest point of exit in Canada. This assists Canadian carriers to compete with US carriers in transporting the goods to the port of exportation.

[3] *The Brussels Agreement Concerning Dutiable Value*, 15 December 1950. The Australian system of valuation dates back to the introduction of tariffs levied by the Commonwealth Government following the formation of the federation of States in 1901 and before that to the States' systems. From 1901 to 1922 the only method of valuation was the 'fair market value' of the goods plus charges for placing the goods free on board at the port of export plus 10 per cent. The 10 per cent was intended to cover roughly the average cost of freight, insurance and other charges from the place of export to the place of landing in Australia. These conventions, like past and present practices in the USA and Canada, can be traced to early British colonial practice; see R. E. Smith, *Customs Valuation in the United States* (Chicago University Press, Chicago, 1948), pp. 39-40, 329.

In 1922 the alternative selling price valuation was added and the 'fair market value' was changed to 'current domestic value'.

Following the 25 per cent devaluation of the Australian pound in relation to sterling in 1931, the Exchange Adjustment Act provided for a deduction from duty on goods on which there was a British Preferential Tariff. This deduction was normally equal to 12½ per cent of the amount of duty. This had the effect of increasing the preferences to British goods.

In 1947 a combination of changes was made to the system which essentially left the rates unchanged. Previously, the value for duty had been calculated in United Kingdom currency but Australian notes and currency had been accepted in payment of the duties. Thus, the apparent tariff rates were higher than the real rates applying to all goods and this was considered a handicap to Australia in tariff negotiations. Therefore Australian currency values were substituted for UK currency values for value for duty. To compensate for the 25 per cent increase in values for duty, the 10 per cent margin was abolished and all *ad valorem* rates were reduced by about 12 per cent; to avoid small fractional rates of duty all reduced rates were adjusted to the nearest 2½ per cent. Finally, all exchange adjustments were incorporated in the tariffs.

[4] In 1970-71 41 per cent by value of the goods cleared through customs were admitted under an *ad valorem* rate, 7 per cent at other than *ad valorem* rates and 51 per cent were free of duty. These percentages were calculated from Commonwealth Bureau of Census and Statistics figures in 'Customs Clearances at Specified Rates of Duty; Australia, 1970-71', Canberra, 15 December 1971.

'Current domestic values' are values in the country of export. Australia does not, therefore, use domestic values in the importing country, a practice which is prohibited by GATT[5] and widely condemned. The current domestic value is intended to measure the price to all purchasers for consumption in the country of export. In practice, the value is most commonly derived from the invoice figures of current domestic value and selling price. Only about 2 per cent by value of all imports have their current domestic values calculated by direct inquiry by the Department of Customs and Excise in the country of export. The Australian practice conforms with GATT Article VII. The 'actual value' required by this Article is 'the price, at which, at a time and place determined by the legislation of the country of importation, such or like merchandise is sold or offered for sale in the ordinary course of trade under fully competitive conditions'. This has been interpreted to mean either a particular exporter's price or the general price of like merchandise and the 'actual value' may be represented by the invoice price plus any abnormal discount or other deduction from the ordinary competitive price.[6]

There are disadvantages to the Australian system. Customs Department representatives stationed in London, New York, Tokyo and New Zealand are mainly concerned with appraising the current domestic value of exports to Australia and inquiries into these values must be carried out in other countries from time to time. It is often difficult to obtain the co-operation of manufacturers in some countries and the valuations must necessarily be arbitrary. Exporters and importers sometimes do not know the c.d.v. and therefore may not know the duty which they will have to pay, and the onus is on the importer to declare the true value of the imported good. The dual basis also makes the invoice and other documents more complex.

The Australian Government is presently considering changing to the Brussels definition of value. This recognises only one definition of value, the 'normal price' which is 'the price which can be obtained at the time the tariff is due by a sale of goods in the free market to an independent seller'. It is therefore the price of the particular article exported. It includes international insurance and freight. This system would be administratively simpler than the present Australian one because it would involve only one valuation and this could be established from the landed cost in Australia. In addition, the Brussels definition would seem to allow a more flexible determination than the complicated but more rigid dual system operated currently. Under the present system the selling price is less than the current domestic value in most cases where they

---

[5] GATT Article VII (2) (a). The outstanding example is the American Selling Price used for benzenoid chemicals in the US.
[6] GATT, *Basic Instruments and Selected Documents*, vol. IV, pp. 12-13, 65.

differ and on average c.d.v. is about 5 per cent higher than the selling prices.[7] This provides some evidence that a change in valuation alone would lower the levels of protection since the Brussels 'normal price' is roughly equivalent to the selling price (ignoring for the moment the second question of the costs of international insurance and freight). However, the change would not result in lower valuations generally and therefore lower protection, as many Australian manufacturers believe.[8] The government would not change the method of valuation alone. There would almost certainly be changes in rates designed to leave the tariff essentially unchanged, as in the 1947 changes to valuation and the 1971 Tariff Simplification. With a c.i.f. basis the rates would be reduced, presumably on the basis of calculated c.i.f./f.o.b. margins for groups of commodities obtained from the quarterly sample of imports and other sources. Moreover, the Tariff Board could hear any complaints.

On the other hand, there are factors which may induce the government not to change the present system. First, with a c.i.f. basis, the rates based on value would have to be changed as noted above. The change from an f.o.b. to a c.i.f. valuation would have another longer-term effect. It would increase the duty paid on all dutiable goods whose tariff is based on a value for duty which come from the United Kingdom, the EEC and some other countries relative to the duty paid on exports from those countries which are closer and have lower unit freight costs. The present system in Australia, and the system operated before 1947 with the 10 per cent margin for all imports from all sources, have generally favoured the United Kingdom and other distant suppliers compared to the Brussels system. This effect has been used in the past in Australia as a justification for retaining the present f.o.b.-based system but it is doubtful that loyalty to the United Kingdom or historic ties are relevant to the choice today. (It would be possible to adjust all *ad valorem* rates so that United Kingdom exporters did not on the average have to pay higher duty because of the change in method of valuation. They would still be adversely affected by the lower duty paid by imports from sources with lower freight costs. Moreover, this change would imply an overall decrease in the level of protection. This is an unlikely outcome.) Another argument used in favour of the f.o.b. basis is that a change to the c.i.f. basis which left the average duty paid for groups of commodities unchanged would increase the duty paid on commodities imported into some Australian ports.

There is an important economic aspect of the change from an f.o.b. to a c.i.f. valuation that has not received attention in Australia. An

---

[7] In approximately 90 per cent of invoices the selling price and c.d.v. are the same.
[8] Committee for Economic Development of Australia, *Non-Tariff Distortions of Trade* (CEDA, 1969), p. 8.

importer chooses to import a standardised commodity from one source rather than from another potential source because the landed duty-paid cost of the former is less than the latter. But it is the landed cost including international freight and insurance but *excluding duty* which is the social opportunity cost to the country. When the tariff is levied on the foreign price of a commodity but not on the international freight and insurance the private cost to the importer may be lower for one source while the landed cost excluding duty is lower for the import from the second source. That is, an f.o.b.-based value for duty which does not tax the cost of landing the good in Australia may distort the choice of country of origin of imports and result in the importing country paying more in terms of scarce foreign exchange than it would under the c.i.f.-based valuation. This is a source of welfare loss that is exactly analogous to Vinerian trade diversion in the context of a customs union or free trade arrangement.[9] All costs of international freight and insurance should be included, even though they may differ for delivery to different domestic ports, as they represent real costs to the economy. In the valuation case the distortion comes about because of differences in the margins for international freight and insurance[10] rather than differences in the *ad valorem* rates themselves as under preferential tariffs or free trade arrangements. A hypothetical example is given in Table 3.1.[11] The incidence of this diversion to higher-cost foreign

---

[9] The case of valuation differs from that of forming a free trade arrangement in that there is no equivalent to the trade creation that also occurs with a free trade arrangement and offsets the cost of trade diversion unless duties are reduced overall or foreign prices increase with the amounts supplied to Australia.

These basic features of different valuation were considered 30 years ago by Carl Kreider, 'Valuation for Customs', *Quarterly Journal of Economics*, November 1941, pp. 157-9. More recently, they have been considered by H. G. Johnson, 'A Note on Tariff Valuation Bases, Economic Efficiency, and the Effects of Preferences', *Journal of Political Economy*, August 1966, pp. 401-2; H. Giersch, 'The Trade Optimum', *International Economic Papers*, no. 7, 1957, pp. 156-84 and P. A. Diamond and F. Mitchell, 'Customs Valuation and Transport Choice', *Journal of International Economics*, February 1971, pp. 119-26.

[10] There is a possible counter-disadvantage of c.i.f.-based values for duty. (This was discussed by Smith, *Customs Valuation*, pp. 319-20 and Baldwin, *Nontariff Distortions*, pp. 138-9.) Under this system importers take into account the duty on international freight and insurance as well as the cost of this freight and insurance in choosing the port of entry. They may choose a port of entry which minimises their cost of delivering the good to an internal city but this port may not minimise the social cost excluding the duty of delivering the good. This arises because there is a tax on international transport and insurance but not on internal freight and insurance. While this may be a relevant consideration for a country such as the United States, which has several ports of entry for major inland cities, it is not important for Australia because more than 80 per cent of the population lives in port cities.

[11] This example is adapted from a table in Kreider, 'Valuation for Customs', p. 158. Kreider recognised this source of trade diversion. However, the figures in his table are unrepresentative since they depend on transport costs from one country which are 100 per cent of the f.o.b. price.

This table assumes that the domestic costs of production are unchanged by the changes in the quantities that may be produced under the two systems and that the foreign supplies of the good are perfectly elastic. It also ignores the consumption cost due to the duty.

34 *Non-Tariff Distortions of Australian Trade*

Table 3.1 Landed duty-paid prices with f.o.b. and c.i.f. valuations $

	f.o.b.		c.i.f.	
	Country A	Country B	Country A	Country B
f.o.b. price	70	88	70	88
International freight and insurance	30	10	30	10
Foreign exchange cost	100	98	100	98
Tariff (20% of value for duty)	14	17·6	20	19·6
Delivered price (i.e. cost to importer)	114	<115·6	120	>117·6

sources increases mainly with inter-source differences in transport margins and with the height of tariffs.

When an f.o.b. valuation is combined with a multi-column tariff, as in Australia, the f.o.b. valuation may diminish or aggravate the occurrence of trade diversion due to tariff preferences. For example, if in the case above imports from country A pay a general rate of 20 per cent and those from country B pay a preferential rate of say 10 per cent, the choice of the private importer is again the socially correct one (since $98 + 9·8 = 107·8 < 114$). But if the country with the preferential rate is also the country with higher freight and insurance per unit of the commodity, both factors work to produce a diversion of trade towards the higher social cost source. This has been the Australian position with respect to the United Kingdom.

In view of the upward trend in freight costs per dollar of f.o.b. trade, these aspects of valuation deserve more attention than they have received. In Australia in 1970-71 the average margin of international freight and insurance for Australian imports was estimated to be 10·3 per cent of the value of imports.[12] This is almost as great as the total net duty collected as a percentage of the f.o.b. value of imports over the same period, which was 11·2 per cent (Table 3.2). The inclusion of international freight and insurance costs in the value for duty would make only a small change to the duty paid. For example if the rate of duty is 20 per cent and the international freight and insurance are 10 per cent of the f.o.b. price, the increase in duty would be slightly less than 2 per cent of the c.i.f. value. Moreover, as noted, the change to a new basis of valuation would entail some compensating reduction in the rates of duty. The importance of the basis of valuation is that the substantial differences in freight and insurance per unit of import between countries of origin for many of the commodities imported into Australia reinforce the preferences to the United Kingdom and increase the trade diversion to higher cost sources.

[12] This average was computed from the quarterly surveys of imports conducted by the Bureau of Census and Statistics for the first three quarters of 1970-71.

The Complex Structure of the Australian Tariff

This section considers aspects of the Australian Customs Tariff which make it difficult for importers to ascertain the duty that may be levied on an imported good or which may be used to increase the duty over that which an importer may reasonably have concluded from a reading of the Tariff. These same aspects also increase the cost to the Commonwealth Government of administering the Tariff.

In this regard the most notable feature of the Australian Customs Tariff is its complexity. It is relatively complex because of the large number of tariff items, the multi-column tariff structure and, especially by comparison with most other developed countries, the several types of duties and types of rates and the large number of tariff items with composite and/or alternative rates. These complexities are considered in turn below. Another factor which makes it difficult to find the rate applicable to a particular import is that the rates and the interpretation of these rates are contained in several different sources. Since December 1970 the Department of Customs and Excise has published an 'Annotated Tariff' which sets out the rates of duty on goods imported into Australia as they are specified in the five schedules of the Customs Tariff as amended at the time. For later reference, the First Schedule is the basic schedule that provides the tariff classification for all goods and their normal rates of duty. The Second Schedule provides for concessional rates of duty, mainly through by-laws. The Third and Fourth Schedules list supplementary primage duties and support value duties respectively on certain goods. The Fifth lists the special rates under various Agreements applied to certain goods from specified countries. The Customs Tariff also contains annotations and other notes. It is a large two-volume publication of about 2,500 pages. Even this Annotated Tariff is not sufficient. In many cases importers must have recourse to Customs General Orders, or the Consolidated By-Law Reference Book and other departmental and legislative sources for full information.

In the last few years there have been some developments which have reduced in certain respects the complexity of the tariff: for example, the Tariff Simplification noted on p. 28 and the elimination of many primage duties. On the other hand, there have been other developments which have added new or more complications to the tariff; for example, the introduction of preferences for the developing countries in 1966, the introduction of support values for selected chemicals in 1967 and the extension of preferences to New Zealand under the New Zealand-Australia Free Trade Agreement of 1965. Overall these developments over the last six years or so have probably resulted in some net reduction in the complexity of the Australian Tariff but it must still be regarded as a most complex tariff structure.

Within tariff items or sub-items the Australian Tariff is more complex than those of most developed countries because different duties are commonly levied on imports within the same tariff items according to the type of import and country of origin of the import. There are three general types of imports: 'normal', 'government' or 'by-law'. 'Normal duties' comprise the bulk of duties listed in the Customs Tariff and produce over 90 per cent of the total duty collected. They specify the duty applicable to imports of goods within a tariff item and from a particular source. Government imports are goods imported by or for the use of the Commonwealth Government. Government imports enter duty-free. By-law rates are concessional rates. By-law imports are mostly admitted duty-free but about a quarter of them enter at rates of 5, 7½ and 12½ per cent (see Table A.1). The by-law provisions of the tariff legislation are peculiar to Australia[13] though most developed countries have a tariff structure that produces a similar effect in allowing entry duty free or at very low rates for materials, components and capital equipment which are not produced in the country concerned.[14] By-laws are examined more thoroughly on pp. 42-51 as a form of tariff-making by administrative decree. The totals for each type of import in 1970-71 are given in Table 3.2.[15]

There are other less important types of duties. There are support value duties on some chemicals. In addition to ordinary customs duty a primage duty of 10 per cent, and in a few cases 5 per cent, is levied on some imports, mainly luxury items. (These items are set out in the Third Schedule to the Customs Tariff.) These duties were originally introduced in 1930 as a revenue duty but on many items they provide additional protection to Australian manufacturers of the same or substitute goods. Goods which are the produce or manufacture of New Zealand, Fiji, Papua New Guinea and a few Pacific Islands are exempt from primage duties, where applicable. Primage duties are being steadily reduced. Whenever the Tariff Board receives a reference in which

[13] Canada has similar provisions but these are used on a much smaller scale.
[14] The use of by-laws is one of the early recognitions by the tariff authorities in Australia of the essential notion of effective protection, namely, that tariffs on materials and inputs used in the production of a commodity represent an implicit tax on the production of the commodity. Another recognition is in the use of bounties in lieu of tariffs to provide protection for goods which are used by other manufacturers as important inputs. A third example is the exemption of imports not produced domestically from anti-dumping duties. This exemption dates back to the Customs Tariff (Industries Preservation) Act 1921, and the by-laws and bounties pre-date this Act. All three devices increased the effective protection of the user industries.
[15] It may be noted here that the Australian statistics of imports on a tariff item basis do not enable one to calculate the amount of duty collected from many types of duties; for example, it is not possible to find out how much duty was collected from temporary duty, or the amount remitted under drawback, or manufacturing in bond. This is basic information for any analysis of these types of duties. Nor are there any statistics of imports of commodities for many features of the tariff; for example, imports cleared at Preferential rates or imports under the New Zealand-Australia Free Trade Agreement, or quantitative restrictions.

Table 3.2 Customs clearances and duty collected, by type of duty, 1970-71

	Customs clearances $ million f.o.b.	Customs duty collected* $ million	Customs duty/ clearances (%)
Government imports	145·5	0	0
By-law imports	1,184·3	21·3	1·8
Normal imports	2,774·0	482·4	17·4
Total imports	4,103·8	503·7	12·3†

* No deductions have been made for drawbacks and refunds. These totalled approximately $44·2 million in 1970-71.

† When an adjustment is made for drawbacks and refunds, the average rate of duty on all imports is 11·2 per cent of the f.o.b. value of imports.

Source: CBCS, 'Customs Duty Collected at Specified Rates of Duty, 1970-71' and 'Customs Clearances at Specified Rates of Duty: Australia, 1970-71', Canberra, 15 December 1972.

some goods are subject to primage, the Board recommends the abolition of these duties or their incorporation in the normal duties. Primage duties collected $7·1 million in 1970-71. This was 1·3 per cent of all duties collected and they are a nuisance to importers since the importer must fill another column on each invoice for these duties. However, the Department of Trade and Industry has resisted their total abolition since they can and have been used in multilateral tariff negotiations by Australia as a form of concession which does not involve a substantial reduction in the level of protection.

Even less important are deferred customs duties, which are duties recommended by the Tariff Board for application after a specified lapse of time. They are a form of anticipatory protection. Temporary duties and anti-dumping duties are a more important part of the tariff structure but these are discussed later.

Given the tariff item or sub-item and the type of duty, there is still the complication that normal duties, and to a lesser extent, by-law duties are commonly differentiated by the country of origin.[16] The Australian Tariff is basically a two-column tariff with the Preferential

[16] By-law preferences are noted briefly in chapter 3. It should be noted that there are preferences on tariffs other than those applying to normal and by-law imports. Canada and New Zealand effectively receive preferential treatment in the area of dumping duties because dumping duties cannot be imposed on imports from these two countries without consultation. New Zealand exports to Australia are exempt from primage where applicable. The Australian method of valuing imports f.o.b. has given a preference to the United Kingdom and other countries whose exports to Australia pay higher freight per commodity unit. This feature was discussed on pp. 32-4. The United Kingdom also receives preference in Commonwealth and State Government purchases (see p. 78). Some of the sales taxes discriminate by country of origin (see p. 89).

tariffs (PT) applying to imports from the United Kingdom, Canada, New Zealand, Ireland and Papua New Guinea and the General rates (GT) applying to imports from other countries.[17] In addition, certain goods which are the produce or manufacture of Ceylon, Malta and other former colonies or protectorates of the United Kingdom receive a preference. There are special preferences granted to imports from New Zealand under the 1965 New Zealand-Australia Free Trade Agreement applying to goods listed in Schedule A of the Agreement.[18] Finally there are preferences on selected products to the group of developing countries,[19] and to Canada under the Trade Agreement with Canada.

Historically the most important of these preferences are the Preferential rates. These carry over from the former British Preferential tariffs. Under the United Kingdom-Australia Trade Agreement the minimum margin of preference is $7\frac{1}{2}$ per cent on UK goods subject to rates of duty of 10 per cent or less and 10 per cent on UK goods subject to rates of duty greater than 10 per cent, but the actual margins still exceed these in some cases. They have steadily declined in importance as the preference margins have been reduced in the post-war period[20] but are still in 1972 the most important preferences to Australia, both as an importing and preference-granting country and as an exporter receiving preferences in the UK. It is not possible to measure the margin of preference for items to which the preferences currently apply but in 1970-71 the average rates of duty paid on all private normal imports from the UK was $22 \cdot 3$ per cent compared to $25 \cdot 0$ per cent and $28 \cdot 2$ per cent respectively for the US and Japan, which are Australia's two main suppliers of imported goods. These averages are affected by the commodity mix of imports from each country but they reflect also the preferences to the UK. Over all commodity imports the average duty on imports from the UK was $9 \cdot 9$ per cent compared to $10 \cdot 0$ per cent and $20 \cdot 2$ per cent respectively for the US and Japan. This arises because a much higher proportion of UK goods came in as government and by-law imports than for the US and in particular for Japan. Preferences on rates of duty for normal imports from the UK will end some time after the British accession to the EEC in 1973.

[17] On 20 September 1972 the Minister for Trade and Industry announced that after the UK accession to the EEC in February 1973 all future Tariff Board reports and, presumably, actual changes to tariffs would list only one tariff unless there were special preferences with other countries.

[18] For an analysis of these preferences see the author's study, *New Zealand Manufacturing Production*, chapter V.

[19] For an analysis of these preferences see the author's paper, 'The Value of Tariff Preferences'.

[20] A sample carried out by the Department of Trade and Industry for the Vernon Committee found that for items in which the preferential rates were applicable to normal imports the average *ad valorem* equivalent preference margin fell from $13 \cdot 8$ per cent in 1951-52 to $10 \cdot 6$ per cent in 1961-62; *Report of the Committee of Economic Enquiry*, vol. II, pp. 1057-8.

On the other hand the preferences granted to New Zealand have been considerably extended since the Agreement with New Zealand was signed in 1965 and Schedule A has been extended several times since after annual bilateral negotiations on items proposed for addition to the Schedule. However, these preferences still apply to only slightly more than 60 per cent of Australian imports from New Zealand, which represents in turn only 2 per cent of Australia's total imports.[21]

Preference margins, where applicable, vary considerably among the commodities and among the different groupings of preference-receiving countries. The result of this multi-column structure is that imports of goods within a tariff item or sub-item from different sources are admitted into Australia at different rates of duty. There are many tariff items within which normal imports are admitted at four different rates depending on the country of origin. Another result of the multiplicity of rates is that imports of a certain commodity, as defined by a tariff item or sub-item, from the one country may be subject to three or more different rates depending on whether they are government, by-law or normal imports and on whether they satisfy the rules of origin for any preferential rates.[22]

In addition to the complexities of classification, types of duty, and preferences, there are complications in the *type of rate*. Although most of the tariff rates are simple *ad valorem* or specific rates, there are sliding-scale rates levied on some textile, machine and other products and some composite rates (rates having fixed and *ad valorem* components) on chemical, textile and other products.[23] Sliding-scale rates have been used where the prices of commodities vary markedly among the countries of origin or over time. Composite duties have been recommended when the local industry is found to have a basic cost disability, perhaps in relation to prices of its raw materials, and, in addition, a further disability which increases with the quality and price of particular grades of good produced. Both the composite and sliding-scale duties are instruments of protection which impose much higher duties when these duties are expressed as *ad valorem* equivalents on cheaper imports.

There are some 'content plans' which are designed to increase the Australian content of production of the goods so protected.[24] These

---

[21] See Lloyd, *New Zealand Manufacturing Production*, chapter V.

[22] Tariff quotas provide another reason for multiple rates applying to imports from the same country.

[23] In a survey conducted for the Vernon Committee, the Department of Customs and Excise found that in February 1964, 556 out of a total of 3,476 tariff items at that time had composite or a'ternative rates; *Report of the Committee of Economic Enquiry*, vol. II, p. 1046. Most of these still exist.

[24] There is also an Australian content required for the payment of the bounties on agricultural tractors produced in Australia and machine tools (see pp. 96-7), for some sales tax exemptions such as those applied to fruit juices (see p. 88), for excise duties on spirits, and for television programs under the Broadcasting Act.

are small in number but they include the very large motor vehicles and petroleum industries. They are associated with special by-laws in return for specified performances. Thus, imported tobacco leaf used in the manufacture of cigarettes and other tobacco products is allowed concessional by-law entry, provided prescribed quantities of locally-grown leaf are incorporated in the manufactured products. At present the prescribed usage of Australian leaf is 50 per cent. For crude oil and distilled petroleum products penalty rates of duty are levied on imports if the refining companies do not absorb their allotted quota of indigenous crude oil. As a part of the motor vehicle industry scheme entry of imported components used in the manufacture of motor vehicles is allowed at concessional by-law rates if the local content of the complete vehicle amounts to one of the percentages specified in one of the five vehicle manufacturing plans presently operating. There are similar arrangements for peanut oil and brined cherries. In the case of coffee, by-law entry is allowed to persons who during each coffee production year obtain at least 30 per cent of their total requirements of raw or kiln dried coffee for roasting purposes directly from Papua New Guinea. These plans are subject to the objections that they yield high and variable rates of effective protection to the products contained in goods concerned. They are an important feature of Australian tariffs because of the importance of domestic production of automobiles, petroleum and petroleum products.

There are also circumstances in which the rates of duties levied on particular imports may be changed without a change in the Customs Tariff itself. These are considered in the following section.

One aspect of the complexity of the Australian tariffs is that some complicated features of the Australian case have arisen in response to earlier differences in rates of duty. For example, by-law entry at concessional rates arose because of the high rates of duty on some commodities used as inputs in other domestic industries. When the UK preferences were added it was necessary to introduce preferences for by-law imports as well as for normal imports to ensure that the margins of UK preferences were not eroded by the by-law system. Similarly, the complex directions operated by the Department of Customs and Excise relating to goods imported in concentrate form, or as parts, or separate articles, or goods which are substitutes or imitations for other goods carrying a different tariff, all become important because of the substantial differences in rates of duty.[25]

As a final comment one should note that the complexities of the large number of tariff items and sub-items and the great variance among

[25] The regulations and interpretations of these and other features of the Australian Tariff are set out in the Department of Customs and Excise annotated publication, *Annotated Customs Tariff*.

duties on items in the Tariff make it extremely difficult for the Tariff Board itself (which has the main responsibility for examining protection by the Customs Tariff) and for economists analysing the Australian Tariff to understand how the pattern of resource allocation has been affected by the Customs Tariff.[26] This dispersion has been borne out by the Tariff Board's recent calculations of effective protection for thirty-one manufacturing industries. Moreover, there is a great dispersion of effective rates of protection within most industries.[27] Under these circumstances it is difficult to predict the effects of any contemplated change in the tariffs affecting one industry on the level and pattern of production in that industry. The effects of tariffs on output of one industry depend on the tariffs on the inputs in the industry and on the scale of effective tariffs in other industries. Hence, the basic policy of designing 'made-to-measure' tariffs that will give the desired protection to the one industry or sub-industry being considered by the Board (given the existing tariff structure in the rest of the economy) may be defeated by subsequent changes in the tariffs affecting other industries with which it competes for scarce supplies of managerial, technical and other labour or by changes in the tariffs on the outputs of other industries which are inputs of the former industries. (The next section pursues this aspect.) In a similar way the various systems of preferences described above conflict with and partially neutralise each other.[28]

Tariff-fixing by Administration

The department which administers the Tariff, the Department of Customs and Excise, is not authorised to alter the tariffs on various items fixed in the schedules to the Customs Tariff, even in cases where the desire for a change has come about purely because of the development of a new product or material which makes the existing tariff uncertain or redundant. Changes in the Customs Tariff are made by Act, normally after an inquiry and report by the Tariff Board. However, there are three areas in which the administering department may change the tariff applicable to a particular item or items. These are the areas of by-law imports, manufacturing in licensed warehouses and substitute notices. Of the three by-law imports are by far the most important. We shall also consider the provisions in the Tariff for temporary protection which can be imposed without further legislation. (There are two other

---

[26] This difficulty is enhanced when one attempts to calculate the net effects of the Australian Tariff and other explicit and implicit subsidies (differential transport and tax concessions, etc.) on the pattern of production in Australia.
[27] See the Tariff Board's rough calculations of the rates within industries; *Annual Report, 1969-70*, Appendix 2, Table 4.
[28] For an example of conflicts, see the author's article 'The Value of Tariff Preferences'.

areas of administrative authority to decide tariff rates which arise with particular traded goods. Dumping duties are imposed without specific legislative authority for each duty but, like temporary duties, these expire after limited periods unless there is a Tariff Board inquiry and an amendment to the Tariff. There is also provision in the Tariff for drawback of duty on materials which are subsequently exported. Dumping duties and drawbacks are discussed in chapters 4 and 8 respectively.)

Australia's By-Law System

By-law imports are a very important part of the Customs Tariff in Australia. (There are also by-laws for some commodities subject to excise duty which are based on the same principle as by-laws for imports and raise similar issues.) Essentially they provide for entry at concessional rates of duty, either 0 or $7\frac{1}{2}$ per cent, for imported capital equipment and raw materials which are not competitive with Australian produced goods. (There are also by-laws which provide duty-free entry for goods imported by or for the use of religious, charitable and other institutions and persons. Since 1968 by-laws have also been used in certain circumstances in preference to customs drawback for goods for export. These by-laws for export are examined on pp. 119-20.) Before some of the effects of by-laws on the level and structure of protection of import-competing goods can be considered, it is necessary to outline the ways in which goods are admitted under by-law.

The original and primary purpose of by-laws was to provide relief to manufacturers from protective duties on imported machinery and other inputs when such relief is not detrimental to an Australian industry. By-law provisions in the Australian Tariff date from the first Customs Tariff Act 1902.[29] Since then the scope of by-laws has been considerably widened and rationalised on the basis of general criteria. Recently the administrative procedures have been simplified, especially by the introduction of the Supplementary By-law Advice List in 1966 listing the by-law determinations which were used regularly and did not

[29] Actually there were similar provisions in the States' Legislation before Federation.
The Customs Tariff 1902 introduced duties on most imports into the Commonwealth with the exception of 'special exemptions' for materials, components and parts used in the production of goods, which were not 'commercially available' from within Australia. These exemptions were specified in the Customs Tariff itself. There was also provision for 'general exemptions' for 'any machinery, machine tool or parts thereof' which were not 'reasonably manufactured within the Commonwealth' under by-law after Parliamentary approval. These two types of provisions are the ancestors of the by-laws relating to certain goods which are specified in the main First Schedule and those generally provided for under the Second Schedule. The present criteria of 'suitably equivalent' and 'reasonably available' were introduced in 1957. The last general change was in April 1970 when the additional criterion of specified end-uses or 'other essential purposes' was deleted from the Customs Act.

have to be decided on an individual basis. However, the by-law system is still complex.[30]

Concessional rates of duty under by-laws are permitted for goods prescribed by the Minister under the authority of Sections 271 to 273 of the Customs Act. General descriptions of goods which may be eligible for by-law rates are given in the Second Schedule of Customs Tariff which also prescribes the special rates of duty lower than those normally applicable for these goods. There are by-laws for imported goods for the use of the Commonwealth Government, the UN and international agencies, personal effects, philanthropic purposes, theatrical costumes and other special purposes. The most important by-laws, and the only ones to be considered here, are those relating to goods imported for use by Australian producers. There is separate provision for by-laws for vehicle components in the Second Schedule. There are also by-law provisions in the First Schedule of the Tariff. These apply to sub-items, paragraphs, or sub-paragraphs rather than whole items and provide for special circumstances such as where the by-law rates are other than 0 or $7\frac{1}{2}$ per cent, or where the admission under by-law is not qualified by the 'suitably equivalent' and 'reasonably available' criteria. These have usually been incorporated in the Tariff upon a suggestion of the Tariff Board in its report on a reference whereas by-laws under the Second Schedule provisions are generally of departmental origin.

The majority of by-laws are approved under the criteria relating to Items 19 and 20 of the Second Schedule. Item 19 of the Second Schedule states that goods 'being goods a suitable equivalent of which that is the produce or manufacture of Australia is not reasonably available' may be imported under by-law. Item 20 includes the phrase 'or the produce or manufacture of the United Kingdom'.

A by-law is a legal means of reducing or eliminating the customs duty paid in respect of imported goods complying with certain prescribed conditions or criteria. Many by-laws have already been prescribed as effective for an indefinite period and goods falling within these by-laws are automatically eligible for by-law admission. These are known as standing by-laws. Others are prescribed for a limited period. These are known as limited period by-laws. By-law provisions are available to any importer[31] and, unless otherwise specified, there is no limit to

---

[30] It is not surprising that the Labor Party spokesman on tariffs, Dr Cairns, spoke during a Parliamentary debate on a statement by the Minister for Trade and Industry of 'by-law operations with which I cannot make myself familiar', *CPD*, H. of R., 19 September 1972, p. 1532.

[31] In the case of by-laws granted for the admission of imports into Australia from New Zealand which are part of the 'special arrangements' under Article 3:7 of the New Zealand-Australia Free Trade Agreement, the concessions may apply only to the parties to the arrangement. In these cases the Customs Tariff, in effect, gives the companies concerned a company tariff preference over their competitors. It is impossible for another Australian importer or user of the

the quantity of goods which may be entered under a by-law. The Minister may also make a determination that a by-law applies only to particular goods specified in the determination. These are *ad hoc* decisions which are valid for a specified period and may refer to a specific quantity of goods and may be issued to one importer.[32] By-laws and by-law determinations may be subject to conditions. These may include the collection of securities to ensure that the goods admitted under by-law will not be diverted to other end uses and thereby diminish the tariff protection of other locally-produced goods.

If no by-law is available to an importer of particular goods he may apply to the Department of Customs to have certain goods presented for admission under by-law. The Customs Act gives the power to make by-laws to the Minister but in practice, because of the volume of by-law applications, this power is delegated to certain officers of the By-Law Branch of the Department of Customs and Excise. In 1970-71 there were 20,247 applications for by-laws received by the department.[33] The department decides whether the application will be granted as an *ad hoc* determination or as a standing or limited period by-law or refused altogether. Subsequently, if an Australian manufacturer of goods admitted under by-law begins production, the manufacturer may apply to the department for cancellation of the by-law. The application will be investigated and, if it is found that a suitably equivalent good is reasonably available, the by-law provision would normally be cancelled.

By-law imports are mostly admitted at rates of 0 or $7\frac{1}{2}$ per cent. Under the most important item, Item 19, the rate of $7\frac{1}{2}$ per cent applies when there is a 'suitably equivalent' good 'reasonably available' from the United Kingdom but not Australia. In this case the import from the United Kingdom enters Australia at the special preferential rate of 0 per cent (free of duty) while imports from other sources pay the rate of $7\frac{1}{2}$ per cent.[34] When there is no 'suitably equivalent' good 'reasonably available' from either Australia or the United Kingdom Item 20 applies and imports from all sources enter free of duty. The by-law preferences accorded the United Kingdom are provided for in the United Kingdom-Australia Trade Agreement which was first reached

---

same product even to find out that a concession has been granted to a competitor. The author has criticised these arrangements in *New Zealand Manufacturing Production*, chapter V.

[32] From 1966 the standing by-laws under the First and Second Schedules of the Tariff were published in consolidated form in the Customs By-Laws book and more recently both by-laws and by-law determinations where practicable have been listed in the *Consolidated By-Law Reference* book.

[33] Department of Customs and Excise, *Review of Activities 1970-71* (Canberra, 1971), p. 27.

[34] On 19 September 1972, the Minister for Trade and Industry announced that as from 1 February 1973, the date of the UK accession to the EEC, all by-law imports will enter free of duty. This will end the UK preferences on by-laws. *CPD*, H. of R., 19 September 1972, pp. 1530-1.

in 1932 and renegotiated in 1957. Before the margin of preference in certain specified areas of the Customs Tariff may be waived for goods admitted under by-law, inquiries are made through the British Department of Trade and Industry to determine whether suitably equivalent goods are reasonably available from British manufacturers. While the final decision is the responsibility of the Australian Government, the margin of preference is normally not waived where there is British production. In 1970-71 the British Department of Trade and Industry made 5,693 inquiries in relation to by-laws. The Australia-Canada Trade Agreement also provides that before certain specified goods of foreign origin, that is, goods other than those qualifying for preferential treatment under the Agreement, may be admitted free of duty under by-law, it must be established that suitably equivalent goods are not reasonably available from Canadian production. Finally, there are by-laws which only apply to goods admitted from New Zealand.

By-law imports are important in the Customs Tariff. There are by-laws or by-law determinations for over 90 per cent of all BTN items, though it should be remembered that many apply only to sub-items, paragraphs, and sub-paragraphs of the appropriate item. While they are distributed throughout the chapters of the BTN there are relatively few in the first twenty chapters of the BTN which cover primary products. Total by-law imports, excluding government imports, amounted to 28·9 per cent of all imports clearances in 1970-71.

Excluding by-law imports for the government, and other special institutions, by-law imports are all capital goods: raw materials, components, parts or capital equipment. They are principally more sophisticated materials, components and equipment, which explains why over 95 per cent by value of the total by-law imports come from the developed countries, the great bulk of this coming from the more advanced industrial countries, the USA, the UK, the EEC and, more recently, Japan.[35]

Understanding by-law admissions hinges on an understanding of the interpretation of the twin criteria of 'suitably equivalent' and 'reasonably available'. These are applied to all imports under Items 19 and 20 of the Second Schedule and, although they are not in the main written into the by-law provisions of the First Schedule, these by-laws are administered where appropriate as if they were. The Department of Customs and Excise has insisted that 'it has neither been practicable nor desirable to precisely define the terms "suitably equivalent" and "reasonably available" '. In one of its publications the department gives this interpretation of 'suitably equivalent';[36]

[35] Some details of by-law imports by country of origin and rate of duty are given in the Commonwealth Bureau of Census and Statistics table 'Customs Clearances at Specified Rates of Duty: Australia, 1970-71' (Canberra, 15 December 1971).
[36] 'Functions', pp. 7-8.

It is not necessary for goods available from local production to be identical with an overseas product for them to be regarded as suitably equivalent. It is sufficient that they be competitive in the general sense of being:
— broadly comparable, or
— reasonably capable of performing the same function or fulfilling the same requirement.

Thus difference in composition or construction (e.g. of material) or marginal differences in performance or capacity (e.g. of machines) do not constitute grounds for by-law entry.

When considering the availability of Australian goods the department first considers the possible delivery of the goods and then if this is reasonable, the price. On the question of delivery they have said:[37]

. . . locally produced goods may still be regarded as being reasonably available even though they are not necessarily in stock for immediate delivery. Individual judgments have to be made on the urgency of the requirement and what constitutes a reasonable time from the receipt of the order to the date of delivery. However, in cases in which a well-established local manufacturer has a demonstrated capacity in a particular field, and has the technical know how (including perhaps licensing arrangements with overseas manufacturers), and can manufacture a machine which represents a logical extension of his existing range of production, then a suitable equivalent may be deemed to be reasonably available from Australian manufacture—even though there has been no previous local production.

On the question of price a number of factors are typically examined— the quality of the good, the conditions of purchase (is the sale dumped or subsidised?), servicing, the retail and ex-factory prices of the local good and other considerations. A locally-produced good may be considered 'reasonably available' though its price is 50 per cent or more higher than the imported good.

By-law entry may also be granted when there is a 'shortfall' of local production in relation to local demand because of seasonal fluctuations in output in primary industry or emergency situations in secondary industry. The basic principles used in determining these by-laws are that the protection to the local industry should not be eroded and all importers should share fairly in the by-law concessions.[38]

---

[37] 'Functions', p. 8. A similar interpretation of 'reasonably available' was noted on p. 17 above in relation to the import licensing of earthmoving, excavating and materials handling machinery.

[38] Ibid. Shortfall by-laws may also apply when concessional imports are not available from other countries; for example when New Zealand paper pulp is not available.

The first aspect of the effects of by-laws we shall discuss is the implications of the wide latitude for the discretion on the part of the administering department to grant and to cancel by-laws. Several criticisms of the by-law system as a case of tariff-fixing by administration are now considered. Controversy arises almost inevitably in the business community because of the double-edged nature of an alteration in a by-law admission. In each decision to cease by-law admission the importer and the user of the good admitted under by-law lose while the local manufacturer gains. (In many cases the importer and user are the same.) Therefore, any decision by the department must offend one of the parties. This double-edged nature of the by-law system is considered again below in discussing the effects of by-laws on the pattern of effective protection in Australia.

In the first place the criteria of equivalence and availability are quite arbitrary and seem to be interpreted broadly in favour of Australian manufacturers of the goods previously admitted under by-law. The notion of equivalence given above is much broader than the economists' concept of homogeneous goods or even close substitutes between which the buyer would have difficulty in choosing. The interpretation of availability to include Australian goods whose delivery lags may be considerably longer than the imported good or whose price (for roughly comparable goods) is significantly higher causes periodic irritation to Australian importers and users. In considering applications for a by-law admission the onus is on the importer to prove that an equivalent Australian good is not reasonably available. This proof is not easy for many importers, especially in view of the vagueness of the concepts of equivalence and availability. In considering cancellations of a by-law or determination the Department tends to rely on the declarations of the Australian producers, especially in cases of potential manufacture by a well-established manufacturer, though it sometimes consults technical experts in other government departments, universities, or research institutions to determine 'suitably equivalent'.

With this kind of tariff-fixing by administration the level of protection received by a producer of a good using a material or component admitted under by-law, or the protection available to an Australian company considering the production of a good presently admitted under by-law, may be changed merely by a change in the administering department's interpretation of what is 'suitably equivalent' or 'reasonably available', without any change in the costs or availability of Australian production. It has been alleged that the department adopted a 'hard line' in 1968, refusing the granting of by-law entry in instances where it was thought previous decisions indicated it would have been granted. The department did in this period begin the publication of a Supplementary By-Law Advice List (now included in the Consolidated

Customs By-Law References) comprising the by-law determinations which were used regularly and did not need to be decided on an individual basis. However, the department introduced these measures to reduce the administration of by-law determinations, which had been increasing rapidly. The department also shifted the onus of initiating investigations on cancellation of by-law entry to the local producer. Previously, the department had begun some inquiries into the possible cancellation of by-laws on its own initiative. It strenuously denies that there was any change in the criteria for by-law entry.

It has also been alleged that the department introduced at this time a new kind of 'front runner' policy which increased the protection to Australian producers. This applies to components only. According to this policy the department conducts a survey of an industry or group of products to determine what components are produced locally. The 'front runner' is the producer in the industry who uses the highest local content of materials and components. When another producer uses a component whose counterpart in the front runner's production is now considered to be reasonably available both components are no longer allowed entry at concessional rates under by-law, even though the local component is recognised not to be suitable for the model or unit produced by the other producer. This principle, but not apparently the name, was used before 1968 in situations where there is more than one local producer of a type of good. The cancellation of by-laws for a counterpart good, following the cancellation of a by-law for a component used by the front runner, is only made when the goods manufactured are directly competitive in their end-uses. It is intended to maintain horizontal equity in the levels of protection received by producers of goods competing in the same end-use by preventing one manufacturer from being handicapped when the particular component he uses becomes reasonably available within Australia and is no longer admitted at a by-law rate.

Another administrative feature of the system is the lack of formal procedures for calling or hearing evidence on by-law decisions, as with Tariff Board decisions relating to non-by-law tariff rates. All by-laws are published in full in the *Gazette* and notices of all determinations are also published. These notices list the kinds of goods, and the item of the First or Second Schedule to the Customs Tariff applying to the goods but they do not give the conditions of the by-law or the name of the importer. No reports on individual by-laws or determinations are published and no reasons for decisions are given. These are precluded by the very large number of decisions—over 40,000 in recent years. Moreover, proprietary information submitted in support of the granting or non-granting of a by-law cannot be disclosed to the importer who is a competitor. There is no formal appeal against decisions. Manufacturers and more frequently importers who are not satisfied with a decision do sometimes approach the department for a reconsideration. The department may qualify the decision; for example, it may reinstate for by-law entry some of the goods included in a cancellation. There is provision under Section 16(c) of the Tariff Board Act for referral of a by-law dispute to the Tariff Board but there have been only four such reports in the last ten years. Alternatively the producer may seek a reference to the Tariff Board for a review of substantive rates of duty affecting his production.

From the point of view of the economy as a whole, the main deficiencies of the by-law system stem not from the exercise of the administrative discretion given to the Department of Customs and Excise but from the principles which underlie the granting of by-laws and the resulting effects on the pattern of protection. The basic principle that has underlain all by-laws since their inception is that a domestic manufacturer should not have to bear the burden of higher costs due to tariffs when the tariffs are levied on goods not produced in Australia.

This principle has rarely, if ever, been challenged inside or outside Parliament. It has always been apparent that lowering the duties on inputs used by a producer increases what is nowadays called the effective protection available to this producer. What has not been appreciated is that it is the level of protection available to the producer *relative* to the levels of protection available for other alternative commodities, and not the absolute level, which determines the allocation of resources in the long-run.

In this context, we note first, all industries have access to and use by-law entry for some materials or components but because the proportion of inputs subject to by-laws differs among industries the system changes the relative effective protection available for industries and individual commodities. The effect of by-laws also differs among industries and commodities for a second reason. The reduction in tariffs following a granting of by-laws is quite arbitrary. By-laws enter at rates of 0 or $7\frac{1}{2}$ per cent but the substantive rates of duty that otherwise apply vary considerably. They may be, for example, 10 per cent or 70 per cent. Thus the reduction in tariffs upon the granting of a by-law entry and, conversely, the increase in the tariff upon the cancellation of a by-law entry, vary greatly and fortuitously according to the substantive tariff that happens to apply. In particular by-laws for automobile parts under the automobile assembly content plans occupy a large part of the administration of by-laws. Estimates on p. 147 confirm that by-law admissions substantially change the pattern of effective protection for Australian manufacturing industries.

The by-law system has a second important effect on levels of protection. It was noted earlier that when by-laws are cancelled the substantive rates of protection which apply are sometimes very high, especially under the 'dragnet' items of the Customs Tariff which determine duties on goods not listed under other tariff items. It has been complained that this results in excessively high rates of protection upon the cancellation of by-laws for such items.[39] When the department cancels a by-law under Items 19 or 20 of the Second Schedule it is required only to examine whether there is a good which is suitably equivalent and reasonably available from local producers. A manufacturer is not required to demonstrate that his production will be 'economic and efficient' as he must before the Tariff Board to gain an increase in protection by a change in the substantive rates of duty. However, the high rates of protection which result from the cancellation of by-laws are the fault of the high substantive rates specified in the Customs Tariff rather than of the by-law system. Moreover, many of the high rates will be reduced, it is hoped, as a result of the Tariff Board's 6-year systematic review of tariffs.

There is another difficulty when the Department of Customs and Excise decides on the tariffs which apply to a significant proportion of total imports at the time of entry while the Tariff Board recommend the substantive rates of duty that apply to normal (that is, non-by-law) imports. The Tariff Board (and the Special Advisory Authority) usually recommends rates of duty which are considered to be necessary for the goods under reference in the knowledge of the availability of the by-law provisions affecting imports of these goods. If the Board considers that the normal by-law criteria should not be applied to specific goods or classes of the goods under reference this is stated in its recommendations. Conversely, some by-laws have resulted from suggestions from Tariff Board reports on references. These include by-laws for some 'dragnet' (residual) item in the Tariff for goods not enumerated elsewhere in the Tariff. Thus there is no substantial conflict over the rates of protection for the goods under reference to the Tariff Board because of department decisions on by-laws for these same goods.

However, this dual, or if the Special Advisory Authority is involved treble, system of tariff-fixing means that some of the levels of protection recommended by the Tariff Board (and the Special Advisory Authority) may be altered subsequently by by-law decisions and the new levels of effective protection may not be reviewed by the Board for some years.

[39] *Report of the Committee of Economic Enquiry*, vol. II, pp. 1047-9. The Tariff Board itself, while deploring the adverse effects of high rates of protection due to the cancellation of by-laws when the substantive rates are high, seems to have accepted the historical Australian view that the payment of duty on capital inputs not produced in Australia is harmful; 'For example, in the absence of by-law entry for goods not produced locally, the competitive position of an industry which uses those goods will be unnecessarily impaired' (*Annual Report for Year 1968-69*, para 34). See also the *Annual Report for Year 1969-70*, para 61, and as an example from a Board report on a reference, *Report on Industrial Chemicals and Synthetic Resins*, 13 April 1966, pp. 30-2.

(On pp. 53-4 we discuss the relationships between the Tariff Board and the Special Advisory Authority.) Goods not previously admitted under by-law may later be admitted following a departmental decision. We have previously noted that when the department cancels a by-law under Items 19 or 20 of the Second Schedule, a manufacturer seeking the cancellation of a by-law is not required to demonstrate that his production will be 'economic and efficient' as he must before the Board to gain an increase in protection by a change in the substantive rates of duty. When considering an application to grant new by-laws the department does not take the effects of its decision on the level of effective protection of producers using these by-law goods except to maintain the equity of by-law treatment among users of components. The Tariff Board cannot foresee such changes. Indeed, much of the time these changes are not known because the particular by-law goods used by each industry and their importance in the costs of production are not known.

These changes in duties levied may go on for many years after the Tariff Board sets the nominal rates of protection for the goods produced and before these rates are again reviewed. They lead to continual changes in the levels of effective protection for many commodities and it is the levels of effective protection for individual commodities rather than the broad averages for industries which determine the allocation of resources and national output. The presence of the by-law system is even more serious in the context of the Tariff Board's proposed systematic review of the levels of protection given by the whole Tariff. It will greatly complicate and could seriously frustrate the Board's proposed rationalisation of the structure of protection. In chapter 10 some measurements are made of the effects of the by-law system on the pattern of effective protection and in chapter 12 alternatives to the by-law system are considered.

Manufacturing in Licensed Warehouses

Under Section 89 of the Customs Act there is provision for manufacturing to be carried out in licensed warehouses.[40] The advantage of this is that the duty paid on imported goods used in the manufacture of goods manufactured in licensed warehouses may be less than the duty normally payable. This may occur under Regulation 72 of the Customs

---

[40] Provision for manufacturing in bond was incorporated in the first Customs Act from similar practices which had applied in different States before Federation. It was intended as an important measure to encourage local manufacture. The initial provisions and interpretations of these are set out in the book by the first Permanent Head of the Department of Trade and Customs, H. N. P. Wollaston, *Customs Law and Regulations* (Sydney, 1904), pp. 56-7. See also the *CPD*, H. of R., 11 July 1901, pp. 2455-7 for a debate critical of this method of fixing tariff rates by administrative decision. Manufacturing in licensed warehouses is now much less important than it was in earlier years.

Regulations because the Department of Customs and Excise allows for waste of materials not incorporated in the manufactured article. Alternatively, such imports are dutiable at the British Preferential rate, if this rate is less than the duty normally payable or the rate with allowance for waste. Either concession may be substantial. Such manufacturing warehouses must be licensed with the Department of Customs and Excise and the goods which may be made under licensed warehouses are specified in the Customs Regulations. The goods manufactured may be sold for home consumption or exported.

The list of items is quite restricted, the main beneficiaries being manufacturers of piecegoods, telephone equipment and dressed timber. For producers of these goods the concession appears to be quite substantial but no statistics of the value of goods manufactured in licensed warehouses or of the duty reductions are compiled. A review of this provision by the Department of Customs and Excise in 1970 found that the duty waived was approximately $2 million annually in 1968-69 and 1969-70 of which one half applied to electrical equipment ultimately purchased by the Commonwealth Government. All of the concessions were for manufacturing for home consumption. Some of the electrical equipment may compete with equipment that is or could be imported duty-free by the Commonwealth Government but the notional duty feature of Commonwealth purchases (when applied) means that the duty reduction under manufacturing in licensed warehouses does result in increased protection for these Australian manufacturers.

Manufacturing in licensed warehouses has effects on the pattern of effective protection which are similar to those of by-laws. By lowering the cost of materials it raises the rates of effective protection for the user industries. This form of protection also resembles by-laws in another respect; it is founded on a misconception. In the case of manufacturing in licensed warehouses, the misconception is that it is unfair for a manufacturer to pay duty on that portion of a material which is not incorporated in the manufactured product; for example, waste timber or textile material. From a national economic point of view it does not matter whether an imported material is incorporated in the product or not. It must be paid for in foreign exchange which could have an alternative use. (A similar confusion concerning the f.o.b. valuation for duty which does not include the costs of transport and insurance was discussed on pp. 32-4.) This provision encourages the overuse of the materials and it raises the effective protection for user industries. It should be abolished and the effective protection of the user industries reviewed. The rates of effective protection can be maintained at the present levels, if this is considered desirable, by increasing the rate of nominal protection of the products or lowering the substantive tariffs on materials. This last option differs from the present provision in that all imports of the materials would pay duty, although at a lower rate than that now levied on the dutiable portion, and it would therefore discourage total imports and encourage reduced waste of the materials concerned.

Temporary Protection

With the removal of import licensing for all but a very small number of commodities in 1960 and the reliance on tariffs for protection and the impending renegotiation of the 1957 Trade Agreement with Japan, many Australian producers and their employees feared that increased competition from imports would jeopardise their incomes and jobs. Provision for temporary protection was introduced by amending the Tariff Board Act in September 1960 to empower the Minister for Trade to make a reference to a Deputy Chairman of the Tariff Board for a recommendation concerning temporary protection within 30 days, pending inquiry and recommendation from the Tariff Board under a normal reference. The industry had to make a *prima facie* case to the Minister that 'urgent action may be necessary to protect an Australian industry' before a reference was made to a Deputy Chairman.[41] If urgent action was considered necessary by a Deputy Chairman, he was required to report whether protection can appropriately be provided by a temporary duty and, if so, at what level. It was intended that temporary duties should be applied only when an industry could show that it would suffer serious injury from imports before the government could receive and act upon the normal reference report from the Tariff Board. The temporary duties automatically lapsed three months after the Minister received the final report of the Board.

This scheme was extended in May 1962 by empowering the Minister to appoint one or more Special Advisory Authorities (SAAs) to undertake an inquiry and report to the Minister whether urgent action be taken to protect an Australian industry, pending report from the Tariff Board on long-term protection as previously. The amendment also explicitly allowed the SAA to recommend temporary protection by means of a temporary duty or, 'if it cannot be so provided' by means of a temporary restriction of these goods, or both. All SAA hearings are in private, unlike those of the Tariff Board. The SAA is required only to consider whether urgent action is necessary to protect an existing industry. It is the task of the Tariff Board, and not the SAA, to consider whether the industry should or should not receive a higher level of

---

[41] No criterion of injury or threatened injury is stated. The Act does not even state that the injury or threatened injury which makes urgent action necessary must be 'not insubstantial' as in the case of tentative and permanent anti-dumping action (see p. 58).

long-term protection.[42] However, there are other conflicts. It normally takes the Tariff Board at least 18 months to complete its report on a reference previously considered by the Special Advisory Authority and several months more before the Minister acts upon its report. That is, temporary protection for more than two years may be given to industries which the Tariff Board considers did not warrant this protection. Moreover, some Tariff Board decisions to reduce duties have been followed by the imposition of temporary duties which restored the previous level of protection.[43] The imposition of temporary duties then means the Board must reconsider protection for the goods concerned.

It has recently been suggested that the SAA function be transferred back to the Tariff Board where it was originally during the period 1960 to 1962. This would reduce the conflict noted above though the different purpose of temporary protection would still lead to temporary tariff changes. This change has been opposed by some industry representatives.[44] In any event, temporary protection has received relatively more attention than the small number of commodities concerned and the shorter duration of temporary duties or restrictions deserve. Temporary protection is much less important than other tariffs such as by-laws and content plans, or than producer subsidies, though it has been important to a few producers, notably the makers of synthetic yarns.

Substitute Notices

Under Section 23 of the Customs Tariff the Minister for Customs and Excise may declare that specified goods are substitutes for or imitations of other dutiable goods and must therefore pay the same rates of duty. Of two tariff items and, therefore, two rates of duty, the higher is always chosen. The Annotated Customs Tariff contains a list of all substitutes and imitations and the goods for which they are substitutes or imitations. These declarations do not change the tariff classification, only the rates of duty. Notices of substitutes or imitations are a reserve administrative power that is used either to prevent customs evasion or to make effective the level of protection on some item which may be defeated by the presence of some substitute or imitation entering at a lower rate under a different item or sub-item. They are less frequently used than they were. The total number of such notices applying in the last few years has usually been less than twenty and they are now unimportant.

[42] The Vernon Committee recommended a clearer distinction be drawn between temporary and permanent protection; *Report of the Committee of Economic Enquiry*, vol. I, p. 397.

[43] For example, the SAA Report on *Industrial Radiographic Equipment*, 5 November 1970.

[44] Australian Industries Development Association (AIDA), *Bulletin*, June 1972, pp. 11-12.

4 Dumping and Support Value Duties

Duties to discourage dumping are not considered to be undesirable non-tariff instruments by GATT and most countries, provided they are properly used. Indeed the GATT regards them as necessary to enforce practices of fair trading among countries. Yet, we shall see that this is a curious case of an instrument which is condoned by GATT, subject to certain rules of application, but which usually harms both the importing and the exporting countries affected.

Dumping Duties and Procedures

Anti-dumping legislation in Australia dates back to the Australian Industries Preservation Act of 1906. The scope of activities covered by the legislation has been steadily widened. In 1957 amendments to the Act provided, for the first time, for action against dumping which injured the trade of a third country with Australia and for countervailing duties. The Customs Tariff (Dumping and Subsidies Act) of 1961 added the highest export price to a third country as another criterion of normal value and widened the definition to include dumping which hinders the establishment of an industry. This revision followed the abolition of most import licensing controls in 1960. The additional criterion of normal value was intended to handle adequately dumping from countries where cost or price information is not available, principally the communist bloc countries. The Customs Tariff (Dumping and Subsidies Act) 1965, introduced provisions against sales dumping and 'package deals'. It is this Act which contains the present legal provisions concerning dumping and anti-dumping duties.[1]

[1] Information concerning the procedures is contained in a booklet published by the Department of Customs and Excise for Australian manufacturers who believe their industry is being injured by dumped imports; *Facts about the Australian Dumping Law*. A list of all goods currently subject to the collection of dumping duties or dumping cash securities is found in the *Dumping Notes* within the *Annotated Customs Tariff*.

The Act now provides for action against the following kinds of dumping:

(i) normal dumping where the 'export price' is less than the 'normal value' of the products concerned;
(ii) third country dumping where the importation of goods at a dumped price is injuring the industry of a third country;
(iii) sales dumping where goods which have not been imported at dumped prices as defined elsewhere in the Act are sold in Australia at prices which do not bear a reasonable relationship to the costs incurred in landing in Australia and merchandising the good;
(iv) freight dumping where goods are carried to Australia freight free or the freight is less than the normal freight.

In all cases two criteria have to be satisfied before any action is taken: it must be established that (a) the selling price is a dumped price and (b) an Australian (or third country) industry is being injured or threatened or the establishment of an Australian industry is being hindered. In case of normal dumping or third country dumping, dumping is considered to have occurred when the export price of any good that has been exported to Australia is less than the normal value of the good. The dumping duty is equal to the full amount by which the export price is less than the normal value. In the case of sales dumping the Minister for Customs and Excise determines and fixes what the export price would have been if the actual price paid for the good was fixed in order to avoid or reduce dumping duty. In case of freight dumping the duty is equal to the full amount by which the actual freight paid is less than the normal freight for the good from the country of export.

For dumping other than freight dumping 'normal value' may be determined by the Minister on any one of four bases:

(i) the fair market value of like goods sold for home consumption in the country of export in the ordinary course of trade, excluding any internal taxes remitted on exportation, plus delivery charges in the country of export;
(ii) the highest export price for like goods from the exporting country to a third country;
(iii) the fair market value of like goods produced and sold in a third country in which costs of production are comparable to those in the exporting country;
(iv) cost of production plus delivery charges plus selling costs and profit in the country of export.

A brief history and discussion of anti-dumping procedures in Australia is given by the *Report of the Committee of Economic Enquiry*, vol. II, pp. 1051-6 and vol. I, pp. 398-401. Crawford, *Australian Trade Policy*, pp. 486-9 reproduces two speeches to Parliament explaining the reasons for the extensions enacted in 1961 and 1965.

The 'export price' is the price paid or to be paid for the goods by the importer, plus any delivery charges in the country of export incurred by the importer or, for goods on consignment, the price that would have been charged if the goods had been sold outright.

There are certain exemptions from anti-dumping action. The most important of these apply to goods prescribed by by-laws when suitably equivalent goods are not reasonably available from Australian manufacturers. Under Trade Agreements with New Zealand and Canada dumping complaints on goods exported from New Zealand or Canada are to be examined and pending the results of the examination, no anti-dumping action is to be taken.

The process of investigating a complaint takes place in five steps:

(i) notification that the goods are the subject of an anti-dumping investigation;
(ii) reference to the Tariff Board when the Minister for Customs and Excise is satisfied that a *prima facie* case of dumping exists;
(iii) interim protection by taking cash securities on goods equal to the full amount by which the export price is below tentative normal values;
(iv) public inquiry by the Tariff Board;
(v) gazettal of a dumping duty after consideration of the Tariff Board's report, if required.

Complaints are initiated by Australian manufacturers of competing goods or, in the case of third country dumping, by the government of the third country. The Department of Customs and Excise encourages complaints to come from the industry as a whole or an important segment of it. The applicant for anti-dumping action must submit an anti-dumping application form which requests information about the description of the goods, the prices, injury and other details.

It is not an easy matter to establish that dumping has occurred. In particular, it is difficult to establish the 'normal value' of commodities. Although both the normal value as stated in the first of the alternative criteria above, and the 'current domestic value' which must be declared for ordinary valuation of the import, are related to the price of the good when sold for consumption in the exporting country, they are not necessarily the same; the current domestic value relates to the specific sale of 'identically similar goods' whereas the normal value for dumping purposes relates to the sale of 'like goods in the ordinary course of trade'. The other criteria are even more difficult to apply.[2]

[2] As an example, the special problems of assessing normal value in the case of dumping by Mainland China have been considered by J. Wilczynski, 'Dumping in Sino-Australian Trade', *Economic Record*, September 1966, pp. 397-415.

The Act does not define injury except to state that it must be 'not insubstantial'. Evidence that the landed duty-paid price of an imported article is less than the price of the domestically-produced good or that the export price is less than the normal value is not sufficient. Injury can be demonstrated by loss of sales, depressed prices or retrenchments and it must be due to imports.[3]

Table 4.1 sets out the statistics of interim protection in the last three years and the subsequent actions.

Table 4.1 Dumping actions

No. of commodities	1968	1969	1970	1971*
Subject to interim protection (cash securities)	3	9	14	5
Referred to the Board	5	10	13	4
Dumping duty recommended	9	4	8	3

* Up to 20 August 1971.

In summary, the position of all commodities (sub-items of the BTN) subject to some anti-dumping action at 1 July 1971, was:[4]

Total number of commodities subject to payment of formal dumping duty	46
Complaints notified as subject to dumping investigations	13
Total number of commodities subject to payment of cash securities	22
Total number of commodities under examination by the Tariff Board	21

Table 4.1 does not give a complete picture since a number of complaints made to the Department of Customs and Excise are dismissed without being notified and reported to the Tariff Board because there is no basis for action, other cases are notified but later found to warrant no action and are dismissed by notice in the *Gazette*, anti-dumping complaints relating to imports from Canada and New Zealand are first discussed with the government concerned and if they are dismissed or an agree-

---

[3] In its report on *Collapsible Sun Lounges* (*Dumping and Subsidies Act*), 14 December 1965, the Tariff Board gave an important interpretation of the injury in the Act; namely, the Board asks whether the exportation of the goods sold below normal value is causing or threatening injury regardless of whether the injury is attributable to the fact that export prices were below normal prices. See also Ethyl Acetate (Dumping and Subsidies Act), 20 June 1968, p. 6. This interpretation appears to be in conflict with Article 3 of the Anti-Dumping Code of GATT.

[4] From the Department of Customs and Excise, Appraisement Circular 1971/no. 23.

ment reached there will be no interim action or reference to the Tariff Board, and finally, some dumping duties are imposed as a result of Tariff Board references relating to ordinary tariff revisions. However, the listing of commodities subject to some anti-dumping action is complete.

Dumping action was recommended by the Tariff Board in every case referred to it. Moreover, the Tariff Board normally accepts the tentative normal values decided by the Department of Customs and Excise. These results are not surprising since the department is satisfied there is a *prima facie* case of dumping before referring it to the Tariff Board and the Board usually accepts the expert evidence of the department on the question of normal values. The Board simply assesses whether the dumping as defined in the Act has caused substantial injury.[5]

All of the dumping relating to the commodities in Table 4.1 was normal dumping. The commodities come from many chapters of the BTN but roughly one-third are chemicals or chemical products. The great majority of dumping actions and declared normal values are against imports from the more industrialised developed countries; principally Japan, the EEC and the USA. A few relate to imports from the communist bloc countries. The only dumping actions against imports from the developing countries apply to textile products such as knitted garments.

From the point of view of GATT Australia's anti-dumping provisions and procedures are permissible since they conform with Article VI and its interpretation.[6] There are unimportant differences in wording; for example, the GATT Article specifies that the injury must be 'material injury' whereas the Australian Act requires 'not insubstantial' injury. There is no provision in the Article for freight dumping and the 'hidden dumping' by associated importing and exporting companies or houses is only one of the cases of sales dumping that may be investigated under the Act. However, the Australian procedures do deviate in some respects from those laid down in the Anti-Dumping Code agreed to at the Kennedy Round of GATT negotiations in 1967,[7] and Australia has not signed the Agreement to implement this Code. Most important, the Anti-Dumping Code states 'provisional measures shall not be imposed for a period longer than three months or, on the decision of the authorities concerned upon the request by the exporter and importer, six months' whereas under Australian law cash securities cannot be held longer than three years after which, if a dumping duty is not gazetted,

---

[5] In its *Annual Report for 1964-65* (Canberra, 1965), pp. 15-16 the Board recommended that the Act be amended so that the dumping duties be decided by the department without a reference to the Board, except where circumstances warranted an independent inquiry. This recommendation was not accepted.

[6] GATT, *Basic Instruments and Documents*, vol. IV, 1969, pp. 14-15. One exception is the Tariff Board's interpretation of injury (see p. 58n above).

[7] GATT, *Basic Instruments*, 15th Supplement, 'Agreement on Implementation of Article VI of the GATT', pp. 24-35.

the security must be returned to the depositor. The Code also provides for retroactivity of duties only for the period for which provisional measures have been applied whereas there is no time limit on the retroactivity of duties in Australia. The special consideration for dumping of exports from Canada and New Zealand is inconsistent with the Code. In practice the inquiries by the Tariff Board which have been reported since 1967 have taken an average of nine months from the receipt of the references from the Minister. Since the reference usually goes to the Board at about the same date as the collection of cash securities becomes effective, this is also the approximate period of interim protection.[8] However, the Board has reduced the length of time between receipt of the reference and its report to the Minister in its last few reports to less than six months and the Board's handling of dumping references may be speeded since the Board was expanded from eight to eleven members in 1972. Concerning retroactivity, dumping duties are normally levied from the date cash securities became payable under the interim protection. In other respects such as the definition of dumping and injury and the giving of evidence the Australian procedures conform to those of the Anti-Dumping Code.

When evaluated from the point of view of what is best for the national economy Australian anti-dumping practice looks rather different. Dumping is a form of price discrimination between markets in different countries. Anti-dumping practice in GATT and in most countries, including Australia, is producer-oriented. It reflects the view that what is harmful to an individual company or business is harmful to the nation. It neglects the benefit to the consumers or users who pay the lower prices for dumped goods. Economists have long recognised that the gain to the consumer-user is more than enough to make it possible for them to compensate the producers for losses of income suffered through dumping.[9] The argument in favour of dumping is the same as the argument in favour of trading with other countries; it is that a country benefits from importing goods from the cheapest source. It is immaterial to the importing country whether an imported good can be landed at a cheap price compared to the locally-produced good because foreign production is technically more efficient or has cheaper labour or material inputs on the one hand, or because of price discrimina-

---

[8] These delays in deciding finally the duty are the only complaint of exporters about the Australian anti-dumping practices, apart from the inevitable complaints that some tentative and final normal values have been set too high. These are less frequent than complaints from Australian manufacturers that these normal values are too low.

[9] The classic study of dumping is Jacob Viner's *Dumping: A Problem in International Trade* (Chicago University Press, Chicago, 1923). For a recent restatement of dumping as an act of price discrimination, see Baldwin, *Non-Tariff Distortions*, pp. 141-2. The exception to this proposition is predatory dumping. This is discussed below.

tion and marginal-cost pricing in favour of the export markets which allow it to be dumped.

In fact, it is clearly in the interests of the importing country if the exporters are prepared to lower the prices of the goods exported, and the lower the better. For example, if an industry uses a capital-intensive method of producing some good which requires a large scale of operation and a substantial annual throughput for least-cost production, it is clearly in the interests of a country with a relatively small domestic demand for such products to import these goods from a larger country with lower overall unit costs and to benefit further if the suppliers in that country are prepared to export at dumped prices in order to utilise fully the potential economies of scale. This situation applies to many industries in Australia, notably the chemical industry, which has been the subject of more dumping actions than any other single industry.

In some recent Tariff Board hearings on dumping complaints the Australian manufacturers have stated that they have excess capacity and that their unit costs would be lowered if they increased total sales after the imposition of dumping duties.[10] This is a variation of a familiar Australian argument that protection from import competition in industries in which there are economies of scale will allow the domestic manufacturers to increase output and lower unit costs. It is very doubtful that the higher prices and reduced competition associated with greater protection will induce greater output and lower unit costs and, even if they do, the high cost to domestic buyers makes this policy undesirable.[11] In recent Australian history there is even an example of the complainant *exporting at dumped prices* the same product as is alleged to be dumped and injuring the complainant in Australia.[12]

If third country dumping arises the argument for no action is, from the importing country's point of view, stronger because there is no harm to any domestic producers. The same applies to dumping which may hinder the establishment of an Australian industry. The harm to the Australian industry is a potential harm only and the argument for considering dumping from the national point applies *a fortiori*.

Some of those who administer the Customs Tariff in Australia have claimed that the main effect of the provision for anti-dumping action is not the collection of dumping duty but that it encourages some exporters to put up their prices for delivery to Australia in order to avoid the possible imposition of dumping duty. This is quite likely.

---

[10] For example, see the Tariff Board reports on *Pneumatic Rubber Tyres*, 8 March 1968, *Pigments and Colour Lakes*, 27 May 1968, and *Dimethyl Silicone Fluids* 12 June 1969.
[11] The reasoning behind this judgment is explained in a paper by G. Pursell and R. H. Snape, 'Economies of Scale, Price Discrimination and Exporting', *Journal of International Economics*, vol. 3 (1973), pp. 85-92.
[12] See the Tariff Board report on *Sorbitol Aqueous Solutions*, 24 June 1969, p. 4.

But any strategy which increases the price of imports in terms of the foreign exchange which must be paid is a cost and not a benefit to the country.

Moreover, evidence put to the Tariff Board in dumping hearings shows that in many cases changes in overseas supplies which are independent of dumping, such as the introduction of new products, contributed to the reduced sales and profits of domestic producers.[13] Evidence put to the Board has also shown that many of the products involved in dumping cases account for a quite minor part of total sales of the producing companies involved. Goods allegedly dumped are almost always within sub-items of the BTN items and mostly within paragraphs or sub-paragraphs of the BTN items or sub-items. In such cases what is injury according to the Act[14] cannot involve a change in the major output of the companies.

Australian legislation has recognised that dumping is not necessarily harmful to the economy in the case of the sub-group of commodities which are not produced in Australia and for which an exemption from dumping can be obtained under the Customs Tariff (Dumping and Subsidies Act).[15] These exemptions should be extended to all dumped goods, with the exception of genuinely harmful dumping as noted in the next paragraph, even if the domestic producers are initially harmed by the dumping. In the event of a change in the definition of dumping as suggested below, adjustment assistance to the industry concerned in the form of grants in aid for labour retraining or relocation and plant reconstruction would more equitably transfer most of the burden of the adjustment to the general taxpayer. This would be a once-for-all problem only as firms would in the future make their production decisions in the light of the new dumping practices.

There is one exception to the argument above that dumping is not harmful to the economy. Dumping in the accepted sense of exporting at prices below the normal values is definitely harmful to the importing country in the cases of 'predatory dumping', that is exporting at low prices with a view to eliminating or reducing local (or third-country) competition and later raising prices. This form of dumping is likely to result in higher prices rather than lower prices in the longer run and thus benefits neither the consumer nor the producers in the importing

---

[13] See, for example, the Tariff Board's reports on *Linoleum (Dumping and Subsidies Act)*, 11 March 1970, *Ethyl Acetate (Dumping and Subsidies Act)*, 12 June 1969, and *Industrial Chemicals and Synthetic Resins*, pp. 24-6.

[14] This accords with the definition of injury in the *Anti-Dumping Code* which defines an industry as the national production of like products; GATT, *Basic Instruments*, 15th Supplement, p. 27. Industries so defined are very much smaller than those at the 2- or 3-digit level of the ISIC.

[15] The relationship of this exemption to the possibility of third-country dumping is unclear. Many by-law imports are supplied by more than one country and some from the United Kingdom enter under by-law preferences that are intended to protect the preferences for imports at substantive rates.

country. It should be prevented. There is no distinction in the Australian legislation between predatory dumping on the one hand and other forms of dumping. 'Sales dumping' is sometimes concerned with attempts to 'break into the Australian market' that may involve these forms of dumping but it is based on an extension of the concept of normal value in the country of export, not on the real sources of loss of welfare indicated above.

The desirable forms of dumping could be permitted in principle and the undesirable prevented if the definition of normal value were changed from the present definition in terms of the normal value in the *country of export* to the normal value in export markets, or, more precisely, the normal value to the *Australian export market*; that is, the non-predatory value. It is the latter value which is relevant to the choice of allowing trade under the normal tariff or not. The export price should also include any refunds or indirect payments to the importer which may be related to the particular transaction, such as concessional prices of other goods.[16] In this concept of dumping, injury to the economy, both buyers and producers combined, has been substituted for the present concept of injury to producers which ignores the welfare of buyers. However, this change is impracticable. It is probably impossible to prove an exporter's intention to raise prices after a period of market penetration.[17]

Another alternative is to abolish completely the present provisions for anti-dumping action in view of the increase in the prices of imported goods which it causes.[18] Any change to the concept of dumping would involve a major difficulty with GATT. If adopted by Australia it would be in conflict with Article VI of the Agreement. Moreover, GATT and other countries would like Australia to sign the Anti-Dumping Code, which is based on the principles of Article VI. It is unlikely that the Contracting Parties could be persuaded to change their notion of dumping or to accept Australia's doing so, even though the latter change would reduce in Australia the number and scope of dumping duties on traded commodities and should therefore be welcomed by exporters of the commodities involved.

Although the basic notion of anti-dumping actions as set out by the GATT is unsound, we must recognise that Article VI and more recently the Anti-Dumping Code have contributed to the freeing of international trade by preventing member countries from using anti-dumping actions, at least on a large scale, as a disguised form of increased protection.

[16] Evidence of these practices was supplied to the Vernon Committee, *Report of the Committee of Economic Enquiry*, vol. I, p. 400. See also the Tariff Board *Report on Industrial Chemicals and Synthetic Resins*, p. 24.

[17] Moreover, this kind of predation requires a world monopoly and it is doubtful that a monopolist would use this method to extend his monopoly; B. Hindley, *Britain's Position on Non-Tariff Protection* (Trade Policy Research Centre, London, 1972), pp. 13-14.

[18] Hindley, *Britain's Position*, p. 18, recommends this policy.

There is also the danger that reducing the scope of anti-dumping practices could lead to pressure from manufacturing producers in Australia for higher tariffs. The Vernon Committee stressed the link between dumping duty and the levels of normal protection.

> There is need for effective anti-dumping legislation which must be regarded as a supplement to the normal tariff-making process. The absence of fully effective legislation may be expected to lead, and in Australia has led, to pressure for prohibitive or nearly prohibitive ordinary tariffs. It is therefore important to review the scope for strengthening the existing law.[19]

In view of this aspect, and the small commodity coverage of anti-dumping actions, it may be better to leave the present provisions unchanged except for the minor amendments needed to bring them into full conformity with the Anti-Dumping Code.

Countervailing Duties

There is provision for countervailing duties, or export subsidy dumping as it is sometimes called in Australia, in the Customs Tariff (Dumping and Subsidies Act) 1961-65. This action is called for when 'there has been paid or granted, directly or indirectly, upon the production, manufacture, carriage or export of any of these goods that have been exported to Australia, a subsidy, bounty, reduction or remission of freight or other financial assistance' and not insubstantial injury to an Australian industry or to those in a third country has been caused or threatened or the establishment of an Australian industry hindered. The steps taken after a complaint are exactly the same as those in the case of normal dumping or any other form of dumping. The amount of duty levied is equal to the amount of the subsidy, bounty or other assistance which is believed to have been paid or granted.

These duties have been used very sparingly in Australia; only seven notices of countervailing duty have been gazetted since the introduction of countervailing duties in 1961 and currently there are no commodities listed as being subject to countervailing duties in the *Dumping Notes*. When the subsidy is a subsidy on exports only, the export price will be less than the domestic price in the exporting country and the normal

---

[19] *Report of the Committee of Economic Enquiry*, vol. I, p. 398. They accepted uncritically the GATT view that dumping is harmful along with the traditional Australian view that goods which are not produced in Australia should be exempted. The Committee also recommended several measures to strengthen and expedite the imposition of anti-dumping duties, including the introduction of 'sales dumping', the retrospective imposition of cash securities, the extension of the retrospective application of dumping duties to dates earlier than the collection of cash securities, and greater co-operation between the Tariff Board and the Department of Customs and Excise.

dumping procedures may be applied. Furthermore, it has been alleged that complaints of injury from subsidised imports are discouraged by the Department of Trade and Industry for fear of inviting retaliation against many of the agricultural exports whose production or export are subsidised in Australia.

The same considerations about the losses or rather the gains to the economy in changing the definitions of normal dumping also apply to 'subsidy dumping'.

Support Value Duties

An example of higher tariffs being used to take care of supposed deficiencies in the anti-dumping provisions is provided by the Tariff Board Report in 1966 on a reference dealing with *Industrial Chemicals and Synthetic Resins*. In this reference the Board was asked to examine possible actions against 'disruptive low pricing' in some chemical products as well as to consider the desirable long-term protection for the products. The Tariff Board recommended, and the government accepted, that imports of some sixty chemicals which are sub-items, or parts of sub-items, of the BTN be made subject to supplementary support duties if the landed cost including duties normally payable on these items is less than the specified support value for the item. (The sub-items and the support values for each are set out in the Fourth Schedule to the Customs Tariff.) The supplementary duty is equal to 90 per cent of the difference between the support value and the landed cost of the item. Support values are 'based on representative duty paid costs of the particular chemical when f.o.b. prices are free of dumping and other elements of price disruption, and when shipping freights and other costs are in accordance with those generally charged for the type of goods concerned'. Support value duties could provide an effective way of maintaining the duty-paid prices of imported goods which would otherwise fall below the support values.

This method of taxing imports was intended to deal with two different kinds of 'disruptive low pricing'. One of these was dumping. The Board considered that dumping duties were not likely to be effective in certain circumstances. Because the government accepted the recommendation for support duties which was based on these arguments it is worth citing the reasons given by the Board:[20]

> There have also been cases of package deals in which an exporter invoices a product at its normal value to avoid dumping duty and undervalues other goods not manufactured in Australia and therefore not subject to anti-dumping action.

[20] *Industrial Chemicals and Synthetic Resins*, pp. 24-5.

The variety of grades and types of some chemicals, particularly synthetic resins, was said to add to the difficulty of detecting dumping. Differences in grade or type cannot be determined readily. For example, Australian manufacturers contended that imported first grade polyethylene is often invoiced as below specification and sold to Australia at an artificially low f.o.b. price.

Quantity discounts were said to provide scope for evasion of anti-dumping action. The Board has evidence that certain chemical exports to Australia have been subject to extremely large quantity discounts. Although these discounts apply equally to domestic and export sales in the exporting country, Australian chemical producers allege that few domestic sales are made in quantities comparable with export shipments and that normal values based upon such quantity discounts are unreal.

Another means of evading anti-dumping action is the routing of chemicals through a non-producing country before re-export to Australia. By pricing such a chemical in the third country at a level much lower than in the country of manufacture, the chemical can be re-shipped to Australia at an f.o.b. price which is equal to the normal value (by the customary definition) in the third country and which is also low enough to make ineffective any protection accorded by the tariff in Australia.

The other circumstance in which support duties may be called for is a 'landslide fall in overseas prices which do not necessarily involve dumping' and which come about because of technological improvements in the supplying countries. The Tariff Board made it clear that it envisaged support values as a means of ensuring the effectiveness of normal protective duties in the event of 'disruptive low pricing' and that they are not intended to provide the local industry with continued insulation from overseas competition or downward price movements in the major chemical manufacturing countries. 'They constitute a form of emergency assistance and will require regular review to determine whether, in the light of cost reductions which have occurred in Australia they can be reduced.'[21]

While these support duties help the tariff to provide protection against dumping in circumstances in which the usual anti-dumping procedures may work slowly or ineffectively, they also provide some additional permanent protection against import competition. They apply immediately whenever the landed cost falls below the support value. The long-term protective effect of the support duties depends first on the levels of the support values and, second, on the frequency and extent of adjustments to these values after reviews and, third, on the extent to which these duties are avoided or evaded. In fact, on the question of review the government accepted the Tariff Board's recommendation

[21] Ibid., p. 26.

that all chemicals subject to support value assistance be subject to one concurrent review each year. A major review of support values was conducted by the Tariff Board[22] in 1968 which resulted in changes to many of the support values. Some were adjusted downwards and some upwards. The Board recommended that support values be discontinued on five chemicals and in the same reference recommended the introduction of new support values on twelve other chemicals. The latter were among a larger group of chemicals which the Special Advisory Authority has assisted by means of temporary support values and which were therefore referred to the Board. In 1969 one support value was altered. The Tariff Board is currently reviewing tariffs on Chemical Industry products and this will probably lead to changes in support values. With respect to the third aspect it has proven difficult to police these support value duties.[23] In 1972 further legislation was introduced to widen the Minister's powers to determine values for duty purposes.[24]

The chemicals case above illustrates the difficulties of trying to reduce competition, whether by anti-dumping measures or by other means, from what is widely regarded in the industry as 'disruptive low pricing' of import substitutes. Strengthening anti-dumping action is certainly preferable to higher permanent tariff protection or import licensing but it is inferior to restricting dumping to cases of predatory dumping as outlined before. The latter alternative should be supplemented by adjustment assistance for producers who are adversely affected by the removal of the present dumping measures or by the development of new products or lower-cost methods of production as in the chemicals industry. In addition to considerations of consumer welfare, adjustment assistance is to be preferred to more anti-dumping action in cases where changes in overseas supplies such as the introduction of new products contributed to the reduced sales and profits of domestic producers. Adjustment assistance might reduce the political opposition to reform but it is not likely to eliminate it. A basic change in anti-dumping and support value measures will be opposed by the same interests that oppose reductions in normal protection.

---

[22] Tariff Board *Report on Chemical Industry-Support Values Review*, 29 April 1968.

[23] As with dumping duties (and also sliding-scale and other duties based on a particular value) it is difficult to prevent evasion and avoidance. In the first place it is difficult to frame the legislation to encompass all practices. In the second place there are many ways in which the importers can evade the duty by over-invoicing the good when imported and recouping this cost by receiving a remission under-the-counter or as a part of a package deal with other goods or, in the case of an association between the importing and exporting companies, by means of some inter-company transfer.

[24] *CPD*, H. of R., 1972, pp. 716-17, 1419-22.

5 Purchasing Policies of the Commonwealth Government

Of all the non-tariff measures examined in this study the area of the purchasing policies of the Commonwealth is perhaps the area about which the least is known.[1] The government is generally secretive about its purchases and purchasing policies and reveals as little as possible.[2] While statistics of imports by the Commonwealth (but not the State or Local Governments) are available by tariff item and chapter of the BTN it is not possible to derive comparable statistics of total government commodity purchases from both local and foreign sources with which the import statistics can be compared. Nothing of an accurate nature is known of the reasons for the decisions which follow.

Attention to the government sector by economists has concentrated on issues of taxation and government employment policy and the effects of aggregate government expenditure on the macroeconomic objectives of full employment and price stability. Here we shall be concerned with a different aspect, namely, whether the goods and services which the government has chosen to provide are provided at the least cost to the economy. The cost of providing given government goods and services may be increased by discrimination against potentially lower-cost foreign supplies (or discrimination among domestic suppliers).

[1] There are two other less important areas about which very little is known, namely industrial standards and voluntary quotas.

[2] One useful source of information is the debates in Parliament and especially the occasional answer by the appropriate Minister to a question. Some of these are noted below. Interesting discussions of the history and operation of Treasury Regulations 52 and 53 which govern most Commonwealth Government purchases are contained in the Parliamentary Joint Committees on Public Accounts' 42nd, 48th and 77th *Reports* in 1959, 1960 and 1965 respectively. Unfortunately, these are rather dated.

There is some further information and discussion of defence procurement in I. Bellany and J. L. Richardson, 'Australian Defence Procurement', *Canberra Papers on Strategy and Defence*, no. 8, Australian National University Press, Canberra, 1970.

Purchasing Procedures

There is no Act of Parliament in Australia which lays down general or specific rules for purchases by the Commonwealth Government. However, Treasury Regulations, especially Nos. 52 and 53, govern Commonwealth Government purchasing and set out rules for tendering. These regulations are made under the authority of the Audit Act. Commonwealth Statutory Authorities and Public Corporations are not bound by the Treasury Regulations and under their enabling Acts are afforded varying degrees of independence in purchasing. These Authorities and Corporations include some which are substantial purchasers of goods, notably the airlines QANTAS and TAA, the Commonwealth Railways, the Snowy Mountains Hydro-Electric Authority, and the Commonwealth Scientific and Industrial Research Organisation. However, many of these follow closely the procedures of the Treasury Regulations. Treasury Department Directions give further instructions on purchasing procedures.

Treasury Regulation No. 52 prescribes that tenders must be called for supplies whose estimated value is more than $1,000. There are two principal kinds of purchases which can be made without calling public tenders. There is a clause which excepts from tenders contracts for 'particular supplies in respect of which the Secretary to the Department of the Treasury, or an officer authorised by him in writing for the purpose, certifies that the inviting of tenders is impracticable or inexpedient'.[3] Most government purchases can be made in this way but the proportion which is made is not known. Purchases made outside Australia on an overseas account at an Australian Embassy or High Commission may also be exempted from the tendering procedures and many purchases, especially of defence equipment, are made without tenders in this way.

The Regulations do not prescribe procedures for advertising tenders. For goods purchased by tender purchasing departments advertise in the *Commonwealth Gazette*, in the daily press in the States where likely tenderers are located, and in some cases in trade journals. Where there is a possibility of overseas firms tendering, details are usually forwarded to Australian Consular Offices in the appropriate countries and to Australia House in London. Any interested contractor, including a foreign

[3] Treasury Regulation No. 52. Treasury Regulation No. 52 was introduced by Statutory Rule No. 21, 1964 and Regulation No. 53 by Statutory Rule No. 77, 1961. Treasury Regulation No. 52 also includes exemptions for supplies authorised by the Governor-General, supplies under an existing contract, and supplies obtained from the Commonwealth Government Printing Office or other Commonwealth factories, a State Government Department or authority or a local authority, and supplies approved by or to be obtained by the Contract Board of the Department of Supply or the Commonwealth Stores Supply and Tender Board which supplies all office machines and other stores to purchasing authorities and makes its own public tenders.

firm not represented in Australia, may bid for a tender and details are available to all prospective tenderers. Treasury Directions on Purchasing Procedures require departments to prepare lists of potential suppliers which may be used to invite specifically likely suppliers to tender. These lists are not made public. Tenders are generally open for a period of 2-4 weeks but are sometimes open for much longer.

Tenders are not revealed to the public. Only the barest information of the name of *the successful tenderer* only for contracts awarded of over $400 is announced in the *Commonwealth Gazette*. This information is restricted to a brief description of the goods purchased, the value of the contract and name and location of the contractor. No information about the number of bids or the reason for the award of the contract to the successful bidder is given and some departments do not notify unsuccessful tenderers of their failure, though in general purchasing departments are prepared to discuss with unsuccessful tenderers the reasons for their failure to win the contract. No information is given generally for defence and other goods when the purchase is made overseas.

All government purchasing authorities are supposed to follow one basic principle: that is to obtain the lowest price consistent with satisfactory quality. This means there should be free and open competition for government purchases to the greatest extent possible, and that the lowest suitable tender should be selected. The lowest suitable tender which is accepted is not necessarily the tender with the lowest price. Other considerations of quality, delivery times, after sales service, the performance of the tenderer in previous government contracts, are all to be assessed in awarding a contract.

There is one other direction to all government purchasing authorities which is important. This is a part of the procedures for comparing tenders received which include both Australian and imported goods which are operated by the Department of Supply. The authority is instructed to include in the tender price for imported goods the amount of any duty and primage which would apply if the goods were being imported commercially and not by the Commonwealth, as well as the cost of freight and insurance for the imported good. No duty is actually paid on such imports since goods imported by the Commonwealth and not intended for sale by the Commonwealth or imported in the national interest enter duty-free under Item 1 of the Second Schedule of the Customs Tariff. The purpose of this notional duty is to give Australian manufacturers the protection in regard to government purchases which is available to them from the Customs Tariff in regard to purchases by the private sector.[4] All cases where the lowest-price acceptable local

---

[4] Where a by-law or by-law determination exists for the goods under consideration, either the by-law or the substantive rate could be applied. It seems more

product is more expensive than an overseas tender price after the inclusion of the notional duty, and the purchase is $15,000 or more, are subject to additional inquiry in the following way. The basic details of the local and overseas tenders are circulated among the Advising Departments which are the Departments of Trade and Industry, Treasury, and Labour and National Service and, in case of dumping, the Department of Customs and Excise. If one of these departments raises an objection to the letting of the contract overseas on the grounds of unemployment in the area of the local tenderer, or the desired development of Australian production of some good, or dumping, the matter is referred to the Cabinet Committee on Government Purchasing Policy for a decision.

All developed countries practise some form of discrimination against foreign suppliers in the purchases of goods by the government sector.[5] The purchasing procedures in Australia compare favourably with those in most other countries in terms of the openness of the tendering. The principal of '*ex ante* publicity' to all potential suppliers is the cornerstone of the guidelines for government purchasing being drafted by the OECD to ensure non-discrimination. All member countries have agreed in principle that discrimination in this area of trade should be ended. Most countries make derogations from the principle of non-discrimination for local unemployment or other reasons as does Australia. However, in other respects the Australian practices compare unfavourably with some countries. The complete secrecy concerning the number and terms of the unsuccessful tenders or offers received, the lists of potential suppliers, the grounds of inexpediency under which a purchase is made without tender and the grounds on which the Cabinet Committee may prefer a locally-manufactured good to a competitive import mean that there is very little '*ex post* publicity'. There is general agreement at the OECD and elsewhere that comprehensive *ex post* information on contracts is essential for surveillances of government purchasing practices but there is disagreement concerning the details which should be published. Certainly in Australia the public and potential suppliers have no way of knowing the extent of preferences in government purchases or of evaluating government purchasing policies. By comparison, in the United States,[6] Japan, Sweden and Belgium, all bids may be inspected by the public after the contract has been awarded.

---

reasonable to believe the by-law rate in such cases is used rather than the substantive rate.

[5] For surveys of policies in some other countries, see *Government Purchasing in Europe, North America and Japan: Regulations and Procedures* (OECD, Paris, 1966), Baldwin, *Nontariff Distortions*, chapter 3, and Johnson and Metzger (eds.), *International Negotiations*.

[6] On the other hand the US has been frequently criticised in GATT and OECD because of the legal preference margins prescribed in the Buy American Act. These are similar to the provision in State Acts in Australia.

72   *Non-Tariff Distortions of Australian Trade*

The Protective Effect Implicit in these Procedures

The statistics in Tables 5.1 and 5.2 give some indication of the effects of government policy. Table 5.1 shows that government imports are a significant proportion of total imports; 4-8 per cent of total import clearances in the four years reported. Table 5.2 shows that defence equipment and materials purchases overseas fluctuate greatly both in total and as a percentage of total defence purchases and total imports. Comparing total government imports with total defence imports we see that defence equipment imports have accounted for roughly 80-90

Table 5.1 Imports for Commonwealth Government, by country of origin ($ million f.o.b.)

Country	1967–68	1968–69	1969–70	1970–71
Countries normally receiving Preferential Tariff				
United Kingdom	60·7	54·2	47·1	43·2
Canada	2·3	1·9	2·6	1·2
New Zealand	1·4	1·3	1·4	0·3
Ireland	0·0	0·0	0·0	0·0
Australian Territories	0·1	0·4	0·4	0·4
TOTAL	64·6	57·7	51·5	45·0
Declared Preference Countries				
Malaysia	0·1	0·0	0·0	0·0
Other DPC	0·2	0·8	1·2	0·3
TOTAL	0·3	0·9	1·3	0·4
Countries normally receiving General Tariff				
USA	120·9	164·8	89·9	59·4
Japan	2·4	2·6	4·1	5·8
EEC	56·2	34·1	31·7	25·8
EFTA	12·5	4·4	4·0	3·9
Other general	0·9	1·0	0·3	0·6
TOTAL	192·9	206·8	130·1	95·4
Australian re-imports	2·5	2·9	5·1	3·2
Origin unknown	2·1	5·0	3·3	1·5
TOTAL CLEARANCES Government imports	262·3	273·4	191·2	145·5
GRAND TOTAL CLEARANCES	3,265·1	3,432·2	3,858·8	4,103·8

Source: CBCS, Tables of 'Customs Clearances at Specified Rates of Duty' for respective years.

Note: These imports do not include goods entering under item 1A of the Second Schedule of the Tariff which are goods which at the time of entry are not owned by the Commonwealth Government but are intended for use by the Commonwealth. These are classified as by-law customs clearances.

per cent of total government imports. This implies that the percentage of imports in total expenditure on imports of non-defence equipment, unlike the percentage for defence equipment in Table 5.2, is quite small.[7]

Table 5.2 Defence procurement expenditures

Year	Defence equipment purchased overseas ($ million)	Overseas purchases as percentage of total
1958-59	39	32
1959-60	46	39
1960-61	53	44
1961-62	60	47
1962-63	67	47
1963-64	111	55
1964-65	111	52
1965-66	131	49
1966-67	191	53
1967-68	279	61
1968-69	246	56
1969-70	150	45
1970-71	112	40

Source: 1958-59 to 1969-70: Statement by the Minister for Defence ex-Question No. 1486, *CPD*, H. of R. 1971, pp. 199-200. 1970-71: Department of Supply.

The main concern in Australia over government purchasing policies has been the defence purchases. The principal source of information in this area is the occasional ministerial statement of new orders or purchases. Criticisms have been made of government defence purchasing. Many of the choices of weapons or aircraft have been disputed. In particular, the government decision to order 24 F 111s immediately before the elections in 1963 has since been the subject of long and intense debate. The decision was apparently made in haste without detailed consideration of alternatives. There is a serious question of the suitability of the aircraft[8] and the contract allowed very substantial cost overruns. These aircraft were originally to cost $US112 million but the modified aircraft to be delivered in 1973 will cost $US344 million, not including $40 million for leasing 24 Phantoms as fill-ins caused by the delay in delivering the F 111s. Other criticisms of defence purchases include the assertions that there are sometimes delays in con-

[7] In the Supplement to the *Treasury Information Bulletin*, 'National Accounting Estimates of Public Authority Receipts and Expenditure', August 1971, Table 2, broad categories of government expenditures are broken down into domestic and overseas outlays. In the category 'War and Defence' overseas outlays were 13·6 per cent of the total net Commonwealth expenditures and on other goods and services overseas outlays were 7·6 per cent of total. Unfortunately, it is not possible to separate the expenditure on goods from that on wages and other services.
[8] One former Service Minister was reported as saying the F 111 could either be regarded as the world's fastest crop-duster or the most expensive flying totem pole.

firming orders, the variability of purchases, the lack of adequate cost-effectiveness methods of evaluating alternative purchases.[9]

The principal government effort to encourage the defence industry in recent years has been the attempts to increase the manufacture of equipment under offset, sub-contract and co-production orders accompanying overseas purchases. This was largely begun by the former Defence Minister Sir Allen Fairhall who called the local defence industry the 'fourth arm of defence'. These efforts have increased. In 1970 the government announced the establishment of a new machinery to work closely with American and other overseas defence industries as an offset against Australian purchases of defence equipment. The machinery consists of a standing committee of the Departments of Defence, Supply, and Trade and Industry plus an advisory committee of leading Australian businessmen. The results of these endeavours have been very small to date.[10] In August 1970 the Minister for Defence stated that the government had entered into only four sub-contract arrangements since 1966 with an approximate total value of $4·6 million, and the largest of these was $1·9 million of meat supplied to the US armed forces.[11] In 1970-71 the value of offset orders placed by the United States in Australia was $7·1 million.[12] The smallness of the value of these offset and sub-contract arrangements negotiated by the government has been strongly criticised by opposition members of Parliament.[13]

In the area of defence purchasing, the idea of offset and co-production agreements which has pre-occupied the discussion of defence purchasing is a misguided mercantilist notion. It is the pattern and level of aggregate imports which is important. Any attempt to use substantial import purchases as a bargaining method to extract offsetting bilateral orders for Australian goods is likely to encourage the production of high-cost goods that are protected from the normal competition with imported goods by the nature of these agreements. If some local production of defence equipment is desirable on defence grounds it is unlikely that the pattern of production that may be negotiated with other countries as offset or co-production orders is that best suited to the defence needs and production capabilities of the country.

The non-price characteristics of many defence purchases, such as the

---

[9] See, for example, the papers by P. Robinson on 'Defence and Australian Industry' and P. D. Groenwegen 'Defence Policy and Procurement' at the Seminar on Defence Policy and Procurement, sponsored by Sydney University Extension Board and the Centre for Continuing Education at the Australian National University, 23 April 1971.

[10] In 1972 the government introduced new proposals for offset purchases for computers and civil aircraft, both fields outside defence purchases. If the idea of offset purchasing spreads this could become an important non-tariff restriction on imports implying high levels of protection (see chapter 10).

[11] *CPD*, H. of R., 1970, p. 237.

[12] *Australian Financial Review*, 8 November 1971.

[13] *CPD*, H. of R., 1970, pp. 787-8 and Senate, 1970, pp. 2082-6.

performance characteristics, maintenance support, benefits to Australian defence industry, compatibility with the equipment of allies, reliability of the source in times of war, are of very considerable importance. They may justifiably override cost differences but should be reviewed critically and weighted against the cost difference. The official policy that Australian defence should be based as far as is practicable on the Australian defence industry would seem to conflict with the 'best value for money' principle which is supposed to apply to all government purchases.

Government encouragement to the defence industry through purchasing policy is certainly small compared to the encouragement given to the manufacturing sector through the protection of the Customs Tariff or other non-tariff measures. The Australian defence industry has filled substantial orders, as Table 5.2 shows, especially in the production of aircraft such as the Mirage and Macchi and naval ships, but more than one-half of the equipment is still purchased overseas, principally in the United States.[14] No doubt many of these purchases must be made overseas because of the small scale of the defence industry productions in Australia and the technological lead in many areas of the United States and other large industrial countries. It should be noted here that the largest part of the industrial-military complex in Australia is the various factories manufacturing aircraft, ordinance and munitions which are owned by the Commonwealth Government itself. These date back to legislation in 1909-11, but they are mainly concerned with small arms and less complex and costly equipment.

The more important question is the extent of the preferences received by Australian manufacturers over overseas suppliers for non-defence purchasing where domestic suppliers account for more government purchases in total value. In the first place the extent of the preference under the notional duty procedure should vary considerably since the substantive rates of duty in the Customs Tariff vary greatly from zero for many items to more than 50 per cent for many other items. Moreover, the extent of preferences is not determined by the notional duty procedure alone. Indeed, preferences given by a purchasing authority to local producers may make imported goods which are comparable in price not acceptable and therefore not even subject to the notional duty procedure and inquiry. While the Treasury Regulations apply to all purchasing authorities, there is no central body overseeing all of these tenders and purchases and these Regulations and Directions do permit considerable discretion to individual departments; for example,

---

[14] In answer to a Question by the Opposition, the Minister for Supply indicated that a total of $951 million funds had been committed for purchases of defence materials and equipment from the United States in the ten years 1960-61 to 1969-70; *CPD*, Senate, 1970, pp. 1082-3.

in the importance attached to differences in quality of goods, delivery or other aspects of alternative bids.

Conflicting statements have been made about the preference or lack of preference for Australian goods in the system of government purchasing. On the one hand we have the AIDA which is a vocal protectionist lobby complaining of 'the absence of a clear and firm policy of preference to local industry',[15] and criticising specific features of the present system, particularly the freedom for purchases to be made of imported goods without tender through the exemptions previously listed. They also assert that the notional duty may not be included in an overseas tender price. Duty is not actually paid by the department concerned and with budgetary limits on its total purchases it is in the interest of the department to import a good if its duty-free price is less than the price of the locally-produced good, other things being equal, although the overseas tender price including the notional duty may exceed the price of the locally-produced good. However, government officials insist the procedure is carried out. Some opposition members of Parliament have complained of the lack of preference and, like AIDA, they have been especially critical of the lack of offset orders in defence purchases.[16]

On the other hand, the Minister for Supply explained to Parliament in 1969 how the procedures for comparing locally-produced and potential competitive imports had been worked:[17]

> Additionally, there are special circumstances in which Australian goods are favoured in any event; for example, if the item is of strategic importance or the industry is depressed. Thus, it will be seen that the Government's purchasing policy procedures ensure that the very closest consideration is given to each case before any suitable Australian product is passed over when government stores are being purchased.
>
> As Chairman of the Cabinet Committee on Government Purchasing Policy, I am in close touch with these matters. I can assure the Senate that there is relatively a very small number of cases requiring attention beyond ordering authority level under our purchasing policy procedures. The point I am making is that where Australian industry has the capacity to meet the requirement it receives orders for the bulk of that requirement. There

---

[15] 'Government Purchasing Policies', AIDA *Bulletin*, November 1970, p. 3. AIDA advocated a Government Purchasing Act making it obligatory for all government purchasing authorities to buy Australian made goods unless there are adequate and specified reasons for not doing so. They also advocated that duty be paid on government imports and as a condition of acceptance of every major contract overseas that it be matched with the maximum possible offset orders and local componentry manufacture.

[16] For example, see the statements by Senator Bishop in *CPD*, Senate, 1970, pp. 609-10, 2081-4.

[17] *CPD*, Senate, 1969, p. 520.

is no real problem in that area. The problem exercising our minds is in the area where the requirement is beyond the capacity of our industry or the numbers required are too few to warrant establishing production in Australia.

We are continuously taking steps to improve the position of our industry in this area of government purchases. For example, senators are aware of the Australian Industrial Research and Development Grants Board which has been set up by the Government. In this way we are encouraging Australian industry to undertake more original research and development work.

We are making overseas governments more aware of our attitude to offset arrangements and our aim to upgrade our technological competence. Let me mention briefly some of the work in the area specific to my own Department. We attempt to give industry advanced notice of projected requirements. We keep industry generally informed of our work by informal contact and through such formal means as the industry advisory committees. We let contracts on industry to develop new capacities in this country.

The real extent of preferences to Australian suppliers must remain unknown until it is possible to examine alternative bids *ex post* and the ways in which choices are made. It seems that some significant preferences come from the deliberate attempts to foster Australian production as well as from the notional duty system. Some departments, and notably the Post-Master General's Department, which is one of the two main purchasing departments and the main Australian purchaser of telephone and telegraph equipment, have fostered local production in different ways. The PMG has entered into agreements with companies to buy specified amounts of equipment over several years and has made it a condition of tender that a tenderer state how much he is prepared to manufacture in Australia. However, this department is still a substantial importer because some of the goods purchased are not available from Australian manufacturers. In other cases Australian manufacturers offer real advantages in the terms of the contracts other than prices; for example, the delivery times may be shorter, or the servicing by local manufacturers superior, or the local company has an advantage in doing repairs or modification of equipment supplied, or the costs of inquiring into foreign contracts may be too high. Yet, there is a real danger that the lack of public inquiry and the large amount of discretion given to the individual department and the Cabinet Committee may be used to give a substantial preference to the local producer under the guise of supposed non-price advantages of local supplies.

The notional tariff, to the extent this procedure is carried out, raises two further important and complex economic issues. The first is whether the (notional) duty paid by the Commonwealth Government should differ among commodities as under the present Customs Tariff or be identical for all commodities, and if the latter, should the rate be zero or some positive uniform notional rate. Clearly applying the rates included in the Tariff, which are largely historical having been determined in an *ad hoc* way over many years, results in an almost haphazard pattern of protection. This issue is similar to that raised by by-laws and is therefore deferred to the general discussion of protection in chapter 12.

The second aspect of notional duty concerns preferences to the United Kingdom, Ireland, Canada and New Zealand under the Preferential rates for many imports which are part of the structure of Australian tariffs.[18] With a multi-column Tariff the application of notional tariffs could mean that Australia imported a good from a Preferential source rather than importing essentially the same (or an equivalent) good from a General source because its 'duty paid' price is less than the other even though the price without duty was greater than that of the other good. With the substantial margins of preference for some goods in the Customs Tariff there are possibilities of significant trade diversion for government imports under this procedure.[19] This aspect will be less important after the British accession to the EEC in 1973.

The only real safeguard against excessive protection to domestic producers in government purchases, and against other practices which do not evaluate all the alternative sources available within the country or allow practices such as late delivery and failure to meet contract terms, is scrutiny by the public of government procedures and individual purchasing decisions. We return to this question in the final chapter.

---

[18] It is not clear what happens when the good could qualify for a by-law admission but even for by-laws imports there are small preferences for goods from the United Kingdom.

[19] The State Governments give preferences to imports from the United Kingdom over imports from other countries but they also give preferences to Australian goods over all imports and in some cases to goods supplied from the State over those supplied from other Australian States. In New South Wales, the State Contracts Control Board which buys stores and equipment for all State Government Departments extends a preference of 10 per cent to goods from all British Commonwealth countries over goods from other countries if the items are not available from within Australia. Local authorities in some States also give preferences. In New South Wales the Local Government Act requires that if Australian goods cannot be purchased or delivered in reasonable time local councils must give at least 10 per cent preference in all cases to British goods over 'foreign' goods. As local authorities pay normal tariffs this preference is in addition to those included in the Customs Tariff. There is some doubt that the local councils are following these mandatory preferences but in August 1971 the Sydney County Council requested the NSW State Government to remove these UK preferences from the Act; see report in the *Australian Financial Review*, 6 August 1971, p. 1.

6 Non-Tariff Barriers Through Government Regulation of Industry

Regulation of imports for quarantine, copyright, technical specifications and related purposes is permitted by GATT but, like anti-dumping action, there is a serious possibility these regulations may be used deliberately for supplementary protection.

Quarantine Regulations

Australia's quarantine regulations of commodities (and persons) are stringent by comparison with all other countries except neighbouring New Zealand. They are derived principally from the Quarantine Act 1908-1969 with some supplementary support from the Prohibited Import Regulations under the Customs Act. They date back to the Quarantine Act 1908, passed shortly after the foundation of the Commonwealth in 1901. In fact, at the time of federation the only health function given to the Commonwealth Government was the power to make laws with respect to quarantine.[1] The coverage of the quarantine regulations has been increased periodically since their introduction.

Under the Quarantine Act the Commonwealth Government regulates the importation into Australia of all goods which may be the possible cause of the introduction of new diseases or pests. These are three sets of regulations under the Act; those applying to animals, those applying to plants, and general regulations.[2] They concern almost exclusively agricultural products, both processed and unprocessed.

---

[1] The Commonwealth Department of Health was formed in 1921 by the extension of the quarantine service. It was not until 1946 that an amendment to the Constitution gave the Commonwealth power to make laws with respect to pharmaceutical, hospital and sickness benefits, and medical and dental services.

[2] In addition to the Regulations, a fairly detailed description of quarantine is provided in Department of Health booklet *Plant and Animal Quarantine: Notes for Importers* (Canberra, July 1968).

Proclamations under the Quarantine Act prohibit imports of the following goods unless specified conditions are met:

Human tissue
Disease germs, microbes, cultures, etc.
Vaccines
Second-hand clothing and rags
Bedding materials

Since 1909 the importation of all plants or parts of plants, whether living or dead, has been subject to quarantine with the object of preventing the introduction of insect pests, plant diseases, and weeds not yet established in Australia. This applies to timber and all articles made of wood, bamboo, etc. and soil as well as to plants, cuttings, seeds, fruit, bulbs, etc. Quarantine inspectors are required to examine all plant material at the first port of entry and to release only material free from diseases and pests. All plant material entering Australia as cargo or passengers luggage or personal effects must be declared. Penalties varying from $200 to $1,000 are laid down in the Quarantine Act for those found evading the regulations. In addition if the good is smuggled or is a prohibited import, the offender may also be liable under the Customs Act to penalties up to three times the value of the goods and two years imprisonment and, which is probably the most severe penalty in many cases, the goods may be forfeited.

Regulations governing plant imports are based on the following general principles. The importation of plants or plant materials likely to be infected with plant diseases or pests, of noxious and poisonous plants and of soil is prohibited. Agricultural seed not restricted must conform to standards of purity and insect and pest freedom. Seeds of commercial crops which are restricted (e.g. wheat, sorghum, maize, sunflower, peanut, cotton) and some pasture crops may be imported only by special permit which is usually issued only to official agencies such as Departments of Agriculture, Commonwealth Scientific and Industrial Research Organisation, and universities. All plant products not specifically restricted, such as timber and logs, are subject to inspection and treatment if necessary upon arrival. Timber and logs may be imported through certain ports only. All nursery stock must be approved, fumigated and grown in post-entry quarantine.

Animal quarantine covers the importation of all animals, parts of animals, animal products and related materials, and goods associated with animals. In general, importation by air is prohibited. Of the domesticated animals, only horses, cattle, dogs, cats and poultry are admitted and then only from a small number of countries in which serious diseases that afflict each group of animals are absent,[3] and they

---

[3] Dogs and cats may be imported only from New Zealand, Great Britain and the Channel Islands, Northern Ireland and Ireland and they must have been

are subject to quarantine detention on arrival. No ruminants may be imported from any country, except cattle from New Zealand. Approved animals for zoos, circuses, and scientific purposes are permitted under strict control. Raw animal products, such as wool, hair, and skins and hides are specially treated when necessary under quarantine control. Other items such as raw meat and eggs, as they are not sterilised, and oysters in the shell, can be imported only from New Zealand. Dairy products (milk, including dried and powdered milk, cream, butter and icecream)[4] may be imported only when produced in and consigned from Canada, New Zealand and the USA, Northern Ireland and Ireland. Other important products such as animal casings and animal fodder may be imported from specified countries only.

The Customs (Prohibited Import) Regulations provide some additional restrictions on imports of animals and plants. Animals of all kinds and the semen of animals, birds of all kinds, live fish and the spawn of fish, are prohibited without the permission in writing of the Minister for Customs and Excise. These broaden the powers to restrict imports under the Quarantine Act which is intended to deal only with the control of diseases and pests. The prohibition against birds was introduced in 1927 following advice that birds which were destructive to crops were being imported into Australia. The restrictions on the imports of seeds were introduced in 1970 to prevent the importation of varieties of wheat and other cereals with undesirable qualities.

The notable feature of the Australian controls on the imports of plants and animals is the stringency of these controls. This feature can be explained basically by the importance of Australian production and exports of agricultural crops and products in the Australian economy and by the geographic isolation and recent settlement of the country which have meant that Australia is relatively free from many exotic animal and plant diseases and pests that are widespread outside Australia. Strict enforcement of the long-standing quarantine regulations since the turn of the century[5] has enabled Australia to remain free of many diseases and pests which have severely affected the crops and animals of many other major agricultural producers and exporters, including others with strict quarantine regulations such as the United States. For example, Australia has remained free of foot-and-mouth disease by virtue of strict quarantine restrictions on importation from any country in which the disease is found. New Zealand has also

---

resident for at least twelve months in any of these countries prior to export and are generally detained in quarantine upon arrival. Horses may be imported from the same group of countries only, subject to certain health certificates and other conditions. Birds may be imported from New Zealand only.

[4] Cheese, except that containing meat or meat products, is not restricted by quarantine.

[5] Prior to Federation the colonies each had effective quarantine controls.

retained strict quarantine controls and freedom from many diseases and pests found in most other parts of the world and this explains the exemption of imports from New Zealand for many products.

The products which are probably most severely restricted by quarantine controls on imports are the dairy products other than cheese, meat and poultry. Quarantine controls have prevented the importation of some agricultural commodities into Australia. For example, wheat and flour have been imported into Australia in substantial quantities only once in more than fifty years. This occurred in 1957-58 when supplies of high protein wheat were not sufficient for domestic requirements because of widespread drought and $1\frac{1}{2}$ million bushels were imported from Canada and elsewhere. As another example imports of pork from New Zealand were included in the duty-free list of the New Zealand-Australia Free Trade Agreement, subject to an annual quota, but in fact no imports have occurred because of quarantine restrictions.

There may be a few cases where the regulations are unnecessarily strict from the health point of view but some of these have probably resulted from over-caution rather than any hidden attempt to provide protection for Australian producers. Strict quarantine is necessary to protect Australian producers of plant and animal crops from disease. Moreover, some countries would not accept Australian exports of certain commodities if some diseases were present in Australia. For example, exports of meat to the US would cease if foot-and-mouth disease occurred. However, it should be noted that there are losses to consumers and users of potential imports because quarantine regulations restrict cheaper imports. We should not automatically accept the view that quarantine regulations benefit the country. Since Australia is an efficient producer of most of the agricultural commodities which have been restricted, the long-run gains to producers have probably more than offset the losses to consumers and users in most commodities.

Standards, Technical Specifications and Goods Descriptions Regulations

This discussion concerns principally those regulations which are applied at the Australian border. Safety, health and other regulations applied within Australia are mentioned briefly.

Prohibition or detainment of goods may also occur under various regulations relating to the marking, description, and specifications of designated goods. Under the Trade Marks Act, the Department of Customs and Excise officers who administer the control of imports of these goods may detain any importation bearing marks identical with, or substantially identical with, a registered Australian trade mark. Action is taken only if the trade mark owner gives notice of his objection and pays a security to cover any expense incurred in the seizure and the goods are in commercial quantity. Similar provisions under the Copyright Act exist in respect to imported goods which infringe copyrights. The regulations relating to prohibited imports specify that imported goods bearing any marking in a language other than that used in the country of origin, must also show in English the country in which they were produced; for example, a Japanese cigarette lighter bearing any wording in English must carry a further marking 'Made in Japan' but if the lighter bears only Japanese wording or no marking at all, no statement is required. The prohibited import regulations also specify for a very small number of goods (clinical thermometers, instruments for indicating specific gravity, and insulating electric conductors) certain markings, sizes and other requirements. The Commerce (Trade Descriptions) Act provides that the Governor-General may, by regulation, prescribe the descriptions and conditions relating to descriptions which are necessary before goods may be imported (and exported). The regulation of imports is set out in the Commerce (Imports) Regulations. Goods specified in these regulations are prohibited unless they have a label which contains the name of the country in which the goods were produced, and for certain goods, a true description.

There are also regulations relating to standards which apply to all goods within Australia, whether imported or domestically produced, which may have some incidental protective effect because the standards are more difficult for foreign manufacturers to meet.

Industrial, health, safety, environmental and other standards have been the subject of little study in most countries. This lack of attention has probably been due to the benign intention of standards, their multiplicity, the lack of public knowledge, and the few complaints received. Yet, these standards may, in some cases, severely restrict trade because of international differences in standards and certification requirements. At the London Conference in January 1972, representatives from all countries asserted there were no serious impediments to imports into their respective countries due to standards requirements but some studies have indicated standards have serious trade-distorting effects.[6]

In Australia, industrial standardisation is the responsibility of the Standards Association of Australia. Standards may relate to one or more of several aspects of industrial practice such as terminology, test methods, dimensions, specifications of performance and safety, etc. These standards are undertaken in response to requests from both industrial associations or firms and government departments. In general, standards derive authority from voluntary adoption by industrial associa-

---

[6] For example, International Chamber of Commerce, *Non-Tariff Obstacles to International Trade* (Paris, 1969), and R. N. Middleton, 'Technical Specifications: A Case Study of Non-Tariff Barriers to Trade', *EFTA Bulletin*, March 1971.

tions or firms, but in special cases where safety of life or property is concerned, there are compulsory applications under statute.

Almost nothing is known of the effects of Australian standards on her trade. One example of standards which restrict some imports, or rather imports from some countries, are the standards relating to markings in non-metric measurements for weights and measures, tools, etc. These require foreign manufacturers outside the United Kingdom or other countries which have the same measurement to incur additional costs because of extra tooling or product modification. This difficulty is diminishing as metrication proceeds in Australia.

7 Discriminatory Features of the Sales and Excise Taxes

The Sales Taxes in Australia

Sales taxes have been imposed in Australia by the Commonwealth Government since 1930 and since 1940 there have been differential rates of sales taxes levied on taxable goods.[1] The Commonwealth sales tax applies to goods only and all goods produced in Australia or imported for consumption in Australia are subject to sales tax unless specifically exempted by the Sales Tax (Exemptions and Classifications) Act or falling within certain general exemptions in the First Schedule to this Act. Goods exported are exempt. The sales tax is designed to fall on the final wholesale sale of the goods which are subject to the tax.

Currently there are four rates of tax levied. A low rate of $2\frac{1}{2}$ per cent applies to household goods covered by the Third Schedule of the Sales Tax (Exemptions and Classifications) Act. A high rate of $27\frac{1}{2}$ per cent applies to goods covered by the Second and Fifth Schedules. These are mostly 'luxury goods' such as jewellery, watches, cameras, cosmetics, and also motor cars other than commercial vehicles such as trucks, buses and vans (which are taxed at the general rate of 15 per cent). Motor cars are the single most important item of sales tax, accounting roughly for an estimated one-third of total sales tax receipts. A 'general' rate of 15 per cent applies to the unspecified taxable goods and the rate of 0 per cent to all exempt goods.

The substantial differentials in the rates of sales taxes on commodities raise important questions concerning the misallocation of resources which are similar to those arising from different rates of protection resulting from tariff and non-tariff restrictions on importables. (There

---

[1] In 1940, in order to raise more revenue for war purposes, a general rate of 10 per cent and a higher and lower rate of 15 and 5 per cent respectively were introduced. A table listing the rates of sales taxes which have applied historically can be found in *Forty-Ninth Report of the Commissioner of Taxation, 1969-70*, CPP, no. 140, 1970, pp. 63-4.

is the obvious difference that the sales tax generally, with the exceptions to be discussed below, applies equally to imported and locally-produced goods.) Sales taxes have other features in common with non-tariff instruments in Australia. First, one of the broad categories of goods exempted are 'aids to manufacture', which includes most machinery and other fixed capital equipment. Similarly, most materials and components are exempted but some inputs such as office equipment and motor vehicles are not. The exemption of 'aids to manufacture' and materials is based on the same principle which underlies the whole Australian system of by-law imports; namely that manufacturers should not have to bear or pass on the unnecessary costs of taxes. This argument is fallacious. It is the level of taxation of a commodity relative to other commodities and not the absolute level of taxation which determines the allocation of resources and real costs of production (see p. 49). Second, all agricultural and other primary products are favoured by a blanket exemption under Item 21 and most agricultural machinery, equipment and materials are exempted.

The distortions of resource allocation and consumer choice due to differential rates of sales taxation must be considerable. Sales tax receipts are the third most important source of Commonwealth taxation receipts following income taxes and excise taxes, and they amounted to $569 million or 8·9 per cent of total net taxation collections by the Commonwealth in 1969-70.[2] The average rate of sales tax on taxable goods, defined as the total sales tax collections as a percentage of taxable sales, was 15·5 per cent in 1969-70.[3] However, collections expressed as a percentage of total final wholesale sales by registered wholesalers[4] are much smaller (4·3 per cent). This is another reflection of the exemptions and the rate differentials. Despite the importance of this tax, in this book I shall be concerned solely with the distortions which come about in the sales tax because of difference in the sales tax treatment of imported goods compared to locally-produced goods.

Sales taxes may affect imports in three ways:

(i) the rate of sales taxation of the same commodity may discriminate between imported and locally-produced supplies;

(ii) the rate of sales taxation may be the same on imported and locally-produced supplies yet effectively discriminate against import substitutes because the imported commodity is classified as a different commodity for the purpose of sales taxation and bears a higher rate of taxation;

[2] Commonwealth of Australia, *Commonwealth Taxation Assessments*, 1969-70 (Canberra, 1971). For comparison total customs duties in the same period amounted to only 6·5 per cent of total net collections.
[3] *Forty-Ninth Report of the Commissioner of Taxation 1969-70*, p. 553.
[4] These do not include final sales by vendors trading only in exempt goods who are not required to register.

(iii) sales taxes which discriminate among distinct commodities change the relative prices to consumers and producers of these commodities and, therefore, the pattern of imports and exports.

Sales taxes also discriminate in favour of exports of taxable commodities because of the blanket exemption of all export sales. This discrimination is not considered.

Although the third category may be important,[5] it is not considered because the discrimination against imports is indirect and therefore outside the scope of this study. The second kind of discrimination has been a major source of complaint by some countries. For example, the US automobile industry has complained of European road taxes which increase with the horsepower of the automobile engine. Japan also levies higher taxes on sales of large-sized cars which are mainly imported than on smaller cars which are mainly produced in Japan.[6] Because Australia has only three positive rates of taxation, each of which is applied to quite distinct groups of commodities, there are no significant examples of this kind of discrimination in Australia. The first kind of discrimination has received little attention in international trade circles, except for the major problem of border tax adjustments,[7] but it is the kind that exists on a fairly small scale in Australia.

The rates of sales tax are determined by nine separate Sales Tax Acts, four of which deal with different classes of goods manufactured in Australia while another four deal with the corresponding classes of goods imported into Australia and the ninth with certain goods in Australia which are leased. These separate Acts are regarded as necessary to comply with Section 55 of the Constitution which provides that laws imposing taxation other than customs or excise duties shall deal with one subject of taxation only.[8] The rates of taxation on imported goods which are taxable are identical in all cases today with the rates levied on the same goods manufactured in Australia since the rates are the same for the four corresponding classes of imported and locally-manufactured goods. However, there is some discrimination between

---

[5] It may even change an export good to an import good or vice versa; see J. R. Melvin, 'Commodity Taxation as a Determinant of Trade', *Canadian Journal of Economics*, February 1970, pp. 62-78.

[6] Kojima, 'Nontariff Barriers to Japan's Trade', p. 26.

[7] The US has complained frequently of border tax adjustments to imports and exports in the EEC countries. These are intended to neutralise the effects of internal value added taxes but may discriminate against imports or have the effect of export subsidies; see Baldwin, *Nontariff Distortions*, chapter 4 and Curzon and Curzon, *Hidden Barriers*, chapter 2.

[8] The detailed general rulings and interpretations by the Commissioner of Taxation of the provision of the 20 Acts relating to the sales tax, together with the 20 Acts and regulations, have been published for convenience by the Commonwealth in *Commonwealth Sales Tax*, Canberra, 1970. These are the Acts and Regulations as in force at 31 July 1970. There have been changes since then, notably an increase in the sales tax rate, where applicable, of 25 per cent to $27\frac{1}{2}$ per cent, which was announced in the August 1970 Budget.

imported and locally-manufactured goods because the exemptions from sales taxes which are set out in the First Schedule of the Sales Tax (Exemptions and Classifications) Act sometimes apply only to the locally-manufactured goods and not to the corresponding imported goods, and in a few cases the converse applies. Some of these apparently discriminatory provisions do not involve any real discrimination either because the imported (or Australian) good which is not exempted under an item in the First Schedule is exempted under another item applying equally to both imported and locally-manufactured goods or because there is no real competition between the imported and locally-produced goods (as for example, with trophies or prizes won outside Australia or anthropological specimens imported into Australia for use by research workers).

There are some remaining exemptions which involve real and significant discriminations against imports and have, therefore, a significant protective effect. These exemptions which apply to Australian manufactured goods but not to comparable imported goods include food for livestock (Item 6 (4)) and poultry (II (2)) other than seeds, bran and pollard and meat imports which are exempted under other items, beer, cider and Australian wine[9] (36) boxes, cases and crates manufactured in Australia for use in marketing goods manufactured in Australia (193).[10] There is also an exemption under item 36(3) for fruit juice products which contain not less than a minimum content of Australian juices or concentrates. In the case of non-alcoholic carbonated beverages the exemption requires a minimum of only 5 per cent by volume of the juices of Australian fruits. This exemption has reportedly increased the demand for the use of Australian fruit juices in the manufacture of soft drinks. For example, apple juice is used not only as an ingredient in apple juice products but also, for the purpose of securing exemption from sales tax, is used in other products which either do not purport to contain fruit juice such as lemonade or cola, or are sold as the product of another fruit such as banana cordial. In these products the cost of small quantities of the fruit juice additive are more than offset by the tax saving. In all of these cases the general rate of 15 per cent applies to imports. Items 100 and 103 exempt goods made in Australia only by small manufacturers whose annual sales do not exceed $1,400, or if the goods are made in the person's own home $1,000, or if the sales tax due would not exceed $100. This exemption may give rise to some discrimination but the intention is to avoid the expense of the registration and collection of the tax and not to protect

---

[9] But, it may be noted, spirits are not exempted.
[10] Before the August 1972 Budget works of art produced in Australia or abroad by Australian artists, were exempt but imports, other than those by New Zealand artists were not exempted from sales taxation.

and it would be administratively difficult and expensive to extend this exemption to small manufacturers overseas.

While these discriminations against imports are small in relation to the total scope of the sales tax, a few are no doubt of substantial value to the producers affected. Unfortunately, no statistics of the value of sales which are taxable or exempt broken down into the commodities affected or even broad commodity groups are available at present and we cannot therefore assess the importance of the discriminations.[11] The one group which probably benefits substantially through protection from overseas competitors in this way are the manufacturers of beer and wine who in effect receive an additional 15 per cent *ad valorem* tariff.

There are also some exemptions which discriminate against imports from particular countries in much the same way as tariff preferences though on a much smaller scale. Item 111 exempts 'goods, the produce or manufacture of New Zealand, Fiji, Norfolk Island, the Territory of Christmas Island or the Territory of Cocos (Keeling) Islands, being goods of the same class or kind as goods upon the sale value of which, if produced or manufactured in Australia, sales tax is not payable'. Imports from these countries therefore are not subject to the discriminatory provisions discussed above.

There is one other way in which discrimination could arise in favour of Australian producers. For the purposes of the sales tax the value of imported goods which are subject to the sales tax upon importation is the sum of the value for duty of the goods plus the duty, including any primage duty, plus 20 per cent. This is a rule of thumb which is intended to obtain a fair wholesale price for imported goods comparable to the fair wholesale price of goods manufactured in Australia. It is intended to adjust, on the average, for the international freight, insurance, and other costs and for the wholesaler's mark-up, which are not included in the value for duty plus the duty. It may sometimes exceed the equivalent wholesale price and sometimes fall short of true fair wholesale price because the actual margins for freight and insurance and wholesale mark-up are less or greater than 20 per cent.

On the other hand, there are a few exemptions available to imported goods but not comparable goods manufactured in Australia. These are all of very minor importance. Under Item 69A imported instruments, apparatus or models designed solely for demonstration purposes are exempted. There are also exemptions for goods imported by or for

---

[11] The only subdivision available to the public is that of net sales taxable at the three rates—$2\frac{1}{2}$ per cent, 15 per cent and $27\frac{1}{2}$ per cent—which enables us to calculate the proportion of sales tax coming from each of these three categories (3·4, 51·5, 45·1 per cent respectively in 1969-70); see *Commonwealth Taxation Assessments, 1969-70*.

It is deplorable that we know almost nothing about the commodities which bear this important tax, let alone the economic effects of the tax.

consular and diplomatic staff and the United Nations and a few other international organisations. These give effect to Australia's obligations under international conventions or agreements with particular countries and are intended to apply to direct imports only and not to purchases of imported goods in Australia.

Excise Taxes

An excise duty is a tax levied on the production or manufacture of goods in Australia. Only a small number of goods in Australia are subject to excise duties but the duties levied on these goods are generally high. Three groups of goods subject to excise, namely alcoholic beverages, tobacco products and petrol and diesel fuel, which account for 99 per cent of total receipts from excise duty, are important items in the budgets of most households in Australia. For this reason, the excise duties collected in 1969-70 amounted to $939 million and were the second most important source of taxation in Australia following the income tax, accounting for 14·7 per cent of total net collections by the Commonwealth in that year.[12] The excise taxes on these principal commodity groups were all intended as revenue duties and the commodities chosen are all the traditional 'luxury commodities'. These commodity taxes distort considerably the prices of these commodities relative to other consumer goods and therefore impose a loss to consumers which is not often recognised. The justification for them in terms of discouraging the consumption of some goods which some sections of the community consider are consumed in excess is questionable but, again, we shall consider only the aspect of possible discrimination between domestic and imported goods.

In considering goods subject to excise tax the rate of excise tax levied on goods produced or manufactured in Australia must be compared with the customs duties on like imports. It is usual for goods which are excisable when produced in Australia to have a higher rate of duty under the Customs Tariff. When excise duty rates are increased or decreased, it is also usual for the same adjustment to be made to the appropriate customs duties to maintain the margin of protection. Thus the difference between excise tariffs on locally-produced goods and tariffs on imports of excisable goods may be considered as a normal tariff form of protection. The margin of protection for excisable goods produced in Australia can be calculated as the level of the tariff less the excise duty. The resulting levels of protection are substantial in some cases but these levels may change significantly from period to period when expressed in *ad valorem* terms because all the excise duties and almost all the customs duties on excisable goods are specific duties.

[12] *Commonwealth Taxation Assessment, 1969-70.*

The only instance of discrimination in excise taxes against Australian production is that of coal, which is duty-free when imported. However, Australia is a low-cost supplier of coal on world markets and no significant quantities of coal have been imported in recent years. Moreover the special excise on coal is only 4·4 cents per ton.

We should note too that two of the three main groups of commodities which are subject to excise tax—namely, tobacco products and petrol and diesel fuel—are produced by industries which the Australian Government has assisted substantially through other non-tariff instruments. The tobacco industry has been assisted by the Tobacco Industry Stabilisation Scheme and the petroleum industry by the petroleum products consumer subsidy scheme, the subsidy on exploration and search and the indigenous crude oil absorption scheme. Imports of petroleum products and some spirits are also controlled by the prohibited imports regulations. However, the levels of protection which Australian producers of crude oil receive under the prices fixed until 1975 have been considerably eroded by the increases overseas in prices for crude oil in the last three years. These commodities provide examples of the offsetting effects of different tariff and non-tariff distortions.

8 Assistance to Producers

The Australian Commonwealth Government, like most other governments, aids industries in very many ways. It is usual to draw a distinction between aids or subsidies which are general in that they are offered on equal terms to all producers who take certain actions and subsidies which are selective, being offered to producers of particular commodities only. Accelerated depreciation and other provisions relating to company taxation are examples of general subsidies. This chapter considers only selective production subsidies. The first sub-group of selective subsidies considered are those based directly on production of specified commodities. In the conventional terminology of public finance theory these are called indirect subsidies. Indirect production subsidies are paid only to domestic producers[1] and therefore discriminate against foreign suppliers. We also consider other subsidies based on income or commodity prices, or on exports. We do not consider the numerous subsidies on inputs such as subsidies on freight, marketing assistance to woolgrowers, or export promotion or petroleum exploration, research and development, etc. other than those paid to producers of inputs. The exceptions to this exclusion are the subsidy on export credit, customs drawbacks and the export market development rebate. As these are subsidies on inputs used in the production of goods for export only they fall within international discussions of non-tariff interventions. The exclusion of other input subsidies is arbitrary. After all a production subsidy is equivalent to a uniform *ad valorem* subsidy on all inputs. But their inclusion would open up too large a field of payments and

[1] If the subsidy is paid on imports of a commodity it becomes a consumption subsidy. Consumption subsidies are not considered although the sales taxes considered in chapter 7 are indirect consumption taxes, that is, negative indirect consumption subsidies. The effect of exemption for domestic producers only from some sales taxation is to convert these sales taxes from taxes on consumption to taxes on imports which discriminate against foreign supplies in the same way as a production subsidy; this is method (i) as described in chapter 7.

taxation concessions. Moreover, it is difficult in many cases to identify the commodities whose production is subsidised by selective input subsidies.

Subsidies and Bounties

Subsidies on Production

There are a number of subsidies paid directly to producers of particular commodities in Australia. Some of the commodities considered in this section are exported on a significant scale, particularly butter and cheese, but the subsidies we consider here are payable on all production, whether sold in Australia or overseas. In all cases other than the very special case of gold bullion one half or more of the total domestic output is consumed in Australia. The largest exports, in both absolute and proportionate terms, of the commodities considered in this section are of butter and cheese. Domestic consumption currently accounts for about 60 per cent and 50 per cent of total butter and cheese production in Australia respectively.[2] Hence the distinction between subsidies paid on exports and subsidies paid to producers is a meaningful one. Moreover, all of the commodities considered here other than gold bullion are import-competing products that receive substantial protection from overseas competitors.

Subsidies to producers are an alternative to tariffs as a means of assisting producers of importable goods. Because they require payments from the consolidated revenue of the Commonwealth Government each subsidy can only be paid in Australia under the authority of an Act of Parliament. The decision by government to enact a bounty[3] or subsidy is made following representations by the industry concerned and in most cases after a reference to the Tariff Board. The Tariff Board Act gives the Board complete discretion to recommend bounties in place of, or as a supplement to, tariff protection in its normal references or in the special references to it concerning bounties or the renewal of Bounty Acts.

The Board and the government have evolved general guidelines indicating when bounties may be used as a form of assistance.[4] The occa-

[2] Since butter, cheese and other dairy products are all made from the same raw material, raw milk, the percentage of raw milk production consumed or used for the manufacture of products consumed in Australia is the more relevant statistic. Some 70 per cent of total milk production is consumed in Australia.

[3] Seven of the current 'subsidies' to producers listed in Table 8.1 are described as bounties in the authorising Acts. The exceptions are the subsidies on shipbuilding, nitrogenous fertilisers and gold bullion. I shall use the term subsidy as the generic term to cover all bounties or subsidies payable to producers and the term bounty when referring to a particular bounty or bounties.

[4] The Tariff Board's view has been stated in the *Annual Report* for 1940-41 (Canberra, 1941), pp. 13-14 and in some comments contained in individual references.

Other discussions on bounties or subsidies in Australia may be found in the

sions on which bounties may be preferred to tariffs all derived from the principal difference[5] between bounties and tariffs as alternative means of protection, namely, that a bounty or subsidy, unlike a tariff, does not raise the price of the commodity to the purchaser. The principal case for subsidies in Australia which is derived from this feature applies to an importable material or capital equipment which is used in the production of an export commodity.[6] A tariff on the capital good will increase the costs of the export commodity and the producer of the export product may bear the whole burden of tariff because the price for his product is fixed on world markets and cannot be increased.

Bounties had their origin in Australia in a desire to protect Australian manufacturers without adding to the costs of producers, especially farm export producers. The bounty under the Iron and Steel Bounty Act was extended in 1922 and the tariff reduced in order to reduce the cost of fencing wire and wire netting and other iron and steel products. In 1923 a bounty on sulphur produced from Australian ores replaced the previous duty on sulphur so that the domestic production of sulphur would be encouraged without penalising the manufacture of superphosphate in which the use of sulphuric acid is an important item of cost. Bounty assistance was first given to the Australian tractor manufacturers in 1922. A similar argument has been applied in support of subsidies rather than tariffs for 'basic commodities which enter into other production to a large extent'[7] or commodities which are a 'raw material for a chain of operations of further manufacture and of distribution'.[8]

The Brigden Committee claimed another practical advantage of bounties: 'The cost of bounties is definitely known and felt; it is not obscured as with duties, and there is a natural and healthy resistance to and criticism of the assistance given'.[9] While this statement has often been cited with approval in Australia the obvious budget costs to which

---

so-called Brigden Committee Report of 1919; J. B. Brigden et al., *The Australian Tariff—An Economic Enquiry* (Melbourne University Press, Melbourne, 1929), pp. 109-11; and in the 1956 Vernon Committee Report, vol. I, pp. 387-99, 355-6, and 178-9 and vol. II, pp. 1061-2, 1079-80.

[5] This is not the only difference. Subsidies in Australia, unlike tariffs, are usually restricted to a specified number of years, are subject to a number of restrictions and may be restricted to particular end-uses (see Table 8.1).

[6] This argument was first spelled out carefully by the Brigden Committee, which listed it as the first advantage of a bounty; *The Australian Tariff*, p. 109. The Tariff Board has repeated the argument several times and recently reaffirmed it in its *Report on Agricultural, Horticultural, etc. Machinery*, 19 June 1970. The Vernon Committee gave it as the 'most important justification of bounties'; *Report of the Committee of Enquiry*, vol. I, pp. 387-8.

[7] *The Australian Tariff*, p. 110.

[8] Tariff Board, *Annual Report for 1940-41*, p. 13. See also the Tariff Board, report on *Industrial Chemicals and Synthetic Resins*, 13 April 1966, pp. 19-22 in which the Board recommended subsidies on seven basic chemicals. The government rejected this recommendation. Recently, the desire to aid shipbuilders without increasing costs to ship operators was, together with defence considerations, one of the reasons for the shipbuilding subsidy; Tariff Board, *Report on Shipbuilding*, 25 June 1971, pp. 6, 17-18.

[9] *The Australian Tariff*, p. 110.

it refers are, on the contrary, the principal objection of the Treasury and government to the widespread use of bounties and, together with the time limits and other restrictions on bounty payments, are one of the reasons why assisted industries have generally preferred tariffs. Moreover, this advantage does not apply to implicit subsidies to producers through subsidies on particular inputs or tax concessions which may not be stated at all as in the case of some tax concessions, though these are not considered.

Other reasons for bounties have been given. Acetate rayon was given a bounty because it was believed a tariff would have made the Australian product vulnerable to imported viscose yarn.[10] The Tariff Board has stated that when a high tariff may reduce the market available to the industry being assisted a bounty may be preferred to a tariff.[11] The Board has also argued that when the output of the Australian industry supplies only a small proportion of Australian requirements it is a ground for preferring a bounty because the tariff will increase the price of the product to all buyers.[12]

It was the intention of the Phosphate Fertiliser Bounty Act and the Nitrogenous Fertiliser Subsidy Act to assist the end-users of these products rather than the producers. Other subsidies paid to the producers will generally benefit the purchasers as part of the subsidy will be passed on, especially where there is a restriction on the net profit that may be earned from the production of the bountiable product as in the cases of sulphuric acid and pyrites, but in the cases of the fertiliser subsidies the Minister of Customs and Excise may stop the bounty payment if satisfied that it is not being passed on to the purchaser. As a means of assisting end-users, subsidies on particular inputs are an inefficient instrument because part of the subsidy goes to the producer of the input and, because some inputs are not subsidised, they encourage the overuse of the subsidised inputs, thereby increasing the costs of production to the economy. The soundness of the main arguments for preferring subsidies to tariffs as an instrument of protection is considered again on pp. 186-7 in the broader context of distortions elsewhere in the economy.

Bounties and subsidies based on production have been used very selectively in Australia. Table 8.1 gives the basic features of the subsidies which are currently payable on the production of certain commodities.[13]

[10] Tariff Board, *Report on Continuous Man-Made Fibres* (*Interim Report*), 2 March 1962.
[11] *Annual Report for 1940-41*, p. 13.
[12] Ibid., p. 13.
[13] The shipbuilding subsidies described in the table are those announced in May 1972 by the Ministers for Trade and Industry and for Shipping and Transport. At the time of writing, it appeared the government would not be able to pass the enabling legislation before the 1972 election. As there is strong opposition to the new plan and as the Labor Party's proposals differ markedly the future of this subsidy is uncertain.

Table 8.1 Commonwealth Government subsidies on production, 1972

Goods on which subsidy (bounty) paid	Date subsidy introduced	Subsidy base and rate	Principal restrictions for full subsidy
RURAL PRODUCERS			
Butter, cheese, and butterfat products with a minimum of 40 per cent butterfat content	1942	The total subsidy for butter and cheese in each production year is determined by Parliament. The rates per pound butterfat in butter and cheese then depend on production. The rates per pound butterfat have been approximately equal for butter and cheese producers	Factories must participate in the dairy products equalisation schemes for these commodities which equalise returns to farmers for dairy products sold in Australia and overseas. The bounty must be passed on to the milk suppliers
Superphosphate and ammonium phosphate sold for use as a fertiliser	1963	$60 per ton of phosphorus pentoxide content	Full benefit of the bounty must be passed on to purchasers
Manufactured nitrogenous substances for use as a fertiliser	1966	$80 per ton of the nitrogen content	Full benefit of the bounty must be passed on to purchasers
MANUFACTURING PRODUCERS			
Tractors used in agriculture	1939	$1,040 per tractor plus $8 for each power take-off h.p. over 20 up to a maximum of $1,600 (for tractors with 90 or more h.p.)	1. Excludes crawler tractors and tractors of less than 20 power take-off horse-power 2. Factory cost of materials and parts wholly manu-

... use in manufacture of cellulose acetate rayon yarn			
Book of a literary or educational character	1969	One quarter of the total cost of production of the book	Excludes books produced by the Commonwealth or a State
Trading ships of over 200 gross register tons for use in Australian coastal or inland waters	1947	A sliding scale of 24 per cent of lowest Australian tender price for vessels up to 1,000 tons plus 2¼ per cent for each additional 1,000 tons up to a maximum of 45 per cent	For vessels whose keels are laid after 31 December 1975 the maximum rate of subsidy will be reduced to 35 per cent, and after 31 December 1978 to 25 per cent
Drilling machines, grinding machines, lathes, special purpose machines incorporating power feeds, and numerically-controlled machinery centres	1972	33⅓ per cent of factory cost	1. Factory cost for bounty purposes is reduced by 1 per cent for each per cent by which the Australian content is less than 85 per cent. Tools with an Australian content less than 55 per cent of factory cost are ineligible for the bounty 2. Only manufacturers in production on 14 April 1972 (when report was signed) will normally be eligible

MINING PRODUCERS

Gold bullion	1954	For small producers whose annual deliveries do not exceed 500 fine oz: $16 per fine oz. For large producers: ¾ of the excess of the average cost of production over $27 per fine oz with a maximum of $12 per fine oz	1. Restricted to producers the value of whose gold output exceeds 50 per cent of the total value of his mine output 2. For large producers who receive an amount in excess of official price of $31.25 per fine oz the subsidy is reduced by 75 per cent of the amount of the excess

Source: Statutes and Regulations.

The bounties on nitrogenous and phosphatic fertilisers are classified as payments to rural producers even though they are paid to manufacturers of these products because of the restriction that the full benefit of the subsidy must be passed on to the purchasers. Table 8.1 excludes subsidies paid for air and shipping services. These are small in relation to the subsidies paid for commodities, only $2·2 million in 1970-71, and in relation to the indirect assistance which the Commonwealth and State Governments give to the air transport industry in particular through the subsidised provision of airport and landing facilities.

These bounties or subsidies to producers have certain features in common. The payments are authorised by an Act of Parliament for limited periods and the extension of these periods requires an Act of Parliament; the exceptions to time limits are the shipbuilding subsidy and the bounty on books. Subsidies are paid to the producers of the goods in Australia, provided the goods are for use in Australia; the exceptions here are that the nitrogenous fertiliser subsidy may be paid on imports of manufactured nitrogenous fertiliser and of natural sodium nitrate where there is no or insufficient local production or where non-dumped imports are sold in Australia on terms more favourable than those on which any Australian producer is prepared to sell,[14] and the book bounty is paid on certain books produced in Australia whether sold in Australia or exported. Several of the bounties are restricted to particular end-uses. This reflects the desire of the government to assist the end-user as in the case of the fertiliser and tractor bounties or to assist the producer of the bountiable products without penalising the producers using the product, as in the cases of pyrites and also sulphuric acid which is used principally in the manufacture of superphosphate fertiliser. Before the bounty is paid, the products must all be of 'good and merchantable quality', except in the cases of bullion, where the problem of quality does not arise, and books.

There are restrictions on the producers of each commodity before the bounty or full bounty is paid. The most important of these have been listed in the table. If these restrictions are not met in full there are provisions which determine the part payment of the subsidy. For example when the Australian content of the parts and materials used in the production of tractors for agriculture is less than 90 per cent the bounty is reduced *pro rata* the Australian content below this level until it is zero at the level of 55 per cent.

In a majority of the cases the subsidy is paid at a fixed rate per unit of quantity or as a percentage of the cost of production (books) but in the cases of ships and gold there is a sliding scale up to the maximum rate. The subsidy rates have normally been fixed upon the recommenda-

[14] Thus this subsidy is a combination of a pure production subsidy and a consumption subsidy.

Assistance to Producers 99

tion of the Tariff Board. The method usually employed by the Tariff Board in fixing the rate of subsidy is to equalise an Australian selling price which provides a reasonable profit margin with the landed duty-free cost of imports.[15] These rates are reviewed before the bounty period expires.

Several of the subsidy rates have been increased substantially over the last ten or fifteen years. The original basic rate of subsidy for phosphatic fertilisers set in 1963 was $30 per ton of phosphorus pentoxide content but by 1969 this had been doubled to $60. Similarly, the maximum subsidy for gold bullion has trebled since its introduction in 1954.[16] The tractor bounty has been increased several times. In 1956 the range of bounties was set at $160-480 per tractor, depending on the tractor's horsepower. The present rates range from $1,040 to $1,600.[17] The shipbuilding maximum subsidy was increased in 1955 from 25 per cent to 33⅓ per cent of the cost of production and to 45 per cent in 1972. Moreover, many of the restrictions have been relaxed. Net profits restraints were removed from the bounties on tractors and gold bullion in 1966 and 1965 respectively.[18] Other earlier restrictions on the tractor bounty such that the bounty had to be reduced if the tariff on imports of the good were increased or if the wages and conditions of employment were less favourable than those under the award or considered reasonable were also removed in 1966. The shipbuilding subsidy was extended in 1972 to cover the non-recognised yards. A new bounty on metal working machine tools was introduced in 1972, following recommendations in the Tariff Board *Report on Metal Working Machine Tools and Accessories*.

On the other hand the original rate of bounty on cellulose acetate flake of 10 pence (that is 16·7 cents) has been reduced by a succession of revisions to only 4 cents. Moreover, bounties have been discontinued on the following commodities (the figures in parentheses are the periods during which the bounties were payable for each commodity): refined

[15] See the Tariff Board, *Annual Report for 1964-65* (Canberra, 1965), also their report *Industrial Chemicals and Synthetic Resins*, 13 April 1966, p. 22 and, most recently, *Shipbuilding*, p. 27.

[16] This statement is incomplete. Under the Commonwealth Banking Act all newly mined gold must be sold to the Reserve Bank. The current free market price of $55 per oz is the price at which, with the maximum subsidy plus 50 per cent of the excess of the sale price over the official price, the price by the producers equals the free market price.

[17] This includes the temporary additional bounty in 1970-71 equal to 100 per cent of the bounty under the Agricultural Tractor Bounty Act 1966, pending a Tariff Board Report on agricultural tractors; statement by the Minister for Trade and Industry, *CPD*, H. of R., 1970, p. 1184. This temporary subsidy was continued in the 1971-72 Budget and again in the 1972-73 Budget of August 1972.

[18] The Tariff Board's *Annual Report for 1964-65* strongly urged the abolition of all profit limitations on bounty payments; *Annual Report*, p. 13. The principal reasons were that these limitations discouraged the producer from increasing production beyond the level of maximum profits, which was the purpose of the bounty, and they provided a disincentive to reduce costs. The Vernon Committee put forward similar views; *Report of the Committee of Enquiry*, vol. I, p. 389.

copper (1958-66), copper and brass strip (1962-65), vinyl resin (1963-66), rayon yarn (1954-62), raw cotton (1951-72),[19] sulphate of ammonia[20] (1966-70), urea (1962-70), sulphuric acid (1954-72) and pyrites (1960-72). In May 1971 the government announced that certain kinds of books would no longer be bountiable.

These changes in the commodity coverage and the rates of subsidy can be used to test the view of the Brigden Committee in 1929 and others subsequently in Australia that subsidies are preferable to tariffs as a means of protection because they are more likely to be reduced or removed after a period. This in turn, it is asserted, will happen because the subsidies must be extended and because the costs of the subsidy to taxpayers are stated clearly each year in the annual accounts of the Commonwealth Government.[21] When the periods for which subsidies may be paid are due for renewal, a reference is sent to the Tariff Board asking it to recommend what means and level of assistance it considers should be given. The government usually accepts the recommendation of the Board on these references though it has rejected or modified them on some occasions.

The general consequence of these review procedures in recent years has been that the number of commodities eligible for subsidies has fallen but the rates of subsidy payable for those commodities which are still subsidised have been increased in more cases than they have been decreased. Total payments for subsidies to producers have increased steadily in recent years, except for 1971-72. (The totals are given in Table 8.2 for the four years 1969 to 1972.) Thus the commonly-held view on the constraints on protection through subsidies must be qualified. Recent experience shows that changes in subsidies depend more on whether the industry is considered to need assistance and whether this assistance should be by means of subsidy, than on the taxpayers' scrutiny of the sums of public monies paid out. In the last ten years the Tariff Board and the government have tended to continue and increase the assistance through subsidy for those commodities which affect farmers' costs of production[22] and to review critically the assistance by subsidy which goes to manufacturers.

[19] From 1951 to 1963 the bounty was paid on the unprocessed cotton seed rather than the ginned cotton.
[20] Producers of sulphate of ammonia may still receive the nitrogenous fertiliser subsidy.
[21] The subsidies on most commodities also differ from tariffs in another related respect. Several of the bounty Acts specify that an annual return must be made to Parliament giving the total bounty payments to individual producers.
[22] The Tariff Board gave an indication of its views on bounties recently in its report on *Agricultural, Horticultural, etc. Machinery*, 19 June 1970, pp. 15-16. It rejected requests from farmer organisations that assistance to farm machinery be by means of bounty rather than tariff for two reasons. First, the tariffs it recommended were small and consequently the cost-saving to farmers by substituting a bounty would be small. Second, the administration of a bounty scheme would be very complex because of the wide range of agricultural machinery.

Table 8.2 Commonwealth Government subsidies on production 1969-72
$000

	Years ending June 30			
	1969	1970	1971	1972
RURAL INDUSTRIES				
Raw cotton bounty*	4,260	3,531	2,973	795
Butter and cheese bounties	27,000	27,000	41,500	39,882
Nitrogenous fertilisers subsidy	11,044	9,876	9,716	9,757
Phosphate fertilisers bounty	31,665	45,820	40,815	45,795
MANUFACTURING INDUSTRIES				
Agricultural tractors bounty	2,249	1,757	2,750	3,160
Cellulose acetate flake bounty	179	276	200	166
Book bounty	—	1,374	3,217	3,181
Shipbuilding subsidy, net	12,551	18,758	18,646	13,396
Sulphate of ammonia bounty*	430	1,081	538	2
Sulphuric acid bounty*	988	740	489	896
Urea bounty*	424	496	449	—
MINING INDUSTRIES				
Pyrites bounty*	385	—	568	1,205
Gold mining assistance	1,791	1,859	2,881	1,852
TOTAL Rural industries	74,329	86,227	95,004	96,231
Manufacturing industries	31,494	40,639	39,381	20,797
Mining industries	2,176	1,859	3,449	3,057
GRAND TOTAL	107,999	128,725	137,834	120,085

* These bounties have ceased.

Source: Adapted from *Budget Speeches*, Statement No. 9.

Another noteworthy feature of subsidy payments is that several of the commodities on which subsidies are paid are commodities which are also protected by other non-tariff barriers to imports. In order to enforce the protection by subsidy of domestic shipbuilders, imports of all ships are prohibited without the permission of the Minister for Shipping and Transport and this is normally only given when the domestic shipbuilders and unable to supply the vessel.[23] Nitrogenous fertilisers have been subject to several dumping actions. On the other hand, the local content requirement for producers of agricultural tractors reduces the value of subsidy at the same time as it gives substantial protection to manufacturers of tractor parts. The Tariff Board has estimated the protection to the manufacturers of parts as equivalent to duties between 25 and 40 per cent.[24]

---

[23] The Navigation Act also requires all ships engaged in trade in Australian coastal waters to be licensed and manned by Australian crews. The level of protection of shipbuilding is considered on pp. 148-9.
[24] Tariff Board report on *Tractors, Engines and Other Parts*, 8 May 1967, p. 16.

Other Assistance to Producers

The government introduced in the budgets brought down in August 1970 and 1971 a number of supposedly temporary payments to dairy farmers and woolgrowers to supplement incomes which fell in these two years. For the fiscal year 1970-71 there was a one-year grant of $17·5 million to butter and cheese producers. (This was in addition to the annual $27 million bounty to butter and cheese and the maximum bounty of $800,000 on exports of processed milk products which had been fixed under the five-year stabilisation plan agreed with the dairy industry in 1967.) This grant more than offset the decrease in payments to dairy farmers in compensation for the 1967 devaluation of pound sterling which fell from $20 million in 1967-70 to $12·7 million in 1970-71. (These bounty and devaluation compensation payments are discussed below.) The special additional grant was renewed for 1971-72, with a reduction of $1·6 million in the bounty on butter and cheese and an estimated reduction of $800,000 in the processed milk products bounty. For woolgrowers there was a one-year scheme of emergency relief in 1970-71 under which $21·3 million was paid to woolgrowers based on the fall in their gross proceeds from wool between 1968-69 and 1969-70, a period during which wool prices fell steeply.

This relief was intended as an interim measure pending action appropriate to the long-term problems of the woolgrowing industry, and in particular the establishment of a reconstruction scheme. Although the reconstruction scheme was introduced in the following budget it was also announced in the August 1971 Budget that a one-year scheme of deficiency payments would be introduced in respect of the 1971-72 wool clip. These payments ensured that growers of shorn wool receive on average a price of 36 cents per lb (79·37 cents per kilo) of greasy wool for the year, with some of course receiving more and some less. Payments each week to all growers are a flat percentage of the actual auction prices for the week. Payments in the 1971-72 seasons were $52·8 million, close to the predicted payments of $60 million. In February 1972 the Commonwealth Government made available an emergency grant of up to $20 million to relieve unemployment in rural areas.

Australia operates price programs for most of the major farm products including wheat, dairy products, sugar, tobacco, rice, eggs and, since 1971, wool and apples and pears. The emphasis is on the stabilisation of the prices of the commodities concerned, though many of them are connected with Commonwealth statutory marketing bodies (wheat, dairy products, eggs, apples and pears) that have a monopoly of export sales and some are combined with bounty or subsidy payments that transfer income from non-participants to the farmers concerned (wheat, butter, cheese and processed milk products, and apples and pears). For

Assistance to Producers 103

some commodities there is a two-price scheme with domestic prices being higher than the average export price realised. Import competition is regulated by quotas (sugar), tariffs or by quarantine and voluntary arrangements (lamb and mutton and butter) and import prohibitions (butter and wheat) as well as by the natural protection of international transport costs from potential foreign sources. The regulation of import competition by means of quotas, voluntary agreements, quarantine and import prohibitions has been discussed elsewhere in this study.

The stabilisation of prices itself has involved some payments. Under the wheat industry stabilisation scheme the government guarantees the prices of exports and fixes higher prices for sales for home consumption and for industrial use. Since 1964-65 the deficiency between average export price realisations and the guaranteed export price has required large annual payments from the Consolidated Revenue Fund. In 1971-72 these payments totalled $58·4 million. The other major stabilisation schemes such as the dairy stabilisation scheme are not intended as a price support measure but since the Reserve Bank advances to the producer boards do allow higher interim payments before the exports of the products are sold overseas than would otherwise be possible, there is a subsidy element implicit in these schemes. For example, advances from the Reserve Bank to the Dairy Produce Board have been around $130 million per annum at concessional rates of around 4 per cent. Even if the rate the Board had to pay from unsubsidised sources were only 9 per cent—a conservative figure—this would be a subsidy of $6·5 million.

The two-price schemes also raise the average market prices (the prices received by the producers are raised further by subsidies). Some of the effects of these multiple instruments are considered on pp. 149-55.

Subsidies on Exports

Export subsidies must increase the welfare of the countries to which the subsidised exports are exported. Despite these effects they are generally outlawed by GATT, in part because of the adverse effects they have on the exports of third countries which compete with the subsidised exports on world markets. Export subsidies will also generally reduce the welfare of the exporting country because they distort the relative prices of exported goods from the relative costs of production.[25] Yet, many countries, like Australia, offer a range of subsidies to exporters through exemption or remission of particular taxes, direct subsidies on export sales, marketing assistance and other instruments.[26]

---

[25] As discussed in chapter 10 the presumption that export subsidies reduce welfare is not certain in an economy with other distortions present.
[26] See Baldwin, *Nontariff Distortions*, chapter 2 and UN, *Incentives for Industrial Exports*, UN Sales no. E.70 II, D.8.

All Australian governments since World War II have sought to promote exports. They have introduced a large number of measures which directly or indirectly assist exporters.[27] During the period of comprehensive import licensing up to the end of 1960 and for a few years after the relaxation of import licensing up to about 1965[28] the main reason for this policy of export promotion was the widespread conviction that the Australian balance of payments continually tended towards a deficit position and consequently exports must be increased to pay for imports that are essential to maintain the rate of economic growth.

In the last six years or so there has been no downward pressure on the Australian dollar and Australia's international reserves have steadily increased due mainly to the very rapid rate of growth of mineral exports and the steady, if somewhat erratic, inflow of long-term capital. In 1972-73 the current account of the balance of payments is in surplus for the first time in many years. Under these circumstances there is an additional source of loss to the economy which is distinct from the resource allocational effects of price distortions. The benefit to the economy of a net inflow of long-term capital such as Australia has had in recent years is that it permits the gross national expenditure on capital formation and consumption to exceed current gross national output. However, the maintenance of an undervalued exchange rate keeps down expenditure on imports and consequently the net inflow of capital is not transferred into real goods and services. Instead in Australia it has resulted mainly in an unnecessary accumulation of foreign exchange reserves; in the calendar year 1972 Australia's official reserve assets increaesd by close to $2,300 million. Export incentives increase the cost of forgoing part of the resources available for spending because they increase the price of exports when the correct policy, given a continued inflow of capital, is to decrease the price of exports and other Australian-produced goods relative to the prices of importable goods and services.

Table 8.3 sets out the expenditures of the Commonwealth Government which are directly related to exports, classified by the method of payment, for the years 1968-72. The totals have been broken down into payments to rural, mining, manufacturing and service industries. In contrast to the direct subsidies and bounties on production already considered, a substantial proportion of payments under all the methods go

---

[27] Crawford, *Australian Trade Policy*, chapter 16 contains a number of important statements by Cabinet Ministers that document successive governments' commitments to the policy of expanding exports and the introduction of some of the measures designed to promote this end up to 1966.

[28] The Committee of Economic Enquiry which reported to the government in May 1965 subscribed to the view that the balance of payments would remain under pressure in the long term but one of the criticisms of their Report was that they had understated the prospective earnings from mineral exports. This criticism has been vindicated by the subsequent boom in mineral exports.

to manufacturers. Tax concessions relate to the year in which the tax was conceded rather than the year in which the income was earned.

Processed Milk Products Bounty

The only subsidy in Australia which is paid directly for exports of a commodity is the processed milk products bounty. This bounty is part of the current stabilisation plan for the whole dairy industry. Since 1947 there have been a succession of 5-year stabilisation plans. Each plan included equalisation schemes which pool the receipts from sales of butter, cheese and casein in all local and export markets into pools for each commodity so that all factories receive the same equalised returns for a commodity. The plan also includes a bounty on butter and cheese produced in Australia. This bounty was first paid in 1942 as a wartime measure to keep down the price of these products in the local market at the same time as encouraging supplies for Australians at home and in the armed services abroad. It was continued after the war to encourage the production of these goods, largely to meet the demands of the United Kingdom consumers during the period of commodity shortages after the war. Today it is one of the measures assisting depressed dairy farmers. This bounty was discussed on pp. 102-3.

The producers of processed milk products (condensed, evaporated and powdered milks, baby foods, etc.) have elected to stay out of the equalisation schemes. Therefore these products have not been eligible for the bounty under the Dairying Industry Act to producers of butter, cheese and other butterfat products stated in the Act. Unlike the principal dairy products, exports of these products are not controlled by the Australian Dairy Produce Board. The main companies are domestic subsidiaries of such international corporations as Nestles and Carnation. In 1962 a bounty was introduced for exports of processed milk products which did not receive the butter and cheese bounty. Before this time producers competing with butter and cheese factories for supplies of whole milk and factory labour were at a disadvantage because of the bounty on butter and cheese produced. Moreover, government programs in other countries subsidised directly and indirectly exports of these products. The subsidy on the exports of these products was introduced to offset the export subsidies of other countries and to divert butterfat from the production of butter which was then in oversupply.[29] Under the Processed Milk Products Bounty Act the bounty was limited to a total of $700,000 for 1962-63. This total limit was increased to $1 million for the next production year and remained fixed at $800,000 until 1970.

[29] See the Second Reading Speech of the Minister for Primary Industry on the Processed Milk Products Bounty Bill 1962; *CPD*, H. of R., 1962, p. 1760.

Table 8.3 Commonwealth Government subsidies based on exports 1968-72 ($000)

	Years ending 30 June				
	1968	1969	1970	1971	1972
Export incentive pay-roll tax rebates					
rural industries	—	—	—	—	—
mining industries	5,831	6,224	n.a.	n.a.	n.a.
manufacturing industries	20,069	21,707	n.a.	n.a.	n.a.
TOTAL	25,900	27,931	33,987	49,356	59,960
Export market development rebate					
rural industries	6	13	16	n.a.	n.a.
mining	126	155	115	n.a.	n.a.
manufacturing	5,268	7,132	10,717	n.a.	n.a.
TOTAL	5,400	7,300	10,848	17,000	n.a.
Devaluation compensation					
rural industries	21,000	35,000	29,000	21,000	7,204
manufacturing industries	—	862	1,069	600	23
TOTAL	21,000	35,862	30,069	21,600	7,227
Processed milk products bounty	743	638	516	2,729	2,052
TOTAL rural industries	21,749	35,651	29,516	23,729	9,256
mining	5,957	6,379	n.a.	n.a.	n.a.
manufacturing	25,337	29,701	n.a.	n.a.	n.a.
GRAND TOTAL	53,043	71,731	n.a.	n.a.	n.a.

Sources and Notes:
Export incentive pay-roll tax rebate:
1967-69: *Taxation Statistics*, 1969-70, p. 198. These statistics are for claims allowed to 31 December 1970 for exports in the years 1965-66, 1966-67 and 1967-68. There may be some upward adjustment to these figures because, until the financial year 1968-69, producers were allowed to make a claim up to three years after the financial year in respect to which the rebate may be claimed.
1970-71: *Budget Speech* 1971-72, p. 71. These are statistics of total rebates allowed during the fiscal years, 1969-70 and 1970-71. Some of the 1970-71 rebates were allowed with respect to exports to the export years ending June 1966, 1967, 1968.
1971-72: *Budget Speech* 1972-73, p. 75.
Export market development rebate: Table 8.5. Manufacturing includes service industries.
Devaluation compensation: Table 8.4.

The Act also specifies that the bounty paid on exports of processed milk products must be the same per pound butterfat as that paid to producers of butter under the Dairying Industry Act. Since much less than one-half of all processed milk products eligible for the bounty is exported the bounty paid is much less per lb of butterfat contained in the total production of these processed milk products than the bounty per lb of butterfat contained in butter and cheese. Moreover, the

Assistance to Producers 107

restriction that the bounty rate per lb of butterfat be equal to that for butter has meant that some of the $800,000 voted annually for the bounty has not been expended. In the case of condensed milk the regulations under the Processed Milk Products Bounty Act 1968 were changed in 1969 to permit bounty to be claimed for condensed milk as a processed milk product when the butterfat contained in the condensed milk has already received bounty under the Dairying Industry Act 1967.

In 1970 the Processed Milk Products Bounty Act was amended to provide for the first time payment of an export bounty of $3,379,000 on certain non-fat milk products, namely, skim milk powder, buttermilk powder and casein, produced and exported in 1970-71. This was a part of the arrangement agreed to by the government for the Australian dairy industry for 1970-71 in response to undertakings by the industry to restrain voluntarily butter and cheese production to 220,000 and 700,000 tons respectively. The bounty was to help maintain the Commonwealth payments to butter factories for non-fat solids which had been increased in the three previous years by devaluation compensation payments.[30]

Export Incentive Grants Scheme

The pay-roll tax rebate for increased exports, along with the export market development allowance, were introduced in 1961. Both were to operate initially for four years but they were extended in 1963 to June 1968. At the end of this period the government considered they had served well their purpose of increasing exports and decided to continue both incentives for a further 5-year period until June 1973. The rebate was replaced in 1972 by a grant to exporters calculated in the same manner as the earlier rebates.

From 1941 to September 1971 pay-roll taxes were collected by the Commonwealth Government. They applied to all employers and local authorities, with exemptions limited only to the Commonwealth Government and government authorities and diplomatic missions, certain charities and a few specified organisations such as SEATO. The tax was $2\frac{1}{2}$ per cent of the total wages paid by an employer with an exemption that is now equal to $20,800 per annum. For the first eight years of the scheme the rebate was determined by reference to the employer's increase in export sales for the financial year over the average level of his export sales for the base period of the two years ended on 30 June 1960. The rebate was equal to the product (increase in export sales/gross receipts for financial year) x $12\frac{1}{2}$ x pay-roll tax for the financial year.

[30] See the Second Reading Speech of the Minister for Primary Industry on the Processed Milk Products Bounty Bill (No. 2) 1970 in *CPD*, H. of R., 1970, p. 1063. Devaluation compensation is discussed later in this sub-section.

Thus, if the value of a firm's exports increased by 1 per cent of its gross business income, the firm received a rebate of $12\frac{1}{2}$ per cent of its pay-roll tax. When the increase in exports reached 8 per cent of the gross receipts the firm was entitled to a full rebate of pay-roll tax.

The Pay-roll Tax Assessment Act 1968 simplified the calculation of the tax. The rebate entitlement is now calculated as $10 \cdot 5$ per cent of the increase in exports for the rebate year over the average annual exports in the base period. The base period was changed to the first three years of the eight years preceding the rebate year. Since the ratio of pay-roll tax paid/gross receipts has been about 1/200 in recent years the earlier method of calculating the rebate was equivalent in the aggregate to roughly 6 per cent of the increase in exports.[31] The possibility of a large increase in rebates was reduced by excluding for the first time exports of minerals, including petroleum and petroleum products. This was done because large increases in exports of these products were foreseen and it was considered that the limited financial ability of the government to pay this subsidy could be used to achieve a greater increase in exports if it were applied to other exports only. Furthermore, the substitution of a moving average base was made because a moving average base gives a greater incentive to exporters to increase exports rather than just sustain them. This substitution was also intended to prevent substantial increases in pay-roll tax rebates as exports increased each year beyond the previously-fixed base period. To contain the increase in payments it would have been simpler to have used, say, the three years previous to the rebate year as the base period with an appropriate multiplying factor but this was considered too sudden a change from the old method. On the other hand, the new definition of the 'value of export sales' was broadened to include the sale overseas of industrial property rights or technological know-how developed in Australia and the supply of services by architects, engineers and a few other selected professional groups in addition to the f.o.b. value of prescribed goods. Provision was also made to allow a producer for export or a supplier of components to carry forward for three years the rebate entitlement in excess of pay-roll tax paid, up to a limit of 50 per cent of his pay-roll tax liability for that year.

A new and different method was introduced for computing the rebate in the case of a 'new exporter'. A new exporter is an employer who did not have a value of export sales in any of the three years ended 30 June 1961. In his first export year the base period amount is nil, in the second year it is $\frac{1}{8}$ of the value of exports in the first export year, and it will normally increase for the next six years according to formulae

---

[31] The distribution of the rebate among individual employers is not the same under the old and new methods since the ratio of pay-roll tax paid/gross receipts varies considerably among the employers.

for each subsequent year which are based on the values of export sales for the first, second and third years after the employer begins to export.[32]

Under the revised scheme, applying to the financial year 1968-69 and subsequent years until 1972-73, the value of rebates allowed has continued to increase each year. Statistics released by the Commonwealth Treasurer state that rebates totalling $49·4 million were allowed in the 1970-71 financial year, and that pay-roll tax rebates amounting to $198·9 million have been allowed from the inception to June 1971. Statistics relating to claims based on exports during 1967-68 which had been allowed up to 31 December 1970 show that of the total pay-roll tax paid in 1967-68 by the employers claiming the rebate, which was $61·9 million, $27·9 million had been allowed as a rebate. The total exports to which these claims related was $1,819·9 million of which $1,205 million were the net increase in export sales for the purposes of the rebate.[33]

The marginal rate of subsidy, from which the total subsidy is calculated, is 10·5 per cent of the increase in exports above the level of the base period. When the pay-roll tax export incentive rebate is expressed as a percentage of these total exports, it represents an average rate of subsidy equivalent to 1·53 per cent of these exports.

In analysing the effects, and therefore the desirability, of this scheme we should note first that it is inequitable between groups of pay-roll tax payers. The sole exclusion of mineral exporters discriminates against this group, but it should be noted that mining companies receive substantial exemptions and reductions in income taxes not available to other producers. The group of 'new exporters' are discriminated against in that from the second to the sixth year of their exports the base against which they may calculate their increase in exports for the purpose of the rebate[34] is higher than it would be if they were treated in the same way as old exporters. Under the moving average base formula they would have a zero base value and all exports would count as a net increase for the first six years. Thus an increase in exports of a given amount entitles an old exporter to a greater rebate than the same increase for a 'new exporter'. It was considered that the object of the scheme was to increase exports and that it was more difficult for a current exporter to increase his export capacity than for a new exporter to do so and, hence, the old exporter needed a greater incentive. However, this distinction between old and new exporters results in the

---

[32] a, b and c are defined as the value of export sales for the first, second and third export years respectively. The bases against which increases in exports are to be calculated are, for the first eight years in order: nil, $a/8$, $(a + b)/8$, $(a + b + c)/8$, $(a + b + c)/6$, $5(a + b + c)/24$, $(a + b + c)/4$, and $7(a + b + c)/24$.
[33] These statistics are taken from *Taxation Statistics, 1969-70*, Commonwealth Government Printing Office (Canberra, 1971), p. 198.
[34] See n. 32 above.

different treatments for equal increases in exports; that is, different marginal subsidies for equal increases in exports.

A more important aspect of the scheme is that it pays a different subsidy to a given value of export earnings depending on whether the value is part of a repetition of past sales or an increase in the total level of exports. There is no economic justification for an export incentive of this kind. The most common reason given for export incentives is the supposed tendency of the Australian balance of payments to a deficit.[35] This argument has not been applicable for several years as the Australian currency has developed into one of the hardest. There is a more subtle and defensible development of this argument that asserts that, with high average protection for importables, the equilibrium free trade exchange rate is higher than the pegged rate (that is, the number of Australian dollars per unit of foreign currency should be higher in order to reflect the true scarcity of foreign exchange) and we should therefore subsidise exports. This line of argument calls for a uniform *ad valorem* subsidy for *all* exports and one, moreover, that should decrease as a currency tends to appreciate.[36] The subsidy through the pay-roll tax rebate involves differential rates of subsidy for different export sales that range from zero for an export sale that does not increase total exports above those of the base period to a maximum of 10·5 per cent for increases in export sales. These differentials in the subsidy per unit of exports distort returns to exporters of these goods and do not lead to an increase in exports, even if this were desirable, at least cost. As one illustration of the inefficiency of the scheme consider the case of one taxpayer (firm) which captures another's export market. Because there is an incentive for the exporter whose sales have increased but no corresponding penalty for an exporter whose sales have decreased, there is an increase in the total subsidy but no change in total exports. If all exporters received the same rate of subsidy on all exports this would not arise.

The pay-roll tax rebate has another, though less important, distorting effect. This export incentive is really a subsidy to a group of producers on the use of one factor, labour.[37] Assuming it is not passed on in full to the labour employed, it lowers the cost of labour to these producers

[35] See the ministerial statements reprinted in Crawford, *Australian Trade Policy*, chapter 16.
[36] This is the other side of the free trade argument for a uniform *ad valorem* tariff; see W. M. Corden, 'Australian Economic Policy Discussions in the Post-War Period: A Survey', *American Economic Review*, June 1968, Supplement, pp. 100, 108 for references to this discussion in Australia. The uniform *ad valorem* export subsidy has received little attention in Australia, unlike the proposal for a uniform *ad valorem* tariff.
[37] More exactly, it is a partial and discriminatory removal of a tax that is distorting in the first place. Since the removal applies only to those producers who are eligible because of increased exports, and not directly to the labour input it is classified as a subsidy on export production rather than an input subsidy though the distinction is blurred in this case.

and distorts factor prices and commodity prices. Since the pay-roll tax is levied initially at the rate of 2½ per cent and the rebates are roughly one half of this, the incentives change the price of labour employed by only about 1 per cent.

The distortions due to this subsidy can only properly be considered as a part of the distortions due to all the export subsidies in combination. They should also take account of differences in tariffs on outputs and on inputs imported by these producers. One notable aspect of the pay-roll tax rebates is that almost one half of these rebates go to producers in the category of industries 'Metals, metal manufactures and machinery'; for rebates relating to 1967-68 exports the percentage was 48·6 per cent.[38] In the Tariff Board's classification the two industries 'Metals manufacture' and 'Machinery' are roughly coterminous with this industry grouping. These are the very two industries out of a total of thirty-one which the Tariff Board specifically singled out as the areas of high effective protection which should be examined first in the systematic review of the Australian Tariff begun by the Board in 1971.[39] These two industries together accounted for 31·8 per cent of the total value of production and the same percentage of the total employment in the manufacturing sector in 1967-68 and they exported a higher proportion of their output (10·6 per cent) in this year than the average for all manufacturing (5·9 per cent).

The high percentage of the total pay-roll tax rebate accounted for by this group of industries is due to the high percentage rate of growth of exports as well as the large base. The Tariff Board has conveniently computed the average rate of growth of the total value of exports of industries between 1966-67 and 1969-70. For the two industries it was 24·0 per cent compared to the average for the whole manufacturing sector of 13·5 per cent.[40] This phenomenon of the most highly protected industries achieving rapid rates of growth of export sales could reflect the fact that these 'import-competing' industries produce some commodities efficiently by the standards of world prices and are able to market these competitively abroad; for example, Australia is a low-cost producer of many basic iron and steel goods by virtue of the large resources of coking coal and iron ore. In this case export incentives encourage the production of commodities in these industries in which Australian producers are efficient by comparison with those in all other countries. If the resources used to produce these commodities come mainly from production of high-cost commodities in the same industries, then the

[38] Calculated from the table relating to 1967-68 exports in *Taxation Statistics 1969-70*, p. 198.
[39] See the Tariff Board, *Annual Report 1969-70*, chapter 2 and Appendix Table 2. The estimated average effective rates of protection for 'Metals Manufacture' and 'Machinery' were 80 and 50 per cent respectively.
[40] The statistics cited above relating to these two industries are all taken from the Tariff Board, *Annual Report 1970-71*, pp. 12, 21.

effect of these incentives is beneficial, contrary to what a hasty judgment based on the average level of import protection in the industries as a whole may suggest. This is an illustration of the importance of intra-industry substitution in production. On the other hand, exporting by highly-protected industries could also be a reflection of the ability to operate profitably by price discrimination, selling goods on the protected markets at high prices and selling abroad at prices that cover the marginal variable costs but not the capital costs.[41] With tax concessions and subsidies the export price need not cover even the marginal costs of production. In the absence of externalities or other substantial special factors such price discrimination clearly represents a misallocation of resources. We return to the problem of distortions throughout the economy in chapter 12.

In 1971 the pay-roll tax was transferred from the Commonwealth Government to the State Governments. It will be entirely up to each State to decide at what rate it will levy its own pay-roll tax and what exemptions it shall adopt. Until June 1973 the Commonwealth will continue to operate the export incentive scheme in the form of export incentive grants so as to give exporters the same rebates based on the pay-roll tax rate of 2½ per cent as before. In September 1972 the Prime Minister announced the government had decided in principle to extend export incentives beyond June 1973. 'The benefits under the new scheme will be comparable in nature and scope to those under the existing scheme' but the details were under review.[42]

Devaluation Compensation

When the United Kingdom devalued the pound sterling by 14 per cent in November 1967 and some other countries in the Sterling Area followed suit shortly after, the Australian Government considered very seriously whether the Australian dollar should also be devalued. Because Australia's international reserves were at the high level of $1,700 million, including $630 million of immediate drawing rights at the International Monetary Fund, and export prospects, especially for minerals, were good, the government decided not to change the official exchange rate. However, there was strong pressure from the farm sector and the Country Party members of the Liberal Party-Country Party Government to devalue and the Prime Minister, Mr Holt, felt it necessary to issue a series of press statements in November and December 1967 explaining the reasons for the government decision. The government noted that the devaluations that had occurred would affect some industries more adversely than others, particularly some primary industries. Of the

---

[41] Government purchasing policies may have the same effect; see Curzon and Curzon, *Global Assault*, p. 24 and Hindley, *Britain's Position*, pp. 19-20.
[42] *CPD*, H. of R., 14 September 1972, pp. 1394-5.

total exports of rural products in 1966-67 of $2,051 some $408 million, or roughly 20 per cent, were exported to the United Kingdom and the other countries which had devalued. It had also been suggested that Australia faced a massive inflow of cheap British goods competing with Australian maufactures but the government noted here that 70 per cent of Australian imports from the United Kingdom already entered duty free and are therefore largely goods not produced in Australia and that for the remainder the export and selective employment tax rebates for exports in the United Kingdom were to be abolished.

To international economists the argument for compensation should be turned around. The pound sterling had been overvalued for some time and should have been devalued before 1967. Hence exporters to the British market had been receiving higher payments in Australian currency than the exchange markets warranted. These compensation payments also illustrate how arguments used in support of some non-tariff instruments are used selectively. After the sterling devaluation some importers received a windfall gain as they paid a lower price in Australian dollars for some goods ordered from the UK and other devaluing countries. If those in Australia who receive lower prices because of the unexpected devaluation of other currencies are considered deserving of compensation, then those who benefit from paying lower prices should be considered to have gained unfairly and the gain should be appropriated by the government. However, in both cases the argument for government intervention is unsound. The risks of exchange rate changes are merely another risk of market change. Traders must accept any losses along with gains that result if they choose not to obtain forward exchange cover or exchange adjustment clauses in sales contracts.[43]

The political pressures necessitated some payments to exporters. Moreover, the pound devaluation came at a time when the government was considering measures to allow the farm sector to adjust to falling overseas demand for some products and it was reviewing the taxation concessions to exporters of manufactures which were due to expire in June 1968. In December 1967, after consultation with primary product exporters and manufacturers, the government announced that it would make 'devaluation compensation' payments to some exporters, principally exporters of farm products.[44]

[43] This argument does not apply, at least in full, to the initial payments for wheat and dairy products because of losses on contracts. In these cases, the government prevented the marketing boards from obtaining forward exchange cover and, in effect, decided to bear the risk of exchange rate changes itself.
[44] In 1968 the government also amended the Pay-roll Tax Assessment Act to provide an alternative and more favourable basis for export sales in the one year 1968-69. Where an exporter could satisfy the Department of Trade and Industry that his export sales in this year were substantially less than they would have been had the devaluations of 1967 and 1968 not occurred he was permitted to substitute the value of export sales in either 1966-67 or 1967-68 for those in 1968-69 for the purpose of the pay-roll tax rebate.

Two kinds of payments were made to primary producers; payments for contractual losses by the statutory marketing authorities and payments based on exports of certain commodities after the devaluation. A Devaluation Reporting Committee of officials was set up in December 1967 and its first priority was to decide on the compensation for identifiable losses, mainly on outstanding sterling contracts for which the statutory marketing authorities had been precluded from obtaining forward exchange cover from the Reserve Bank. The principal losses accepted by the government were $30 million by the Australian Wheat Board and $3 million by the Australian Dairy Produce Board less the amount of premiums that would have been payable had insurance cover been available plus bank interest on these devaluation losses. The United Kingdom had previously received over 60 per cent of the canned fruits exports. Payments were announced in May 1968 of 50 cents per bushel on apples and 53 cents per bushel on pears exported to the devalued markets during 1968. In August and in December 1968 the government announced the basis of compensation payments for a number of other rural products. These payments were for exports during 1968. For most commodities the bases of payments were the differences between the f.o.b. returns from sales immediately prior to devaluation and the actual f.o.b. returns after devaluation. They were subject to a maximum rate of 15 per cent (roughly equal to the $14 \cdot 3$ per cent devaluation of pound sterling) or 20 per cent in the case of dairy products because competitors from New Zealand on the United Kingdom markets had benefited from the 20 per cent devaluation of the New Zealand currency.

The general principle on which these payments to primary producers had been calculated was that 'it would not be unreasonable in the short run to attribute to devaluation the whole of the fall in export returns where it appeared that devaluation had been an important factor and that losses were demonstrable and unavoidable'. In December 1968 it was announced that devaluation compensation would be continued for another year to cover the 1968-69 production of the same commodities, essentially on the same bases as the previous year, and in October 1969 the Prime Minister announced that the policy of providing compensation for primary industries would be continued for 1970 production on the same basis as in 1969. In March 1971 it was announced that devaluation compensation would be continued for 1971 but payments would then be terminated because 'it had become increasingly difficult to differentiate between the effects of other forces in the market and the residual of Sterling devaluation'. In the case of dairy products the government had made a special increase in bounty payments of $19 \cdot 3$ million for the 1970-71 season and in the case of apples and pears the government had decided to set up a price stabilisation scheme.

Assistance to Producers 115

These arrangements obviated any devaluation payments for these commodities for the 1970-71 season. (The special one-year grant to dairy producers has been continued for the two following years.) Devaluation compensation was paid during the 1971-72 fiscal year, thus extending for some primary commodities the payments to cover four production seasons after the event of the devaluation of sterling.

A somewhat different method was used to calculate the compensation paid to exporters of manufactured goods. A Manufactured Exports Devaluation Committee was set up in February 1968 to investigate the problems of individual firms exporting manufactures and advise the government. The government announced in August 1968 that compensation would be paid on losses made by exporters of manufactures in order to regain or retain their competitive positions in overseas markets in respect to 'eligible exports'. Normally eligible exports were current exports of goods which had been exported to the devaluing countries or to third countries in the base period 1966-67 before the sterling devaluation. The compensation payable in relation to post-devaluation price reductions for these eligible exports was 100 per cent for goods exported from the date of sterling devaluation to the end of June 1968. Exporters had to make a claim for compensation to the Department of Trade and Industry. In May 1969 the government announced that devaluation compensation was to continue at diminishing levels for exports made during the three successive periods of six months starting in July 1968. The payments were to be 75 per cent of eligible exports, then 50 per cent and finally 25 per cent for the last period from 1 July to 31 December 1969. At the time of this announcement also the definition of the goods eligible for these compensation payments was liberalised to include the export of services which were ancillary to manufactured products and, for manufacturers who exported new products between the end of the 1966-67 base period and the actual date of devaluation in November 1967, they introduced an alternative base period from 19 November 1966 to 18 November 1967. Later the Minister for Trade and Industry announced that claims for eligible exports in the period ending December 1969 would be accepted up to June 1970. When payments on all of these claims had been made there would be no further devaluation compensation payments to exporters of manufactures. Some details of the payments made to manufacturers for eligible exports during the fiscal years 1968-69 to 1971-72 are set out in Table 8.4.

The status in GATT of the single most important form of assistance considered in this section, the pay-roll tax rebate, is doubtful. Two-thirds of the rebates by value have gone to producers of goods other than primary products. Under Article XVI of GATT any form of subsidy to such products which directly or indirectly 'results in the sale of such

Table 8.4 Devaluation compensation payments ($000)

	Years ending 30 June				
	1968	1969	1970	1971	1972
Rural industries					
Apples and pears	1,971	379	2,061	2,595	—
Canned deciduous fruit	—	4,261	825	90	30
Copra	—	236	—	—	—
Dairy products	889	12,875	20,012	12,698	2,631
Dried vine fruits	—	217	168	119	1,039
Eggs	—	189	246	36	46
Honey	—	145	21	7	—
Sugar	—	5,919	5,563	5,423	3,424
Wheat	18,140	10,485	—	—	—
Other	—	294	105	31	34
TOTAL rural industries	21,000	35,000	29,000	21,000	7,204
Manufacturing industries					
Textiles	—	0	307	200	—
Food	—	117	262	257	—
Light and electrical engineering	—	6	106	79	—
Heavy engineering and metals	—	687	310	3	—
Chemicals	—	2	14	3	—
Building materials and miscellaneous	—	51	171	56	—
TOTAL manufacturing industries	—	862	1,069	600	23
TOTAL ALL INDUSTRIES	21,000	35,862	30,069	21,600	7,227

Source: Rural industries: Budget Speeches, 1971-72 and 1972-73, Statement No. 9. Manufacturing industries: Department of Trade and Industry.

product for export at a price lower than the comparable price charged for the like product to buyers in the domestic market' is prohibited. No information is available on the commodities for which the rebate is granted or their prices in Australia and abroad. Since the payment of the rebate is related to the increase in export sales alone, the return to a producer per dollar of sales is higher in the case of export sales which increase his total exports than for sales on the domestic markets. It is likely therefore that exports will be pushed to the level where the *market* price for exports is less than the market price for domestic sales but the total receipts per unit of export including the rebate is roughly equal between the export and domestic markets. More than 96 per cent of the total payments under the devaluation compensation scheme have gone to producers of primary products and these would appear consistent with the provision that such subsidies 'shall not be applied in a manner which results in that contracting party having more than an equitable

Assistance to Producers 117

share of world export trade in that product',[45] especially since these payments were intended to restore in part the payments received by Australian producers in the *status quo ante* before the devaluation of sterling. The bounty on processed milk products would seem to contravene GATT.

Subsidies on Inputs used in Exports

Three forms of subsidies which are based on the value of particular inputs used in export production will be considered, namely, the export market development rebate, drawbacks and export credit subsidies.

Export Market Development Rebate

When the government introduced the export market development allowance in 1961 it was intended to encourage the development of new export markets, especially for manufactures.[46] Under Australian tax law expenditures on overseas market development is an allowable deduction from company income. The incentive introduced a double deduction, subject to a maximum limit for the tax saving of 80 per cent of eligible expenditure. This special deduction was applicable to expenditure primarily and principally in the promotion of exports of Australian goods and services and for expenditures to promote the grant or assignment of rights outside Australia in patents, trademarks, designs and copyrights. In the case of overseas visits only the fares qualified for the allowance. The allowance applied to all products in all export markets. In 1968 these provisions were continued for another five years, as were those relating to the pay-roll tax rebate but the amendments were less substantial than those to the pay-roll tax rebate. The special deduction was replaced by a tax rebate of 42·5 cents per dollar expended, subject to the new limit of a total tax saving of 87·5 cents for each dollar expended. For public companies the tax rate applicable to income in excess of $10,000 rose from $42\frac{1}{2}$ per cent to 45 per cent for income earned in the financial years ending in June 1968 and 1969 and further to $47\frac{1}{2}$ per cent for 1970 and 1971. For private companies the tax rate applicable to income in excess of $10,000 rose from $37\frac{1}{2}$ per cent to 40 per cent for the financial years ending June 1968 and 1969 and then to $42\frac{1}{2}$ per cent. The effect of the new $87\frac{1}{2}$ per cent tax saving limit is to reduce the rebate that would otherwise be payable to a

---

[45] Australia has frequently complained at GATT of the inadequacy of this provision concerning export subsidies to primary products, especially when they are used as a means of disposing of domestic supplies resulting from high support prices. See, for example, the statement reprinted in Crawford, *Australian Trade Policy*, pp. 153-4.

[46] See the statement by the Minister for Trade and Industry reprinted in Crawford, *Australian Trade Policy*, pp. 539-42.

118 *Non-Tariff Distortions of Australian Trade*

public company paying the maximum rate (47½ per cent for these two years) to 40 per cent and the total tax saving that would otherwise apply from 90 per cent (47½ + 42½ per cent) to 87½ per cent. As a result of the increases that have taken place in company tax rates, a company now paying the public company or the maximum private company tax rate may enjoy a tax saving in excess of the limit of 80 per cent which applied under the double deduction system. At the same time the classes of expenditure eligible for the concession were extended to include capital expenditures incurred in promoting outside Australia rights in relation to inventions, designs and certain classes of know-how developed in Australia.

In Table 8.4 I have estimated the tax saving to industry groups from the export market development rebate (but not including the primary tax saving due to the deduction from taxable income of these same expenditures under the normal provisions of the Income Tax Assessment Act). For the year 1969-70, which covers income earned and deductions made in the income year 1968-69, I have applied the rate of 40 per cent to the total amounts subject to rebate by all private and public companies on all taxable income.[47] The statistics of expenditures

Table 8.5 Export market development rebates 1967-70 ($000)

Industry group	Fiscal years ending 30 June			
	1967	1968	1969	1970
Agriculture, forestry and fishing	6	5	11	16
Mining	159	118	129	115
Manufacturing	3,329	3,886	4,092	6,364
Electricity, gas, water, etc. services	—	—	—	—
Building and construction	9	27	29	45
Transport, etc.	6	2	880	2,858
Commerce	880	830	708	1,102
Finance and property	28	40	39	313
Service industries	15	12	14	26
Amusement, hotels, etc.	13	22	21	9
Industry not stated*	204	134	106	498
TOTAL	4,649	5,076	6,029	11,337

Source: Computed from statistics of export market development expenditures subject to deduction from taxable income or rebate; *Taxation Statistics*, 1966-67 to 1970-71.

* This includes the deduction from taxable income or rebates for co-operatives and non-profit companies. Co-operatives and non-profit companies paid the same marginal rates of taxation as public companies, i.e. 42½ per cent up to 1966-67 and then 45 per cent in 1967-68 and 1968-69.

[47] In this year the marginal rate of taxation for public companies, which accounts for ¾ of taxable income, was 47·5 per cent. With a primary tax saving due to the deduction of 47·5 per cent and a total allowable tax saving of 87·5 per cent, the rebate is reduced to 40 per cent.

subject to the rebate are published by the Commonwealth Taxation Office.[48] For earlier years I have multiplied the statistics of expenditures in each industry group subject to the double deduction by the maximum tax saving of 80 per cent less the weighted average of the marginal rates of taxation applied to income of public and private companies in the respective years.[49] The totals calculated in this way are somewhat less than the estimates given in the annual Budget Speech; for example the figure for 1969-70 is given as $12 million compared to my estimate of $11·3 million. One factor which may account for this is that the published figures for each industry do not include the carryover of rebates from previous years in which some companies had no taxable incomes.

The tax concession has grown very rapidly in recent years and is now quite substantial, totalling $17 million in 1970-71. More than one half has gone to producers of manufacturing goods.

Drawback and By-Laws for Exports

There are two provisions in the Australian Tariff, both administered by the Department of Customs and Excise, which allow producers freedom from customs duty, and where applicable sales tax, on imported goods which are subsequently exported. These are drawback and by-laws for export.

Drawback of import duty is allowed under Section 168 of the Customs Act on the exportation of all goods other than spirits, wine, beer, tobacco, cigars, cigarettes or opium. Drawback applies both to imported materials which are used, or have been subject to a process or to a treatment or mixed with like goods produced in Australia, in the manufacture of a good which is exported and to goods which are exported in the State in which they were imported. The only imported goods which are excluded are second-hand goods which have been used in Australia, goods exported in the State in which they were imported and the value of which for home consumption is less than the amount of drawback, and materials used as an aid to manufacture, for example sandpaper or cleaning materials. The second exclusion is designed to exclude from the concession goods such as fashion clothes which have not been sold to the ultimate user and are re-exported for disposal abroad.

Item 34 of the Second Schedule of the Tariff provides for the duty-free admission under by-law of goods which are imported with the

---

[48] *Taxation Statistics 1969-70*, pp. 162-5.
[49] The weights were the percentage of taxable income earned by public and private companies: from *Taxation Statistics* for the respective years. The weighted average rates of taxation were 41·1 per cent, 41·2 per cent and 43·8 per cent for the fiscal years 1966-67, 1967-68 and 1968-69 respectively. Hence the factors used in the multiplication were 38·9 per cent, 38·8 per cent and 36·2 per cent respectively.

intention that they be later exported and which would be eligible for drawback of duty. These by-laws are available both to importers who export the good in which the imported material is used and to importers who are under contract to supply the material to the ultimate exporter. Whereas the provision for drawback dates back to the very first Federal Customs Tariff in Australia, the provision for by-law for export entry was only introduced in 1968.[50] The advantages to an Australian producer using by-law for exports rather than drawback are that he does not need capital to pay the duty for the period from the time of importing to the time of drawback payment and the amount of documentation is less than in the case of drawback. The first advantage does not always apply. While the by-law entry may be granted before the good is exported in the case of exporters who are entering a new export market or establishing a new contract, in the case of exporters who already have an established export clientele the by-laws are granted on a replacement basis after the goods are exported. The exporter must be able to substantiate that an identical quantity of goods was used in the manufacture of goods exported within the 12 months preceding the application. This feature principally accounts for the continued use of drawbacks by most exporters.

In 1970-71 drawbacks amounted to close to $7 million. There are no records kept presently of concessions under by-laws for exports but on the basis of a sample in late 1971 the value of these concessions was running at annual rates of about $2 million for 1971-72.

Under the interpretation of Article XVI of GATT the concessions to exporters under customs drawback and the by-laws for exports scheme are not regarded as a subsidy and are, therefore, permitted.

The analysis of drawbacks and by-laws, like that of other forms of tax remission, is complicated by the fact that the initial tax itself distorts trade and production. Drawbacks and by-laws for exports are considered further in chapter 10.

Subsidies on Export Credit

For more than ten years the commercial banks, encouraged by the Reserve Bank, have been giving preferences to production for export, both in terms of the availability of loans and the interest rates for bank advances. While this finance is not 'export credit' it has aided the production of goods for export, especially farm products, and probably has had as great an effect on exports as the direct credit assistance to exporters. The Commonwealth Development Bank of Australia has

[50] The Tariff Board recommended a system of by-laws for industrial chemicals used wholly in the production of goods for export in its 1966 report on *Industrial Chemicals and Synthetic Resins*, p. 31.

Assistance to Producers 121

provided since 1960 loans for the development of enterprises in the primary and secondary industries which would otherwise be unable to obtain development finance on reasonable terms. The Australian Resources Development Bank set up in 1967 is a new source of export production finance through its direct lending or equity investment in large-scale mineral ventures for periods up to ten years.

The supply of export finance[51] is not a major problem for Australian exporters of agricultural and mineral products and consumer goods which are either sold directly for cash or have satisfactory access to short-term credit of up to 180 days. The trading banks are the main source of export finance in Australia. Exporters are allowed preferences in the interest rates and conditions of bank advances and loans. Bank finance is generally considered adequate for short- and medium-term periods. Medium-term finance in the form of term loans is available for exports of capital goods from the trading banks' Term Loan Funds, which were established by arrangement between the trading banks, the Commonwealth Government and the Reserve Bank. These loans are usually for periods of three to eight years. In 1964 the eight major trading banks of that time established the Australian Banks' Export Re-Finance Corporation. This Corporation strengthened the banks' ability to provide medium- and long-term export finance by refinancing exports of a capital nature sold on terms in excess of 12 months. The principal area in which finance for exports is a recurring problem is that of long-term finance, especially of the more expensive manufactured capital goods, for which the terms of export credit have tended to lengthen in world markets.

The government's participation in export credit services is limited to two areas. The Reserve Bank has provided loans to the Australian Banks' Export Re-Finance Corporation. But the most important measure which the Commonwealth Government has taken to increase the supply of export finance was the establishment in 1956 of the Exports Payments Insurance Corporation (EPIC).

EPIC is an autonomous statutory body which is financially guaranteed by the Commonwealth Government. It provides, upon payment of a premium, comprehensive or specific insurance policies against all risks of non-payment for exports which are not covered by commercial insurance. These risks comprise buyers' defaults, political risks such as exchange transfer blockages (but not devaluation), and catastrophic risks not normally insurable. The Corporation also guarantees export loans. While the Corporation does not itself make loans this protection

---

[51] The *Annual Reports* of the Australian Banks' Export Re-Finance Corporation and the Exports Payments Insurance Corporation contain useful statements of recent developments as well as the activities of these Corporations.

against non-payment of overseas accounts also provides collateral security which increases exporters' access to export finance.

The scope of the Corporation's policies has been extended several times. In 1961 a provision was added enabling EPIC to refer to the Commonwealth Government insurance proposals which it considers are not commercially acceptable but which may be desirable in the 'national interest'. These policies are administered separately and the government, not the Corporation, is responsible for any losses. An amendment was necessary because the Corporation is required by the Export Payments Insurance Corporation Act to secure revenue to cover all its expenditures. In November 1964, the Act was further amended to allow EPIC to offer guarantees to the lending institutions which finance export transactions valued at £100,000 or more on credit terms of two or more years. The following year the Act was amended to authorise the EPIC to insure certain types of Australian investment in overseas countries against 'non-commercial' risks in these countries. Specifically, the Corporation was authorised to insure Australian investors against risk of expropriation, damage or destruction of property caused by war, riot, insurrection, and similar happenings, and inability to transfer capital or earnings back to Australia. Overseas investment policies are also kept in the government account. It was indicated at the time this amendment was before the House that such insurance would be restricted to Australian companies or other private or public bodies whose investment brings either current or potential commodity exports from Australia. Thus it was intended, like the other extensions of export insurance, as part of the export drive.[52] At the same time the capital and maximum contingent liabilities which the Corporation could accept under contracts of insurance and guarantees were increased. Again in 1970 the maximum contingent liability which the Corporation may underwrite in its own account was raised from $200 million to $300 million and the maximum contingent liability for overseas investment insurance was raised from $40 million to $100 million. In 1971 the exchange control regulations were amended to permit the granting by Australian lending institutions of 'buyers' credit' loans to the overseas buyer rather than to the Australian supplier. The Export Payments Insurance Corporation Act was then amended so that EPIC may guarantee the repayment of such loans. Guarantees will be issued subject to loans satisfying three criteria. The export goods must be capital goods for which the credit terms are longer than five years, the Australian content must normally be at least 65 per cent, the loan guaranteed must represent no more than 80 per

[52] The reasons behind the introduction of the Corporation in 1956 and the amendments of 1961 and 1965 are set out in statements by the Minister for Trade and Industry which are reproduced in Crawford, *Australian Trade Policy*, chapter 16.

cent of the contract amount and the amount of the loan after down-payment must be at least $200,000.[53]

These increases in the scope of the Corporation's insurance policies and in its maximum contingent liabilities have enabled its supply of these services to keep ahead of the demand by Australian exporters. Indeed in the first ten years or so little use of the services was made by manufacturers. However, there have been some major changes in the use of these services since then. In the five years from 1965-66 to 1969-70 the maximum contingent liability on policies written on the Corporation's own account doubled, reaching $190 million in 1969-70.[54] Policies insuring or guaranteeing exports of manufactures have rapidly increased until in 1969-70, for the first time, manufactured goods constituted more than one half of the business underwritten on its own account in terms of the face value. Insurance of exports of capital goods has increased but the value of contracts for capital goods in 1969-70 was still only a meagre $11 million. In addition the contingent liabilities on the government account totalled $17·6 million and $2·2 million respectively for overseas investment insurance and national interest insurance.

These increases in the value of exports insured by the Corporation partly reflect the rapid increase in recent years in exports of manufactures. They also reflect the increase in demand for exports because of the world-wide trend towards longer credit terms, even for raw materials and consumer goods exports for which the conventional maximum credit used to be 180 days, and the desire to remain competitive in respect to credit terms on the world markets.

Adjustment Assistance

The main discussion of the case for adjustment assistance and the criteria for desirable assistance is left until chapter 13. This section merely describes the hesitant efforts that have been made in Australia and gives some criticisms of the agricultural adjustment assistance programs.

There is no provision for adjustment assistance in the Australian tariff legislation and no financial assistance is given to companies or their employees who may be adversely affected by a reduction in the level of tariff protection following a change in the normal tariffs or by-laws or other non-tariff barriers to imports. When import licensing for a wide range of goods ceased in 1960, the government introduced provision for temporary protection, pending a review by the Tariff

---

[53] The last three restrictions are set by regulation. The terms and rationale for these new guarantees are set out in the Second Reading of EPIC Bill (No. 2) 1971 in the *CPD*, Senate, 1971, pp. 1174-8.
[54] All statistics of EPIC's activities have been taken from the *Annual Report for 1969-70* (Canberra, 1971).

Board. This provision has been used to raise duties which have been lowered after a Tariff Board inquiry but it has been used sparingly for this purpose. Under the Australian Trade Agreements with the United Kingdom, Canada, New Zealand and Japan there is provision for revocation of duty concessions but these have been used very rarely. The only action in the nature of adjustment assistance which the Tariff Board has recommended in a few of its tariff revisions is a phasing of duty or subsidy reduction to give the industry concerned more time to adjust to lower protection.[55] Apart from the possibility of dumping or a change in by-laws if the good is an input there is no other recourse open to an Australian manufacturer who has been adversely affected by a reduction in the level of protection for the goods he produces.[56]

In contrast to the absence of adjustment assistance for manufacturers whose protection has been altered, the Commonwealth Government began in 1970-71 two programs for rural reconstruction which involve quite substantial outlays.[57] This assistance was in response to changes in overseas market conditions rather than domestic protection. Farm incomes fell from $1,270 million in 1968-69 to $1,076 million the following year and fell again to $892 million in 1970-71.[58] Average income per farm operator declined to less than $4,500. In real terms this was about 45 per cent below the peak level in 1963-64.[59] It should be noted

---

[55] As recent examples the Tariff Board *Report on Knitted Shirts and Outergarments*, 29 April 1971 recommended a temporary duty in place of import licensing and the *Report on Shipbuilding*, 25 June 1971 recommended a supplementary interim subsidy at the same time as it recommended the cessation of import prohibitions of ships. Both sets of adjustment assistance were accepted though other features of these two reports were not accepted by the government.

[56] The Department of Labour and National Service does operate labour retraining schemes but they are restricted to persons displaced by technological change, an employment training scheme for Aborigines and one for women, and a rural retraining scheme. The last is discussed in this section. The others are very small in scale. The largest scheme has been that for women. The retraining of persons displaced by technological change schemes began on 1 July 1971 but by 17 February 1972 only 11 personal applications had been approved. Eligibility for the scheme was broadened as announced in the *Budget Speech, 1972-73* (Canberra, 1972), p. 11.

[57] All States have a State Bank and also one or more specialised agencies providing adjustment assistance to rural producers.

The existing State programs, incomes and debt in the rural sector, and the possibilities of increasing the four main forms of rural adjustment assistance—debt reconstruction, long-term credit and increasing farm size, and assisting those who want to leave the industry—are all discussed in some detail in the report by the Bureau of Agricultural Economics, *Debt Reconstruction and Farm Adjustment* (Canberra, 1971). Special reference is made in the Report to the sheep industry.

[58] Commonwealth of Australia, *National Income and Expenditure, 1971-72* (Canberra, 1972), p. 9. These figures include company income for farms but exclude wages, depreciation, net rents and interest paid. They include production subsidies but not $21 million of emergency assistance to woolgrowers.

[59] By contrast average weekly earnings per employed male in Australia rose by 26 per cent in real terms between 1963-64 and 1970-71. Many farmers are now earning less than $2,000 annually for their labour, management and own capital investments; see *Debt Reconstruction*, Attach. J. This compares with average earnings for male employees of almost $5,000.

too that a substantial part of this income received by farmers is direct payment by the government through bounties and other income supplements or indirectly from the consumer through import protection and two-price schemes. There are many other indicators of considerable financial difficulty. For many farmers debts equal or exceed the present value of their assets. In 1971 the Bureau of Agricultural Economics estimated that at least a third of the sheep industry is facing significant economic or financial problems.[60] The fall in incomes in the last two years was much greater than had been predicted. However, the estimated 1971-72 figure of $1,108 million showed a substantial recovery, largely due to the 16 per cent increase in average wool prices over the previous season.

Although the Commonwealth Government had decided to introduce the marginal dairy farms reconstruction scheme in April 1967 at the request of the Australian Dairy Industry Council[61] it was not until April 1971 that the last States, New South Wales and Victoria, finally signed the Agreement to introduce the Commonwealth Government scheme. The first year in which the scheme operated in all States was 1971-72. The Commonwealth agreed to provide $25 million over a period of four years. The scheme specifies that only one-half of the financial assistance from the Commonwealth to the States will have to be repaid and that over a period of 25 years at 6 per cent per annum.

A larger rural reconstruction scheme was also begun in 1970-71 under the States Grant (Rural Reconstruction) Act 1971. This scheme is intended mainly for woolgrowers who had been severely affected by sharp falls in wool prices in 1970 and 1971. Under the scheme the Commonwealth was to pay the States $100 million over four years to finance schemes of rural debt reconstruction, farm build-up and rehabilitation. Payments by the States to farmers are in the form of loans to be repaid over a maximum of 30 years,[62] except for grants in the case of farm build-up to cover losses in the disposal of 'redundant assets' which are not useful for the built-up property. Farm build-up occurs when a farmer whom it is considered could become 'economically viable' is lent or granted money to buy adjacent property which is not considered economically viable. The rehabilitation loans provide limited assistance to those obliged to leave the industry and whose properties have been purchased by an adjoining owner under the farm build-up provisions. The rates of interest on each loan are decided by the State administering

---

[60] *Debt Reconstruction*, p. 39.
[61] Australian Dairy Produce Board, *Annual Report for 1966-67*, p. 33. In 1960 the Dairy Industry Committee of Enquiry had recommended a number of measures to eliminate uneconomic dairy farms; *Report of the Dairy Industry Committee of Enquiry* (Government Printer, Canberra, 1960).
[62] The initial 20-year limit was extended to 30 years after the review of the scheme in early 1972. Repayment conditions for rehabilitation loans are very flexible.

authority but they must average not less than 4 per cent per annum for all debt reconstruction loans and not less than 6¼ per cent for farm build-up loans. The element of subsidy in these loans is very great, as one of the conditions of eligibility for both debt reconstruction and farm build-up loans is that the applicant is unable to obtain the finance from any normal source. There is a clause in the Agreement that includes a guideline suggesting that the aim is to use 50 per cent of funds for farm build-up and another clause imposes a limit of $3,000 (initially $1,000) per farmer on rehabilitation loans.

After the review of the scheme in early 1972 the terms of the loan were substantially eased.[63] The Commonwealth agreed that the $100 million allocated one year earlier for a 4-year period ending June 1975 should be paid in the two years ending June 1973. It was also agreed that the estimated proportion of funds going to farm build-up should be increased from the 10 per cent it was expected to reach in June 1972 to 30 per cent during 1972-73. This is well below the previously-agreed guideline of 50 per cent for the whole period. The total amount provided by the Commonwealth to the States for reconstruction until June 1973 was increased to $118 million, including $3 million under a supplementary grant to Queensland because of drought in that State.

The August 1971 Budget Speech also announced that the Commonwealth Government would introduce a retraining scheme for eligible farmers to supplement these two reconstruction schemes. Eligible farmers are farmers who have been occupying and working farms for which an application for reconstruction assistance under the State Grants (Rural Reconstruction) Act or the Marginal Dairy Farms Agreements Act has been or is likely to be refused, or farms acquired by other farms under the farm build-up provisions of these two schemes. The training scheme applies to farm workers as well as to farm owners and members of their families. In 1970-71 the Commonwealth Government also provided $6 million for relief of long-term indebtedness problems of canneries in Victoria, New South Wales and South Australia. As another reconstruction measure the Commonwealth Government is to make an advance of $10 million in the 1971-72 financial year to the Commonwealth Development Bank to assist the Bank's lending to farmers for the acquisition of additional land in order to build up the size and operational efficiency of their farms.

In view of the poor market prospects for wool and dairy products the need for adjustment assistance to producers of these products has not been seriously questioned, although precise and adequate reasons for this assistance have not been given. The equity argument to assist the

---

[63] See the statement by the Minister for Primary Industry, *CPD*, H. of R., 12 April 1972, pp. 1498-502.

farmer whose fall in income is largely the result of changes in overseas market conditions is weaker than the parallel case of manufacturers affected by changes in tariffs or non-tariff barriers to imports which were imposed by the Australian Government. It has been argued that, because of government calls for increased farm production in the war and post-war years to which farmers responded by committing more resources to farm production, there is a moral obligation on the present government to assist farmers now in difficulty. It should be noted that the government has not in recent years rescinded any of the financial or tax encouragements.[64]

The primary economic argument for assistance to farmers derives from impediments to the movement of resources into new forms of farming or out of farming. These may be substantial in the rural sector, particularly because of the price support schemes for some products which equalise prices and therefore pay the farmer for all his production of these products a price substantially above the value of the product to the economy. Moreover, most farmers do not have an alternative skill or professional training and need retraining if they are to find ready alternative employment outside the farming sector. However, the government should provide such retraining services or finance only if these are not already available (see chapter 13).

It is important to note that the presence of a difference between the low incomes currently earned by some farmers and higher earnings available elsewhere does not itself demonstrate that an impediment to resource movement exists or provide an argument for assistance. If a farmer has an occupational preference for farming under these circumstances then he should not be encouraged to move or be assisted (in the absence of true impediments). Similarly, there is no case for assisting farm amalgamation, even if it is true that farm size is an important determinant of farm efficiency, unless there are imperfections in the private capital market which hinder the transfers of farm land.[65] The

---

[64] Two other apparent equity arguments are often mentioned. One is that 'woolgrowers have provided over many decades benefits to the country as the mainstay of export income without any form of price support or stabilisation plan' (Second Reading of the States Grants (Rural Reconstruction) Bill 1971), *CPD*, H. of R., 29 April 1971. However, no government is obliged to compensate any sector of the economy for its past mistakes (in this case the maintenance of an overvalued currency). The second argument is the cost-squeeze on farmers because of rising domestic labour and other costs and the constant or falling overseas prices for the products. The special difficulties of farmers due to these conditions reflect the change in comparative advantage of Australia in selling overseas and are the underlying reason for adjustment. They do not justify subsidies or income supplements as a form of adjustment.

[65] The nature and the qualifications to the efficiency argument for adjustment assistance to Australian farmers have been argued cogently by G. W. Edwards, 'Rural Reconstruction: Theory and Principles', a paper presented to the 43rd Congress of the Australia and New Zealand Association for the Advancement of Science, Brisbane, May 1971.

fact that interest rates are higher than farmers want to or can pay is not sufficient; they must be higher than the opportunity cost of the borrowed capital.

There is another argument for assisting some farmers analogous to one of the arguments for assisting import-competing manufacturers and their employees. If farmers are not assisted to move, the forces of free markets and low incomes will not be permitted to force some farmers eventually off the land since there would be irresistible pressure for expanded farm subsidies and income supplements. The adjustment to new market conditions on farms may be more difficult in one respect than the adjustment in a manufacturing firm. Firms typically produce hundreds of products and there are, therefore, opportunities for shifting production to new or expanding lines. Farmers are more specialised. There are considerable opportunities for shifting to new crops or forms of livestock farming but in a large-scale adjustment many farmers must leave their present farms and some must leave farming altogether. Such movements are less likely in manufacturing. Adjustment assistance may be the only way of reducing the aggregate value of subsidy outlays to agricultural producers.

From the point of view of achieving the desirable movement of resources the present farm reconstruction plans have been criticised on several grounds.[66] The guideline in the farm reconstruction scheme that a maximum of 50 per cent of the loans be given for debt reconstruction has been criticised by farm organisations and State Governments as too low but from a national point of view it is too high since it does little to encourage farmers to increase their farm size or leave the land. This is a vital part of a successful farm reconstruction program but it is a difficult and unpopular task. The demand by farmers is for debt reconstruction first, farm build-up second and last, rehabilitation. The Commonwealth Government has capitulated to these demands for greater debt reconstruction as a proportion of the programs. A related criticism is that the total funds for rehabilitation and the (expanded) limit of $3,000 for rehabilitation loans are far too small, both absolutely and in comparison to the average loans for farm build-up and debt reconstruction which were, at the end of April 1972, $26,500.[67] Indeed, there appears to be a basic confusion in the program. If farms are to be amalgamated and built up the number of farms must be reduced and along with this amalgamation the number of farmers must be reduced. However, in introducing the legislation to Parliament the Minister for

---

[66] Some aspects of farm adjustment assistance are considered in greater detail in C. D. Throsby (ed.), *Agricultural Policy* (Penguin Books, Sydney, 1972); K. Campbell, 'Rural Reconstruction', *Current Affairs Bulletin*, August 1971. The paper by Edwards, 'Rural Reconstruction', gives a more analytical criticism of adjustment assistance.

[67] *CPD*, H. of R., 1972, p. 3358.

Primary Industry stated 'This is not a policy of "get big or get out". It is not a policy of forcing people off the land'.[68] Assistance to the less efficient farmers to change their production or leave farming is a necessary complement to assistance to those whose farms are 'viable'.

Moreover, there is a direct conflict between a reconstruction program which should be designed in part to encourage some farmers to leave farming and the increases in subsidies and income supplements to farmers which are designed to increase their incomes and encourage them to continue their present farming. This conflict is particularly acute if such subsidies and income supplements and other assistance go principally to low-income farmers, since this makes the adjustment assistance still more difficult by keeping downward pressure on the prices received and the incomes of efficient producers. Some payments such as the bounties on cheese, butter and processed milk products are paid on current production and therefore encourage sub-marginal producers to increase their current production. Similarly, other policies such as the marketing quotas on wheat are biased in favour of smaller farmers. No doubt some of these farmers deserve assistance for the reasons outlined above but the assistance should not be of a kind which aggravates the long-term difficulties of efficient producers. Fundamentally, these criticisms stem from the habit of calling farm adjustment assistance 'farm reconstruction' and interpreting this to mean the reconstruction of individual farms whereas we are really concerned with the *movement* of resources within the farming sector and between this sector and other sectors.

The full difficulty of achieving an effective adjustment program can be appreciated when it is noted that for twenty years after World War II the successive governments introduced numerous measures to increase farm production, first to relieve a shortage of foodstuffs and materials in the United Kingdom and Australia and later to increase earnings of foreign exchange.[69] It was not easy in the mid-sixties to recognise the basic changes in market prospects for some of the principal farm products and it will not be easy to reverse a long-standing policy of encouraging farm production.

---

[68] *CPD*, H. of R., 1971, p. 2234.
[69] See the numerous statements by Ministers and farm organisations on the need for and the measures to increase farm production made in the 1940s and 1950s, which are reprinted in Crawford, *Australian Trade Policy*, chapter 13.

9 General Features of Non-Tariff Distortions in Australia

Although the non-tariff distortions to trade in Australia vary widely in terms of the commodities affected, the departments by which they are administered, the reasons behind their introduction, the legal instruments that enforce them and in other respects, there are a number of common features that apply to most of the distortions or to important sub-groups of them. These are listed below as an introduction to the analysis and discussion of some of these general features in the following chapters.

1. There are important non-tariff distortions of both import and export trade.

2. Non-tariff distortions are more numerous and more important in Australia than is widely believed. The voluntary quotas on manufactures and on lamb and butter, by-laws for exports and manufacturing in licensed warehouses and discriminatory sales taxes are examples of distortions not commonly known outside of those concerned with their administration. The ways and the extent to which the value for duty procedures, the by-law system, and government purchases affect imports have not been well appreciated.

3. The importance of individual distortions has changed significantly over the last ten years. This has been the result of a number of changes relating to the administration of individual restrictions or regulations rather than any systematic policy on the part of the Commonwealth Government. Direct and indirect subsidies to exporters of both manufactures and primary products have become relatively more important. Assistance to Australian dairy farmers and woolgrowers has been markedly increased in the last two years mainly through adjustment assistance schemes and new income supplements for both groups.

In 1972 two new non-tariff restrictions on imports emerged. These are restrictive tariff quotas on knitted textiles and small-pitch chain, and the extension of offset purchasing outside defence purchases to civil aircraft and computer equipment.

4. Most of the commodities subject to low rates of duty or tax or financial assistance are materials or capital equipment, machinery or components used in the production of other goods rather than final investment or consumption goods. By-law imports are almost all capital goods. Bounties have been used mainly to assist the producers of some goods without penalising producers of other goods which use the bountiable products as important inputs. Farmers in particular benefit from bounties on tractors and nitrogenous and phosphatic fertilisers. Virtually all of the imported goods purchased by the Commonwealth Government and entered free of duty, other than defence procurements, are capital goods used by the Post Office or other government department or statutory authorities to provide services to the public.

This feature has important implications for the effective rates of protection or subsidy of Australian production which are considered in chapter 10.

The subsidies on exports and export credit, and the subsidies on butter and cheese, and the wool price deficiency scheme all benefit producers of final goods, principally primary producers and exporters. Some of the voluntary agreements, dumping and temporary protection and the import licensing of knitted shirts, coats and the like, benefit producers of final manufactured goods consumed in Australia.

5. Many of the non-tariff distortions we have examined date back several decades, several of them to the first Australian Customs Act 1901 and Customs Tariff 1902. For example, the antecedents of the present by-laws go back to the Customs Tariff 1902. The systems of manufacturing in licensed warehouses, prohibition of imports of butter substitutes, and drawbacks can all be traced clearly to the first Customs Act of 1901. The basis of the present system of plant and animal quarantine was established soon after the introduction of the first Commonwealth tariff. The introduction of anti-dumping legislation in 1906 made Australia one of the first countries to act against what it considered to be unfairly-priced imports. Bounties became an important form of protection for several Australian industries in the 1920s.

Other non-tariff distortions are of more recent origin. Temporary protection was not introduced in Australia until 1960. Import-expanding tariff quotas for goods under the tariff preference scheme for the Developing Countries and those under the New Zealand-Australia Free Trade were both introduced in 1966. Import-restricting tariff quotas on textiles were introduced in 1972. Support value duties for some chemicals were introduced in 1966. Export credit insurance and other measures to promote exports, in particular the pay-roll tax rebate for exports and the export market development allowance, began in the early 1960s.

Adjustment assistance to dairy farmers and woolgrowers and price support for woolgrowers began only in 1970-71.

6. Most of Australia's non-tariff distortions seem permissible under the Articles of GATT of which Australia is a member. The import licensing restrictions on the three commodity groups certainly breach the spirit and intention of GATT but these commodity groups are unimportant. The bounty on processed milk products would seem to contravene GATT. The status of the pay-roll tax rebate for exports is doubtful. Australia's anti-dumping provisions conform to Article VI of the GATT but they deviate in some minor respects from those laid down in the Anti-Dumping Code.

The following generalisations relate only to non-tariff distortions of *import* trade:

1. Non-tariff distortions of imports are more numerous and more important in Australia than is widely believed. This is true even if we exclude the para-tariff aspects of the Customs Tariff such as the by-law system and dumping which have been defined in this study as non-tariff distortions but which are normally regarded as purely tariff matters.

The accepted view in Australia is that almost all Australian industries receive their protection through the Customs Tariff. The official government view is that the 'Customs Tariff is the normal and accepted instrument for protection of Australian Industry'.[1] This view was accepted, for example, by the Committee of Economic Enquiry in 1965.[2] The Tariff Board itself in its recent review of the structure of protection in Australia reached the general conclusion that 'these non-tariff barriers as a whole are of minor importance in determining the protection afforded at the industry level in this study'.[3] While the substantive tariffs are more important for most industries, para-tariff and other restrictions to Australian import trade are more important than these statements indicate.

One aspect of the importance of non-tariff distortions of imports is that by-law imports and imports by the Commonwealth Government together comprise more than one-third of total import clearances. That is, only two-thirds of total actual imports enter Australia at the rates of duty laid down for all tariff items in the Customs Tariff. A further significant proportion of these are affected by quarantine,

---

[1] From the statement by the Minister for Trade in 1952, reprinted in Crawford, *Australian Trade Policy*, p. 477. Statements to the same effect have been made periodically since that date.

[2] Apart from dumping, bounties and temporary protection, the Committee devoted only one page each to import licensing and EPIC and a passing mention of import prohibitions and quarantine. The Committee made no mention of many instruments discussed here. The Committee does not seem to have appreciated the significance of by-law imports.

[3] *Annual Report for 1969-70*, p. 25.

quantitative restrictions, discriminatory sales taxes, dumping and other actions that fall within the group of non-tariff instruments.

What public discussion there has been in Australia of non-tariff distortions of imports has generally concentrated on less important instruments such as temporary protection, import licensing or less important aspects of other instruments such as the supposed unfair trading aspects of dumping. Little attention has been paid to some significant instruments such as discriminatory sales taxes and voluntary import restrictions or to the protective effects of other instruments such as dumping and government purchases.

The lack of appreciation of non-tariff forms of protection may reflect in part the concentration of public discussion on the decisions of the Tariff Board since the ending in 1960 of comprehensive import licensing which had been the main form of import regulation. It may also be due to the fact that many of the non-tariff areas of decisions that affect imports of commodities, such as by-law imports, government imports and voluntary agreements and manufacturing in bond, are decided administratively and the public is largely ignorant of the decisions and the reasons behind them.

2. For the import-competing sector perhaps the most important form of 'non-tariff' protection is the system of by-law imports which allows entry duty-free or at relatively low rates for all materials, components and fixed capital goods which are not produced in Australia. The effects of the by-law system on the pattern of effective protection have not been well understood. They are considered below in chapters 10 and 12.

3. Excluding the by-law system and other para-tariff restrictions such as dumping, most import-competing manufactured goods are protected by tariff rather than by non-tariff barriers.

However, some manufacturing industries, notably shipbuilding, chemicals, textiles and telephone equipment, receive substantial protection from a combination of non-tariff barriers to imports. The interrelatedness of non-tariff distortions is considered further in chapter 10 since it has an important bearing on the prospects for reducing non-tariff barriers in Australia.

4. Comparing Australian practice to that of other developed countries, one feature of the non-tariff restrictions to trade in Australia is that little use is made of direct quantitative restrictions to protect Australian industry; import licenses, import prohibitions, voluntary agreements and tariff quotas apply in each case to only a small group of commodities and except for the restriction of imports of ships and possibly also those on lamb and butter they are unimportant. Little deliberate use is made too of health, or technical or safety regulations or customs valua-

tion or tariff classification to restrict imports or impose higher duties to protect Australian producers.

On the other hand, there are many subsidies in Australia and there is much more discretion available to Customs officials in determining duties actually levied in Australia than in most other developed countries. Several provisions give important discretion in Australia—the alternative values for duty, granting and cancelling of by-laws, manufacturing in licensed warehouses, alternative duty rates specified in the Customs Tariff, and import prohibitions.

The particular list of six categories of non-tariff distortions agreed to in the London Program and studied here with a few additions has probably given an upward bias to the extent of Australian trade-distorting non-tariff instruments compared to those of other developed countries because it includes all major trade-distorting instruments in Australia while it omits several instruments which are known to be widespread in some other countries and to seriously distort world trade. For example, in Australia there are no exchange controls on commodity imports, or prior deposits, or State trading other than in primary commodities, or minimum import prices, or border taxes, all of which are important in some developed countries.

10 The Costs of Non-Tariff Distortions

The Nature of Distortions

A distortion is defined as any relative price which is different from the corresponding relative price in the optimal situation with complete freedom of production, consumption and trade in the country concerned,[1] except for interventions in price or production decisions by means of taxes or subsidies which can be justified by the presence of some externality or special objective. These interventions are not themselves considered distortions. In this chapter we shall be concerned solely with distortions.[2] It is possible for a quantitative restriction on trade or domestic production not to result in a distortion by this definition if domestic prices are also fixed at the free trade level. In Australia all quantitative restrictions on production or trade distort prices. The relationships between the distortions of prices and the distortions of quantities produced and traded is discussed below on pp. 159-63.

Some forms of protection of domestic producers have the characteristic that they create a difference between the price received by the producer of the commodity and the price paid by the consumer, or in case of an input, the price paid by the user. For example, subsidy payments may

---

[1] Baldwin defines a non-tariff trade-distorting policy as 'any measure (public or private) that causes internationally traded goods and services, or resources devoted to the production of these goods and services, to be allocated in such a way as to reduce potential real *world* income'; *Nontariff Distortions*, p. 5. Hindley, *Britain's Position*, also considers some effects of non-tariff instruments on the welfare of countries other than the country imposing the instrument.

In a study of the possible choices open to a country it seems preferable to take distortions in the rest of the world as given and to consider the effects of its own instruments on the welfare of this country alone.

[2] In the case of an objective other than protection such as the need for quarantine or defence or the protection of public morals, there are efficient and inefficient methods of achieving the objective. Inefficient methods entail avoidable costs. Some suggestions concerning the instruments for other objectives are made in chapter 14.

increase the price received by the producer without changing the price to the consumer or user. Or the consumer may receive some of the benefit of the subsidy as well as the producer. In either case there is a difference between the distortion of the prices to the producer and the distortion of the price to the consumer.

We shall in general need to distinguish between these two different distortions. Even in the case of simple *ad valorem* tariffs the distinction should be made. In this case a tariff on a final commodity raises the price of the commodity to the producer and the consumer by the same amount. However, tariffs or subsidies or any other instruments which change the cost of inputs to the producer of the commodity will also change the price net of these materials costs to the producer. It is these net prices which determine the decisions of producers. For a commodity protected by a tariff, therefore, the nominal tariff which determines consumer choice will normally differ from the effective tariff which determines producer choice.

There is a third kind of distortion, the distortion of the relative prices of inputs to producers. This causes inefficient or high-cost production by encouraging the greater use of inputs whose prices are below the cost to the economy.[3]

The last kind of distortion is the result of export subsidies, two-price schemes and other price discrimination which result in the domestic producer receiving a lower price from foreign buyers than he receives from domestic buyers of the same commodity. There is a similar cost when dumping policies raise the price in foreign exchange which importers of a commodity must pay.

One important feature of all distortions in prices is that they result in a redistribution of the real incomes of different groups in the economy. Those which result in high nominal tariffs or implicit nominal tariffs harm consumers of the commodities whose prices are distorted upwards. Those which result in high levels of protection or those which raise prices received by exporters benefit these producers and harm producers in the rest of the world. Tariff and non-tariff restrictions on imports transfer real income from the consumers and producers of other commodities with lower protection in Australia and from foreign producers to the producers of the protected commodities and the labour and factors which they hire intensively. Some distortions, such as export subsidies, harm domestic consumers of the commodities whose prices are raised on the domestic market while they benefit the domestic

---

[3] In terms of a general equilibrium analysis of international trade, the third distortion represents the movement to an inner transformation surface. The distortions of prices to producers and consumers give rise to the familiar production loss and consumption loss of welfare; see, for example, H. G. Johnson, 'The Cost of Protection and the Scientific Tariff', *Journal of Political Economy*, August 1960, pp. 327-45.

producers and the factors which they hire, and consumers or users in the rest of the world.

There is another important feature of distortions. The pure theory of international trade has shown that the harm from any distortion outweighs the benefits to the country imposing the distortions and, therefore, the transfers of real income leave the country as a whole worse off.[4] The net costs of distortions can be understood more concretely by breaking them into two categories. Either the distortion reduces the value of national production, or it reduces the consumer welfare derived from this production, below that which is attainable. I have endeavoured throughout the study to isolate the nature of the costs of individual distortions. I indicate, for example, how taxes and subsidies which distort relative prices of inputs increase the real costs of production, and thereby reduce the value of national production.

These distortions have arisen for several reasons. Many are survivals of historical antecedents whose justification no longer holds or needs to be modified. Some arise because of misguided policies and false arguments. Others arise because different government authorities are responsible by law for different instruments and they act independently and sometimes in conflict with each other. They should be reviewed by the policymakers. The rest of this chapter describes one important feature of these distortions in Australia and then provides some measurements of price distortions.

The Interrelatedness of Non-Tariff Distortions in Australia

One feature of the tariff revisions which are referred to the Tariff Board is that they are largely concentrated in a few areas of the tariff classification. Moreover, many of the items or groups of commodities within these 'trouble areas' have been subject to several reviews in the last ten years. They are also areas which have high levels of protection. The two principal areas of Tariff Board activity are in the tariffs relating to the products of the chemical industry and the textile industry. For example, there have been more than a dozen Tariff Board reports on

---

[4] This proposition only applies strictly if there is only one distortion. If there are additional distortions in the economy affecting other commodities to which the commodity subject to a distortion and under examination is related as a substitute or complement, either in production or consumption, it is possible that a distortion to this commodity which partially offsets distortions to its substitutes or complements may bring a net benefit to the economy. This aspect is considered in chapter 12.

The traditional terms of trade argument, and related arguments concerning discrimination among export markets or multilateral tariff bargaining, are the only valid argument for trade restrictions as the first-best instrument; see J. N. Bhagwati, *The Theory and Practice of Commercial Policy: Departures from Unified Exchange Rates*, Special Papers in International Economics, No. 8 (Princeton University International Finance Section, Princeton, 1968), chapter II. Such trade restrictions are not distorting.

polyethylene and polyethylene products alone in the last ten years[5] and these products account for only a small part of the chemical industry's production and imports. There have been five major reviews of the nitrogenous fertiliser industry over the last ten years. There were nineteen interim reports by the Tariff Board preceding the important *General Textile Reference—Final Report* in October 1967.

While compiling and studying the non-tariff instruments to Australian imports, it became more apparent that many of these barriers were concentrated in the 'trouble areas' of the Customs Tariff. Many of the commodities in these areas were subject to more than one non-tariff restriction.[6] Thus the impact and the history of various non-tariff instruments are closely related to each other and to the history of tariff reviews in these same areas. Because of the complexity of the Australian Customs Tariff and the frequency of changes in normal tariffs, by-laws and by-law determinations and non-tariff instruments in these areas, it is a major task even to trace the recent history of tariffs and non-tariff instruments affecting single tariff items.

Three cases are reviewed briefly below to show some of the interrelationships. No attempt is made to give a detailed history or analysis of these cases, though estimates of protection are made in the next section for shipbuilding and dairy products. In these cases I do not examine vertical relationships between the commodities concerned on the one hand and on the other the changes in the protection of the inputs used due to by-law changes, dumping, other non-tariff instruments or tariff revisions. Nor do I consider the effects of protection on the user industries to which they supply their output. Similarly ignored are the horizontal relationships between changes in the tariffs and non-tariffs affecting these commodities and those affecting close substitutes made from different materials or imported in a finished state. Frequently the changes to tariffs or other restrictions affecting one commodity are caused or followed by changes in the tariffs affecting close substitute commodities, or by changes to the tariffs on important inputs used by producers of these commodities. There are many such relationships affecting the three commodity groups considered here.

As the first case we shall briefly reconsider the recent history of the tariff and non-tariff restrictions on imports of 'Knitted Shirts, Mens' and Boys' Shirts'. These are currently imported under paragraphs 60.04.1 (Undergarments, such as dress shirts) and 60.05.4 (Outerwear such as

[5] For comparison the Tariff Board has done an average of about 40 reports per year over the period 1960-71.
[6] In a study of the identifiable non-tariff barriers to imports in fifteen developed countries, not including Australia, significant correlations were found between the height of tariffs in industries and the incidence of non-tariff barriers; I. Walter and J. W. Chung, 'The Pattern of Non-Tariff Obstacles to International Market Access', *Weltwirtschaftliches Archiv*, Bd 108, 1972, pp. 122-34. These authors also observed the 'multi-stacking' of non-tariff instruments in some industries.

casual shirts). As noted on p. 16 imports of these commodities were made subject to import licensing from July 1969. At that time the operative duties were 57½ per cent or, if this rate is higher $1.57 per dozen, plus 5 per cent primage, from General sources and 22½ per cent from Preferential sources. Knitted shirts from Hong Kong, Macao or Mainland China became subject to dumping duty from 23 November 1967 and those imported from Poland from 8 July 1968. Since the import licensing had followed the recommendation of the Special Advisory Authority in his report on 14 May 1969, the matter had to be referred to the Tariff Board for inquiry into the permanent protection for the products. The Tariff Board's report was sent to the Minister for Trade and Industry in August but Cabinet did not accept the Tariff Board's recommendation that import licensing be ended. Mr Anthony, the Leader of the Country Party and Deputy Prime Minister, who is also the Minister for Trade and Industry, stated in Parliament that Cabinet did not want to reduce the tariffs because the industry provided substantial employment in rural centres which were already severely hit by the recession in the wheat and wool industries.[7] Moreover, the proposed reduction would conflict with the Coalition's policies of decentralisation. The Minister also announced that the government intended to negotiate voluntary restraint agreements with the principal low-cost Asian suppliers. When these negotiations did not succeed tariff quotas with additional specific duties on imports in excess of the quotas were introduced in 1972.

The second case is shipbuilding. The arrangement that applied before May 1972 was that a government agency, the Australian Shipbuilding Board, bought all vessels from the shipbuilders and sold them to the shipowners at previously-agreed prices. Thus, the government paid a subsidy on each ship equal to the difference between the purchase price and the sale price. The purchase price is intended to equate the price of the locally-built vessel with the estimated cost of the vessel if purchased from the United Kingdom. The subsidy was subject to a maximum of 33⅓ per cent of the cost of the locally-built vessel. The local industry is protected from imports which might still undersell the Australian-built vessels despite the subsidy by the prohibited imports regulations which prohibit the import of any vessel, new or second-hand, without the permission of the Minister for Shipping. In addition, the tariffs that commonly applied were 40 per cent General and 30 per cent Preferential. The Minister announced new arrangements in May 1972 but at the time of writing these were still under discussion with the industry.

The producers of butter and cheese in Australia are assisted by almost the whole gamut of different types of non-tariff instruments, as noted in several sections. Producers of butter and cheese (and other

[7] *CPD*, H. of R., 1971, pp. 813-14.

solid butterfat products) receive a *production subsidy*. *Export* receipts were increased directly over the years 1968 to 1970 by payments to compensate for the devaluation of sterling in 1967. The production subsidy was limited to $27 million until 1971 when payments were increased to $41·5 million and the devaluation compensation for butter and cheese producers averaged over $9 million for each of the three years. To reduce competition from margarine *substitutes*, under the prohibited import regulations imports of margarine and similar butter substitutes must be coloured a distinct pink and branded with the name of the contents to distinguish them clearly from butter. Under the Dairying Industry Act the State Governments impose quotas on the domestic production of table margarine. *Imports* of butter are also prohibited under the animal quarantine regulations unless they are produced in and shipped directly from Canada, the USA, New Zealand, Northern Ireland or Ireland. Further, there is an agreement between the Australian Dairy Produce Board and the New Zealand Dairy Board that New Zealand butter will not be exported to Australia. In response to the falling prices for exports of dairy products and the uncertain prospects of the industry when the United Kingdom joins the EEC, the government in the last two years has made supplementary bounty payments and introduced an *adjustment assistance* scheme under which it will provide $25 million in loans and grants to assist farm amalgamation and debt reconstruction in the industry. From 1973 there will probably be *production quotas* as part of the industry stabilisation arrangements. All of these non-tariff barriers assist producers, the gross value of whose milk produced and used for butter and cheese production, including the subsidies, was $217 million in 1970-71.[8]

Several other goods are subject to more than one non-tariff barrier. The case of nitrogenous fertiliser is another that is particularly difficult to disentangle as it involves important subsidies and bounties under three different Acts, support values and support value reviews, changes in by-laws, several dumping actions, quotas for the developing countries since 1966 as well as four major tariff reviews. Moreover, events in the nitrogenous fertiliser industry are closely associated with developments in the whole chemical industry.

One notable feature is that the industries that are subject to multiple non-tariff instruments in Australia are generally the industries that are more subject to non-tariff instruments in other developed countries. In their recent study of non-tariff instruments in fifteen developed countries, Walter and Chung found: 'Sectors which emerge as particularly heavily subject to NTBs are processed foods, beverages and tobacco products,

[8] Annual Report of the Dairy Produce Board, for the Year Ended June 1971, *CPP*, no. 97, 1971, table 37. Dairy and other farmers are also assisted by bounties on inputs of nitrogenous and phosphatic fertilisers and on tractors, and they receive numerous farm income tax concessions.

certain chemicals, pharmaceuticals, starches and allied products, cotton and synthetic textiles, electrical and electronic apparatus, motor vehicles and clothing'.[9] Similarly all countries in the London Program subsidise their shipbuilding industry. In addition to the non-tariff instruments affecting textiles, shipbuilding, butterfat processed foods, and chemicals mentioned above, we have noted elsewhere in this study non-tariff instruments in Australia affecting the other industries in this list. These include the discriminatory sales tax exemption for alcoholic beverages, government purchasing preferences and manufacturing in bond for electrical and electronic apparatus, and the content plan and by-laws for motor vehicle assembly in Australia. This similarity across countries in the incidence of non-tariff instruments by industry reflects the greater competition in world markets for these commodities, either from other developed countries as in the case of chemicals or from developing countries principally as in the case of textiles.

The multiplicity of instruments affecting some commodities has important implications for the level of protection, which is discussed in the next section and for multilateral and unilateral changes in policies.

Rates of Distortion implied by Some Non-Tariff Instruments

The multiplicity of non-tariff instruments that apply to some commodities poses a choice. Should we examine each instrument or each distortion? In other words, should we measure the effects of one non-tariff instrument alone or should we measure the joint effects of the combination of non-tariff instruments which apply to the commodities in question? And in either case should we include in our measurement the effects of the tariffs which apply to the same commodities? It is only the joint or net effects of all instruments affecting each commodity which matter in determining the extent of the distortions of prices in the economy. This suggests that we should look at all tariff and non-tariff instruments jointly. On the other hand, several of the significant non-tariff instruments apply to large groups of commodities and are administered without regard to the effects of other instruments that may jointly determine the effective protection available to producers of the commodities. Some of these instruments, such as the rules of government purchasing, are periodically subject to review. In the conclusion, I recommend the abolition of several instruments and their replacement by simple *ad valorem* tariffs where necessary. Where the instrument itself is or may be reviewed, it is important to have some idea of the net effect of this instrument alone on the pattern of protection or assistance to producers.

To compare different non-tariff instruments, either singly or in combination, it is necessary to reduce them to some common standard of

[9] 'The Pattern of Non-Tariff Obstacles', p. 126.

comparison. The most obvious device is to calculate the *implicit nominal ad valorem tariff* for the non-tariff instrument(s) applying to a commodity or set of commodities.[10] The following discussion of implicit tariffs is in terms of commodity price distortions but the same principles apply to the analysis of individual instruments.

For an importable commodity subject to non-tariff-induced distortions, the implicit tariff is usually defined as the percentage by which the domestic price exceeds the landed duty-free price of the import commodity which is a perfect substitute. Assuming that the price of the imported commodity is fixed on world markets, the implicit tariff defined in this way is also the percentage change in the price to the domestic consumer or industrial user brought about by the distortion.[11] This is the implicit price change relevant to the consumption loss of the distortion.

If there is any domestic production of the importable commodity, this implicit tariff is for some distortions also the percentage change in the price received for the commodity by the domestic producers. However, in the case of distortions involving subsidies, which create a difference between the commodity price to the consumer and the price to the producer, this identity is no longer true. The change in the price to the consumer is less than the change in price to the producer. If the world price is fixed, a production subsidy will have zero effect on the price to the consumer. For the purpose of measuring the price change relevant to the production loss, one should define the implicit price change as the percentage change in the price for the commodity received by the producers. For an exportable commodity, the export price which is received by the producers may differ from the landed duty-free price of an importable substitute because of international transport and insurance costs.

To distinguish these two price changes, I shall refer to the *implicit price change to consumers* and *the implicit price change* (or the implicit rate of protection) *to producers* rather than the ambiguous term the 'implicit tariff'. The implicit price change to producers is the nominal rate rather than the effective rate unless otherwise stated. One seeks to estimate the effects of tariffs and non-tariff instruments on producers' incomes rather than on the price received for the commodity produced;

---

[10] Alternatively we could express each instrument or combination of instruments in terms of one of the non-tariff instruments. Calculations have been made in Australia of the (production) 'subsidy equivalent' of some tariffs but for our purposes of examining the restrictiveness of these barriers the implicit tariff is preferable to the subsidy equivalent. The former gives an indication of the effect of the instrument on producer prices alone.

[11] If the world prices are not fixed, the percentage change in the price to consumers and the percentage by which the domestic price exceeds the foreign price differ. In this event it is preferable to use the change in the price to consumers: see J. N. Bhagwati, 'More on the Equivalence of Tariffs and Quotas', *American Economic Review*, March 1968, pp. 142-6.

that is, one should calculate the implicit effective tariff. This takes into account the changes in the prices of inputs. We shall consider some implicit effective rates below. No attempt is made in this section to measure the effects of changes in the relative prices of inputs on the real costs of production. These are the third source of loss due to distortions in the economy.

Another major aspect of measuring the implicit price changes for most non-tariff instruments is that the levels of price changes often vary considerably, both among the commodities which may be subject to the instrument and for each commodity over time. This variation occurs for two reasons. First, many non-tariff instruments, unlike the tariffs which are specified in the Schedules to the Customs Tariff and normally remain fixed for many years, are changed frequently. Some are subject to a large degree of administrative discretion (for example, value for duty, and by-law imports), or are decided *ad hoc* in each individual case (for example, government purchases and dumping actions). Quotas may be varied.

Even if there is no change in the instrument itself, it is inherent in the nature of most non-tariff instruments that the level of nominal protection implied varies with the domestic demand or some other variable. It is clear that the level of the implicit protection implied by a fixed quota increases as demand for the commodity or domestic costs increase.[12] The same applies to other quantitative restrictions, including import prohibitions. The level of protection implied by other non-tariff instruments varies with, for example, the landed duty-free cost of the particular shipment of imports (as in the case of support value duties) or with the domestic costs of production (as in the case of subsidies on gold bullion or ships) or with the source of the imports (as in the case of some quarantinable goods).

An illustration of the variability of the nominal rates of protection for producers is provided by the shipbuilding subsidy as it operated before the changes announced in May 1972. In this case the variation in the implicit price change to the producer arose from three separate features of the subsidy scheme. First, as noted earlier, the subsidy varied as the amount necessary to equate the price of the locally-built vessel with the estimated cost of the vessel if purchased from the United Kingdom, up to a maximum of 33⅓ per cent of the cost to build the vessel in Australia. Second, the level of implicit protection should be

---

[12] The basic reference is to the paper by J. N. Bhagwati, 'On the Equivalence of Tariffs and Quotas', in J. N. Bhagwati, *Trade, Tariffs and Growth* (Weidenfeld and Nicolson, London, 1969). See also M. Kreinen, 'More on the Equivalence of Tariffs and Quotas', *Kyklos*, 1970, pp. 75-8.
An example of the sharp changes in levels of protection due principally to import licensing in only one year is given for India by J. N. Bhagwati and P. Desai, *India: Planning for Industrialisation* (Oxford University Press, London, 1970), chapter 17.

obtained by relating the Australian price to the cost of the import from the cheapest foreign source. There is a variable difference between the cost of the United Kingdom potential import and the cheapest potential import from some other country. The United Kingdom costs were used as a base for the subsidy from 1947 because the United Kingdom was at that time the likely source of Australian purchases of imported ships.[13] Third, the UK prices which the Australian Shipbuilding Board (ASB) used for calculating the subsidy were in most instances assessed from knowledge and advice available to the ASB and were not based on actual quotations.[14] The higher costs of the UK shipyards and the import prohibitions have meant that they do not even tender in most instances.

The multiplicity and variability of non-tariff instruments make it much more difficult to measure the effects of these instruments on prices than it is to measure the effects of tariffs. The multiplicity of instruments means that they must be looked at together and with instruments such as import prohibitions it is likely that some of the protection available will not be used. Therefore one must measure the implicit price changes directly in most cases by a comparison of the landed duty-free price of imports or the export price on the one hand with the domestic prices to producers and consumers of the locally-produced substitutes. The resulting measures are averages that may hide considerable variance for individual orders and may differ substantially from the average level of implicit protection for the same commodities in the previous or subsequent years.

It is not surprising that few measurements have been made of the effects of non-tariff instruments in any country. The few estimates that have been made mainly relate to quotas and other quantitative restrictions.[15]

It is not possible to estimate the effects of most *individual non-tariff instruments* in Australia for several reasons. For some non-tariff instruments such as manufacturing in licensed warehouses, dumping and support value duties, some voluntary quotas, export subsidies by means of the export incentive scheme or the export market development

---

[13] If UK prices are used, the implicit protection is understated considerably. Since 1947 UK costs have risen steadily relative to those of some other shipbuilding countries, notably in recent years, Japan.

[14] Tariff Board, *Report on Shipbuilding*, 25 June 1971, p. 13.

[15] The most notable effort to date to measure the production effects of non-tariff instruments is that by Baldwin who measured for a selection of non-tariff instruments in the United Kingdom and the United States the effective rates of protection for industries: *Nontariff Distortions*, chapter 7. Economists in some countries have made estimates of the nominal rates of protection implied by import licensing systems; for example, Bhagwati and Desai, *India: Planning for Industrialisation*, chapter 17 and W. Candler and P. Hampton, 'The Measurement of Industrial Protection in New Zealand', *Australian Economic Papers*, June 1966, pp. 47-58. None of the other country studies in the London Program have estimated rates of protection for non-tariff instruments.

rebates, the payments or duty concessions cannot be traced to the individual commodities from the statistics presently collected. For some other non-tariff instruments data is collected that would enable the estimation of implicit nominal rates of protection but it is not available to the general public. The outstanding example of this problem is the whole important area of government purchases by tender.

For a few non-tariff instruments there is some information readily available which gives us an indication of the protective effects of these instruments. The most simple of these is the discriminatory sales taxes discussed in chapter 7. The tariff implied by all of the discriminatory exemptions of Australian-produced commodities subject to sales taxation is a constant 15 per cent *ad valorem*. This additional implicit protection applies to all beer, cider, wine, fruit juice products (with a minimum local content in this case) and to boxes, cases and crates. The export incentive payments are equal to 10·5 per cent of eligible exports.

For three methods of tariff duty concessions—manufacturing in licensed warehouses, customs drawback and by-laws for exports—we have statistics or estimates of the value of the duty waived. A review of manufacturing in licensed warehouses in 1970 by the administering department, the Department of Customs and Excise, found that the duty waived was approximately $2 million annually in 1968-69 and 1969-70 of which one half applied to electrical equipment. This department also estimated that in 1971 the value of concessions under the by-law for export scheme was running at an annual rate of about $2 million, and under the customs drawback provisions it was $6·8 million in 1970-71. Regrettably statistics are not kept of the value of imports of the commodities to which these concessions are applied and, therefore, no estimates can be made of the implicit tariff reductions.

Many non-tariff instruments result in the total or virtual exclusion of all imports and are, therefore, equivalent to prohibitive tariffs. In Australia the most significant prohibitive restrictions relate to primary products such as wheat, butter and lamb as noted elsewhere. The prohibitive effect of these instruments does not measure the implicit protection but in the case of butter and wheat, these import prohibitions account for part of the implicit protection reported in Table 10.2.

Further estimates of the effects of one instrument on the pattern of nominal and effective rates of protection were made in the case of by-laws and by-law determinations. On p. 49 we noted that one general effect of granting concessional entry under by-law to non-competitive imports is to increase the effective protection for producers, using as inputs the goods imported. Because the percentages of importable materials which actually are admitted under by-law, the differences between the by-law rate and the normal duties otherwise payable and the ratio of the value of importable materials to the value of output all differ among producers we expect the use of by-law to affect the pattern of effective protection.

Table 10.1 reports estimates of effects of by-laws and by-law determinations on the pattern of effective protection among Australian manufacturing industries in 1967-68. These figures were computed at my request by the Tariff Board, using data prepared by the Tariff Board for its 1970 study of effective protection in the manufacturing sector.[16] This table reports the rates of effective protection previously published by the Board and an alternative set of rates which were obtained by applying the tariff rate for normal private imports under each tariff item to by-law imports as well as normal private imports, and then substituting the higher average tariff on importable materials in each industry in the expression for the effective rate of protection for the industry. In all other respects the assumptions used for the alternative set of estimates are precisely the same as those used in the original Tariff Board computations. Thus the alternative set estimates what the effective rates would have been if all materials imported under by-law in each industry had paid the substantive rates of duty. This method of estimating the effects of by-law entry of materials ignores the substitution among inputs that might occur if the by-law system were abolished and no further changes made to the Customs Tariff but such input substitutions are unlikely to be sufficiently large to alter significantly the estimates.

These estimates confirm the prediction that the Australian system of by-laws significantly changes the scale and the rankings of effective protection to Australian manufacturers. According to these estimates the abolition of by-law entry by itself would lower the effective protection for twenty-five of the thirty-one Tariff Board industry groupings of manufactures. While many of the changes are small, in the case of seven industries the adjustment is quite large and definitely significant. The seven industries which receive substantially higher average effective protection because of the widespread admission of their materials at concessional rates under by-law are the group of three chemical or chemical-based industries, 'Pharmaceutical and toilet preparations', 'Paints, polishes and inks' and 'Plastic products', the group of two transport industries, 'Motor vehicles and parts' and 'Vessels and other transport equipment' and the 'Machinery' and 'Jewellery, toys and other products' industries. This result is consistent with other evidence,[17] which shows that the three largest groups of imports in terms of value of the imports cleared under by-law are the products of chemical and allied

---

[16] The Board's estimates of effective rates of protection were published in its *Annual Report for Year 1969-70*, Appendix 2.

[17] An unpublished tabulation prepared by the Bureau of Census and Statistics shows normal, by-law and Commonwealth Government imports for 1969-70 classified by the 100 chapters of the BTN.

Table 10.1 Effects of by-laws on the pattern of Effective protection of manufactures

Industry	Average nominal rate on importable materials used		Ratio of value of materials to value of output	Average effective rate	
	Actual	By-law imports at substantive rates		Actual	By-law imports at substantive rates
1.1 Glass and clay products	2	5	44	29	26
1.2 Bricks	1	1	31	48	47
1.3 Cement and plaster products	1	2	32	28	27
2.1 Chemicals and fertilisers	3	5	54	36	33
2.2 Pharmaceuticals and toilet preparations	5	16	53	68	56
2.3 Soaps and detergents	3	7	49	35	31
2.4 Paints, polishes and inks	13	25	48	62	50
2.5 Oil and fuel	1	1	71	3	3
3.1 Metals manufactures	5	7	57	80	77
3.2 Machinery	16	29	45	50	38
3.3 Motor vehicles and parts	17	39	62	67	25
3.4 Vessels and other transport equipment	9	46	42	71	44
4.1 Yarn and cloth	4	7	41	42	41
4.2 Clothing	13	15	54	74	72
4.3 Rope, canvas and sacking	7	7	73	120	119
5.1 Wool scouring and fellmongering	0	0	68	0	0
5.2 Leather goods, handbags and cases	9	10	58	63	62
6.1 Footwear	18	19	55	68	67
7.1 Confectionery	34	35	46	39	38
7.2 Brewing, winemaking and distilling	8	8	51	16	15
7.3 Animal and vegetable oils	4	4	62	5	4
7.4 Food and drinks	9	9	42	19	18
7.5 Tobacco products	70	70	46	30	30
8.1 Timber milling	10	10	57	22	22
8.2 Wooden products	17	17	48	30	30
9 Furniture	19	22	50	54	50
10 Paper stationery and printing	4	7	27	37	36
11 Tyres and other rubber products	15	16	57	33	33
12 Plastic products	21	29	54	55	46
13.1 Optical and scientific instruments	17	20	39	6	4
13.2 Jewellery, toys and other products	5	16	53	68	56

Source: Tariff Board.

industries and plastics, machinery and mechanical appliances, vehicles and other transport equipment.

The total effects of the by-law system on the distortion of prices to producers are substantially greater than indicated in the table. First, the method ignores all imports of fixed capital equipment under by-laws and these are probably more important in total value than imports of materials used up in the process of manufacture.[18] Second, these estimates are averages for large industries producing many commodities but it is the rates of protection for individual commodities rather than the industry averages which determine producer decisions. The by-law system has certainly changed significantly the relative prices to producers of some commodities within industries, and resources such as skilled and managerial labour and some multi-purpose machines may be switched quite readily within a range of processes in an industry. Third, the tens of thousands of administrative decisions to grant, extend or cancel by-laws and by-law determinations each year must result in an unstable level of protection for those producers whose materials, fixed capital equipment or own products are substantially affected by these decisions. In particular, attention was drawn to the last category of producers and especially the Australian producers of machinery who receive very high levels of protection under 'dragnet' items of the Customs Tariff when by-laws are cancelled. On pp. 181-2 some suggestions are made to reduce the costs of the distortions which are due wholly or in part to the by-law system.

We now consider the distortion of prices of some individual *commodities* due to non-tariff instruments.

In its last *Report on Shipbuilding* the Tariff Board has supplied figures which enable us to estimate the implicit price change to the producers resulting from the subsidy arrangements and import prohibition affecting shipbuilding in Australia. The Tariff Board received evidence comparing local tenders for large ships such as tankers, bulk carriers, and specialised cargo units, with quotations and other prices received from a number of other countries between 1965 and 1970. These showed that large ships

> which are a large segment of the local demand, could have been obtained from shipbuilders in several overseas countries at contract prices which were only 50 to 65 per cent of the prices charged by Australian builders . . . Further advantages offered by overseas

---

[18] No classification of by-law imports into materials and fixed capital equipment is available but the statistics of by-law imports by chapter of the BTN permit a rough division. The tools, machinery, mechanical appliances and transport equipment of chapters 82, 84-9 inclusive, which are primarily fixed capital equipment, amounted to 72 per cent by value of total by-law imports in 1969-70. These chapters include some materials but offsetting this there are fixed capital imports under by-law in other chapters.

builders in the form of extended credit, low interest rates and shorter construction times were estimated by the Board to be equivalent to a subsidy within the range of 5 to 10 per cent.[19]

A subsidy expressed as a percentage of local cost ranging from 55 to 75 per cent gives an implicit rate of protection of between 122 and 300 per cent.[20] The ASB also estimated for the Board that the materials and components were on average 50 per cent of the construction costs of the recognised yards. If the percentage of value added is taken as one half and the tariffs on the materials and components are ignored, this yields estimates of the effective rate of protection which range from 244 to 600 per cent.[21] The Board stated in one place that their estimates of effective protection ranged from 150 to 300 per cent and elsewhere in the Report it gave a different estimate of 300 to 400 per cent.[22] Whichever estimate is used, some of the rates of effective protection implied by these arrangements are very high. As many of the smaller ships built particularly by the non-recognised yards over this period received no subsidy and some were exported, the levels of effective protection ranged from near zero to the upper limits calculated above.

Moreover, it is possible in the case of shipbuilding to break down the implicit nominal rates of protection to the separate contributions of the tariffs, subsidies, and the import prohibition. The nominal protection available from tariffs alone in this period was in most cases the 40 per cent General tariff rate. The implicit nominal protection available from the subsidy alone was 50 per cent at the maximum rate of subsidy of 33⅓ per cent of local cost. If there were a maximum subsidy of 33⅓ per cent plus a tariff of 40 per cent, then the nominal protection available would be 110 per cent.[23] In this case the effect of the tariff is to allow the domestic subsidised price to rise to the foreign landed price including the tariff. The excess of the nominal rate of protection actually observed and noted in the previous paragraph over this rate of 110 per cent is attributable to the import prohibitions, as the Tariff Board observed.

Direct estimates were made of the price distortions implied by the *joint* effects of numerous instruments affecting selected agricultural commodities. Tables 10.2, 10.3 and 10.4 report the estimates of the implied nominal rates of protection for producers of the commodities and the implied price change to consumers which are due to the com-

---

[19] *Report on Shipbuilding*, p. 13.
[20] If s is the rate of subsidy expressed as a percentage of local unit cost, the rate of implicit protection defined as the increase in the producer price above the landed cost of the overseas vessel is $g = s/(1-s)$.
[21] Strictly speaking one should use the free trade value added percentage.
[22] *Shipbuilding*, pp. 13, 17-18.
[23] In this case if t is the nominal tariff, the nominal protection which alone is implied by both the nominal tariff and the subsidy is $g = (s+t)/(1-s)$.

binations of tariff and non-tariff instruments affecting each commodity. These estimates were made at my request by the Bureau of Agricultural Economics. Two distinct sub-groups of commodities are considered. The first is the group of commodities which are currently exported but whose domestic sales are substantially in the hands of marketing boards which fix or implement agreed prices. The second is a selection of commodities which have not been exported on a substantial scale. Further information on the data and methods used is given in the Appendix.

In computing the estimates of the effects of these instruments on producer and consumer prices, there is a problem in choosing the base price that would prevail if there were free international trade between Australia and other countries in the commodity concerned. In particular, should one use the import parity or the export parity price? The answer seems clear in principle. If the commodity would be exported if there were no interventions in the market for this commodity, then one should use the export parity price, and if the commodity would be imported one should use the import parity price. In each case these are the prices that would prevail if there were completely free trade. For import commodities there is an element of dumping in that some of the import parity prices are below the comparable prices in the country of supply. However, for this purpose one should use the estimate of the import price if the commodities were or could have been supplied to Australia, whether or not it is a dumped price. (See pp. 60-1.) Moreover, the export parity prices are dumped prices; Table 10.4 measures for the export commodities the percentage by which the average price received by Australian producers exceeded the average price realised on export sales. For the calculations in Tables 10.2, 10.3 and 10.4 it has been assumed that the present international trade prices would not change with the changes in Australian trade and production and that the commodities presently exported would continue to be exported under free trade in these commodities.[24]

Increases in the prices received by producers of a commodity may be due to two distinct sets of policies or instruments. First, the prices received by producers of some agricultural commodities are increased by subsidies paid directly to the producers. Second, import prohibitions, quarantine and other restrictions on imports, such as the voluntary agreements between the marketing Boards of Australia and New Zealand, permit the domestic prices to be maintained substantially above the

---

[24] The latter is not as safe an assumption as it may seem for two reasons. First, production or export subsidies may convert a good which is importable under free trade into a good which is exportable under protection. Second, when one considers the possibilities of shifting resources from one farm commodity to another when the prices of all major farm commodities are changed after the freeing of trade, it is not clear which commodities would be exported and which imported in this situation. Both of these complications are discussed in the next section.

import parity prices that would otherwise prevail. The first set of policies transfers income from taxpayers to rural producers while the second set transfers real income from the domestic consumers to the domestic producers of these commodities.

Table 10.2 shows the contributions to the total price changes of direct subsidy payments based on production or exports for those selected commodities receiving subsidies. The subsidies paid to producers of each commodity have been expressed as a percentage of the export or import parity prices. Payments included in this table were the butter and cheese bounty, the raw cotton bounty, the Commonwealth payments under the wheat stabilisation scheme and devaluation compensation payments to producers of dairy products, dried vine fruits, sugar, wheat and eggs for the years 1968-71. They do not include adjustment assistance to dairy farmers or woolgrowers, or subsidies on fertilisers, tractors, rail transport, export credit and other inputs or income tax concessions. Subsidies paid to producers of butter and cheese, cotton and wheat

Table 10.2 Rates of subsidies for selected agricultural commodities, 1946-47 to 1970-71 (percentages)

	Butter	Cheese	Cotton*	Wheat	Sugar	Eggs	Dried vine fruits
1946-47	14·6	11·8	—	—	—	—	—
1947-48	14·5	14·7	—	—	—	—	—
1948-49	11·9	9·0	—	—	—	—	—
1949-50	15·0	14·7	—	—	—	—	—
1950-51	26·7	22·1	—	—	—	—	—
1951-52	31·9	16·7	—	—	—	—	—
1952-53	21·8	15·7	—	—	—	—	—
1953-54	22·4	15·3	5·8	—	—	—	—
1954-55	20·5	15·6	11·5	—	—	—	—
1955-56	18·4	12·1	21·5	—	—	—	—
1956-57	22·0	15·7	66·1	—	—	—	—
1957-58	30·1	26·1	49·9	—	—	—	—
1958-59	19·4	10·8	56·3	2·6	—	—	—
1959-60	18·5	14·2	41·8	5·3	—	—	—
1960-61	26·3	13·5	63·7	4·6	—	—	—
1961-62	21·5	12·9	46·1	5·9	—	—	—
1962-63	18·8	11·5	53·1	0·4	—	—	—
1963-64	18·0	11·2	46·1	3·9	—	—	—
1964-65	17·9	10·1	64·4	4·9	—	—	—
1965-66	19·6	11·0	65·8	2·4	—	—	—
1966-67	19·2	10·8	43·8	1·3	—	—	—
1967-68	33·6	27·5	45·2	4·5	0·5	—	—
1968-69	37·4	36·6	26·2	8·6	4·4	3·5	2·5
1969-70	33·4	30·4	23·0	10·0	4·6	3·3	0·9
1970-71	43·6	17·7	22·2	13·2	2·2	4·2	1·3

* Import parity price used. For all other commodities export parity prices were used.

Source and Notes: See Appendix.

have all been substantial in recent years when expressed as a percentage of the product price. Moreover, butter and cheese and wheat are major agricultural commodities in terms of the value of production.

In comparing the distortions of prices among agricultural commodities or the distortions of prices of agricultural commodities with those of manufactures, we must include the effects which restrictions on imports have indirectly on domestic prices. Table 10.3 reports the estimates of increase in average prices to producers of the selected agricultural commodities which are due to both sources of increased prices, the direct subsidies and the higher prices paid by buyers. These estimates follow one of the methods employed by Stuart Harris in an earlier pioneering paper on the levels of protection for Australian rural industries.[25]

Producers of all of the agricultural commodities examined have received positive assistance from the instruments operated by the Commonwealth Government in recent years. There is a steady upward trend in the levels of protection and assistance to producers of some of these agricultural commodities throughout the post-war period in Australia but I shall concentrate solely on the pattern in recent years.

The extent of this assistance to agricultural producers varies greatly among producers of the different commodities. Thus, there are substantial distortions of resource allocation within the agricultural sector. The price increases are greatest for producers of eggs, tobacco and dairy products but they are also substantial for producers of all the other agricultural commodities except barley.

Another important result is that all of the commodities exhibit substantial annual variations in the degree of nominal protection or assistance to producers. This variation is due to variation in either of the two sources of higher prices (see Appendix). First, the export or import parities themselves fluctuate significantly for some commodities, especially sugar and dairy products, while some of the instruments such as the butter and cheese bounty give assistance to producers whose level is changed or is fixed in terms of units of quantity and therefore varies as a percentage of price. Second, the insulation of the domestic markets from the world markets by means of import restrictions allows prices on the domestic markets to fluctuate with changes in domestic supply and demand conditions or to remain constant when the foreign prices fluctuate; this occurs, for example, with the annual fixing of dairy product prices in Australia. These variations illustrate the instability of the distortions of prices which result from instruments other than *ad valorem* tariffs or subsidies.

[25] S. F. Harris, 'Some Measures of Levels of Protection in Australia's Rural Industries', *Australian Journal of Agricultural Economics*, December 1964, pp. 124-44.

Table 10.3 Implicit price changes to producers for selected agricultural commodities, 1946-47 to 1970-71 (percentages)

	Butter	Cheese	Wheat	Sugar	Eggs	Dried vine fruits	Barley	Rice	Cotton	Linseed	Tobacco
1946-47	1·4	5·9	−44·3	1·6	3·0	7·5	n.a.	−1·0	n.a.	n.a.	n.a.
1947-48	1·2	4·5	−16·7	−15·6	1·1	9·8	−23·9	−4·0	n.a.	−8·7	n.a.
1948-49	−0·2	1·8	−18·0	−9·5	−5·2	12·0	−16·7	−4·4	n.a.	43·9	n.a.
1949-50	−0·1	1·9	−17·9	−9·2	−5·5	12·8	−15·7	−3·5	n.a.	9·4	n.a.
1950-51	4·4	6·1	−21·2	−14·2	2·4	2·3	−18·0	−14·2	n.a.	−1·2	n.a.
1951-52	11·4	15·6	−17·6	−6·6	21·6	2·9	−14·5	−7·2	n.a.	9·8	5·5
1952-53	24·1	25·8	−7·6	3·7	8·8	4·0	−1·2	−0·8	n.a.	0·8	22·2
1953-54	22·2	24·1	−0·1	9·9	9·9	6·8	4·1	5·9	3·2	26·1	58·2
1954-55	22·9	30·3	4·3	10·6	30·9	6·5	0·5	10·7	−2·6	11·1	79·5
1955-56	32·0	13·0	1·2	10·0	35·0	4·2	4·5	10·1	5·4	−2·8	48·4
1956-57	53·5	50·1	−2·1	13·1	31·6	4·1	3·7	8·9	30·3	12·0	46·4
1957-58	89·8	100·5	1·4	7·7	48·8	3·7	−0·4	9·9	30·9	17·7	45·7
1958-59	43·0	11·5	2·5	15·4	57·0	4·1	2·2	12·8	23·8	18·6	58·2
1959-60	40·0	35·4	6·6	17·8	46·3	11·9	10·6	15·3	43·3	9·4	56·4
1960-61	78·9	34·6	8·2	22·9	58·2	11·0	3·8	13·8	42·9	16·7	29·2
1961-62	58·4	40·2	6·9	27·9	41·8	11·5	3·2	11·6	−2·1	5·3	64·0
1962-63	44·8	30·9	8·9	16·9	59·6	11·6	5·5	13·9	34·2	18·6	57·3
1963-64	41·4	31·9	0·6	−2·6	55·6	7·5	2·1	17·2	93·2	17·2	44·1
1964-65	41·8	27·7	5·9	14·2	94·0	6·8	0·9	18·5	92·3	12·8	40·0
1965-66	51·1	32·6	7·1	26·6	138·2	11·7	1·7	13·0	106·0	17·1	62·4
1966-67	51·4	38·4	3·4	30·5	100·0	13·4	2·2	10·5	86·8	18·2	46·1
1967-68	94·4	89·9	18·8	38·9	129·5	15·2	13·2	11·4	75·5	7·4	48·3
1968-69	107·2	105·6	8·2	37·4	187·9	32·5	2·9	15·7	61·4	4·9	52·6
1969-70	88·6	85·8	12·8	30·6	150·6	21·3	1·8	23·4	39·8	15·5	47·0
1970-71	92·2	60·2	15·6	19·2	119·3	37·1	−0·6	16·2	46·1	17·3	46·5

Source and Notes: See Appendix.

Periodically comparisons are reported in the financial press of the several hundred millions of subsidies paid to agricultural producers with the $2,700 million estimate by the Tariff Board for the subsidy equivalent of protection to the manufacturing sector in 1967-68.[26] This comparison is illegitimate since it does not compare like with like. The manufacturing figure combines the effects of both subsidies and higher prices due to tariffs. The comparison is obviously unfair to the manufacturing sector.

The estimates of the nominal rates of protection for agricultural commodities in Table 10.3 may be compared with like estimates of nominal rates of protection for the manufacturing sector. Yet there are other differences between the two sets of estimates which should be kept in mind. In the first place, the estimates for agriculture relate to commodities whereas the estimates which have been made by the Tariff Board and others[27] for manufacturing relate to industries which commonly produce a great variety of different commodities. Aggregation of commodities into industries reduces the variance and the apparent cost of distortions. There are important differences in nominal levels of protection within industries as well as between industries as the previous table for agriculture shows. These intra-industry differences may be as important in determining misallocation of resources as differences in the average levels between industries or sectors. A second difference is that, because of the method of estimation, the estimates of the implicit price changes for the agricultural commodities are all direct estimates of the 'protection used' rather than the 'protection available' in the terminology of the estimates for the manufacturing sector. The estimates of the protection used by the manufacturing sector are much lower than the more commonly-quoted estimates of the protection available.[28]

Bearing these two differences in mind, the distortion of producer prices for these agricultural commodities is greater than the Tariff Board's estimates for the manufacturing industries both in terms of the levels of protection and the intra-sector variance of these rates.[29] On the other hand, the main pastoral export commodities—beef, lamb and

---

[26] *Annual Report for Year 1969-70*, para 38.

[27] See the Tariff Board, *Annual Report for 1969-70*, Appendix 2 and H. D. Evans, *A General Equilibrium Analysis of Protection: Effects of Protection in Australia* (North Holland, Amsterdam, 1972).

[28] One estimate, on the basis of Tariff Board data for 1967-68, is that 'water in the tariff' reduces the average rate of effective protection available for the manufacturing sector of 46 per cent to an average effective rate of protection used of only 18 per cent; see F. H. Gruen and H. D. Evans, 'Tariff Policies and the Tariff Board', *Australian Economic Review*, 2nd Quarter, 1971, p. 41. However, the estimates of water in the tariff on which these calculations of effective rates are based may not be very good because of the small sample and differences in the qualities of domestic and imported goods compared.

[29] Nominal rates of protection for 31 manufacturing industries are given by the Tariff Board in its *Annual Report for Year 1969-70*, Appendix 2, Table 3, column 2. The nominal rates of protection available to manufacturers in 1967-68 averaged 28 per cent.

mutton, and wool—have received few production subsidies and, with the exception of lamb and mutton, are not significantly protected from overseas suppliers. Nevertheless, in view of the results above for other agricultural commodities, one cannot say that the protection of the manufacturing sector is overall greater than that of the agriculture sector. Moreover, a comparison of corresponding elements in Tables 10.2 and 10.3 reveals that producers of most of the agricultural commodities considered here receive more of their higher prices from the effects of import and other restrictions than they do from direct subsidy payments. The common characterisation of agricultural production as being assisted by direct government subsidy in contrast to manufacturing production receiving higher prices from consumers because of import protection is basically untrue.

The implicit *nominal* rates of protection or assistance to producers in Table 10.3 should be adjusted for the effects of protection or assistance on the cost of inputs to the producers and converted into implicit *effective* rates of protection or assistance. It is the effective rather than the nominal rates which determine producer choices in the allocation of resources. No estimates of effective protection for these commodities were made for several reasons. There are some basic conceptual problems in the definitions of effective rates of protection. These include the treatment of non-tradable inputs such as services and inputs of fixed capital equipment and machinery and the problem of negative value added under free trade, all of which may be important for some agricultural commodities. There are also some problems in obtaining the data on input price distortions. The data that has been used by the Tariff Board are on an industry basis rather than a commodity basis. For estimates of the effective protection of commodities it is necessary to estimate the costs of materials used in each commodity and the distortions of their prices.

Nevertheless, the estimates of nominal rates of protection to producers can safely be said to indicate that there is significant distortion of price incentives to produce different commodities within the agriculture sector. One feature of the agricultural sector is that the tariffs on importable inputs of materials and equipment used by farmers are on the average low compared to most tariffs in the Customs Tariff. We noted on pp. 94-5 that subsidies have been used in preference to tariffs to protect the Australian manufacturers of tractors and fertilisers used on the farms, in order to keep farm costs down. The Vernon Committee estimated that the tariffs on farm materials, plant and improvements increased the total costs of the woolgrower by about 8 per cent.[30] The Tariff Board has estimated the cost of farm machinery to wheatgrowers

[30] *Report of the Committee of Economic Enquiry*, vol. II, pp. 1079-80.

to be about 4·5-5·5 cents per bushel.[31] Moreover, these added costs are partially offset by subsidies to farm producers on production credit, irrigation, freight, disease control and other inputs. The low average tariff-subsidy distortion of the price of inputs relative to the implicit nominal tariffs on the commodities[32] means that the effective rates of protection are higher than the implicit nominal rates of protection but it also means that the inter-commodity variation in effective rates is determined chiefly by the variations in the nominal rates and, probably to a lesser extent, variations in the percentage of value added in production under free trade conditions.[33]

Table 10.4 reports estimates of the percentage change in prices to consumers or buyers of the agricultural commodities which are implied by the combination of instruments affecting each commodity. These estimates are the estimates relevant to the consumption loss of the distortions. It is apparent that consumers are paying much higher prices for some agricultural commodities than they would if there were no government interventions in the importing and marketing of these commodities. Non-tariff restrictions on trade in these commodities result in substantial real income transfers from the consumers to the producers of these commodities.

A second obvious result is that for some commodities and years the percentage change in the prices to consumers differs substantially from the corresponding changes in the prices to producers. It is necessary, therefore, to consider both implicit price changes in evaluating the welfare losses of these distortions.

It is notable that, for some observations, the price change to the consumers or users of exportables is greater than the price change to producers. This is an unusual result that does not arise in estimates of the effects of tariffs on importable commodities. The argument that production subsidies should be preferred to tariffs because a subsidy does not impose a distortion of prices to consumers (see p. 186) does not apply to exportables. The explanation of this phenomenon

[31] *Report on Agricultural, Horticultural, etc., Machinery*, pp. 14-15. Neither the Tariff Board nor the Vernon Committee estimates made allowance for partial usage of tariffs. They are, therefore, maximum estimates.

[32] In its much-publicised estimates of the effective protection for manufacturing industries, the Tariff Board estimated the average tariff on materials used by manufacturing industries as a group was only 10 per cent; *Annual Report for 1969-70*, p. 31. In the manufacturing sector this is due mainly to the system of by-law imports for non-competitive inputs.

[33] One other complication that may affect both nominal and effective rates for agricultural commodities is the change in the exchange rate that would follow a movement to free trade. This is discussed in the next section. We may note here that this adjustment would increase both the nominal tariff on the outputs of commodities and the nominal tariff on their inputs. It is illegitimate to make the adjustment for the tariff on the output of a commodity without making it also for the tariffs on inputs, as the Australian Wool Board has done in its report, *Secondary Industry Protection and the Wool Industry* (Australian Wool Board, Canberra, March 1972).

Table 10.4 Implicit price changes to consumers for selected agricultural commodities, 1946-47 to 1970-71 (percentages)

	Butter	Cheese	Wheat	Sugar	Eggs	Dried vine fruits	Barley	Rice	Cotton	Linseed	Tobacco
1946-47	-23·4	-13·1	-74·9	1·9	4·2	22·3	n.a.	-3·5	n.a.	n.a.	n.a.
1947-48	-26·9	-19·9	-65·9	-19·0	1·6	30·0	-72·4	-20·2	n.a.	-8·7	n.a.
1948-49	-21·9	-16·9	-53·0	-18·0	-7·9	27·2	-44·2	-18·6	n.a.	43·9	n.a.
1949-50	-29·0	-24·4	-58·9	-17·3	-8·1	31·2	-50·3	-8·8	n.a.	9·4	n.a.
1950-51	-32·9	-27·8	-53·3	-25·2	3·2	5·4	-52·7	-26·7	n.a.	-1·2	n.a.
1951-52	-23·2	-2·0	-42·2	-8·4	27·6	10·7	-41·3	-18·1	n.a.	9·8	5·5
1952-53	3·3	20·1	-22·8	7·4	14·0	20·2	-5·4	-2·6	n.a.	0·8	24·2
1953-54	-0·3	16·6	-0·2	23·9	16·1	34·3	19·1	13·3	-2·5	26·1	58·2
1954-55	3·9	28·3	11·6	25·8	46·2	28·8	1·4	29·0	-14·1	11·1	79·5
1955-56	23·7	1·6	3·8	21·6	50·6	15·0	21·0	18·9	-16·1	2·8	48·4
1956-57	50·6	60·7	4·0	29·7	41·9	15·3	14·1	20·2	-35·7	12·0	46·4
1957-58	88·9	96·7	2·1	18·1	65·1	20·3	-1·1	24·1	-18·9	17·7	45·7
1958-59	39·7	1·8	9·3	38·9	65·1	18·9	9·7	50·9	-32·5	18·7	58·2
1959-60	36·1	36·8	12·0	40·0	54·1	40·6	27·1	47·0	1·5	9·4	56·4
1960-61	82·9	34·2	13·3	56·6	75·3	45·7	37·7	38·5	-20·8	16·7	29·2
1961-62	64·5	49·8	10·2	65·9	54·4	57·1	10·2	29·9	-48·2	5·3	64·0
1962-63	46·2	40·0	16·7	52·6	71·8	39·8	13·8	35·4	-18·9	18·6	57·3
1963-64	40·7	35·1	0·9	-7·2	62·0	35·5	7·3	49·2	17·1	17·2	44·1
1964-65	43·5	32·6	9·1	44·0	110·8	41·5	3·5	46·4	27·9	12·8	40·0
1965-66	58·2	37·7	7·7	81·4	159·2	51·0	3·5	44·2	40·2	17·1	62·4
1966-67	61·9	48·9	7·2	111·1	114·5	53·8	7·3	31·2	43·1	18·2	46·1
1967-68	101·2	118·4	21·1	140·5	159·3	51·1	17·7	37·5	30·3	7·4	48·3
1968-69	119·7	133·8	34·4	127·9	230·6	71·7	21·6	48·6	39·6	6·6	54·6
1969-70	109·0	105·1	22·3	73·7	189·1	83·8	24·3	53·0	28·3	15·5	47·0
1970-71	87·1	75·1	25·8	57·9	147·3	95·7	-6·9	86·3	38·2	20·2	46·5

Source and Notes: See Appendix.

is that we are considering exportable commodities for which two-price schemes and associated import prohibitions and restrictions result in substantially higher market prices for sales on the domestic markets than the average prices realised for the same commodities in foreign markets. Subsidies based on exports also push up domestic market prices. The higher domestic prices can more than offset the effects of excluding direct subsidy payments to producers, especially where the proportion of total production sold on the home market is small, and results in greater distortions of consumer prices than of producer prices.[34] This has applied particularly to wheat, sugar and rice for recent years in Tables 10.3 and 10.4.

Two-price schemes and export subsidies which result in the domestic producer receiving a lower price directly from the foreign buyer than the domestic buyer impose a cost on the economy in addition to the cost of distortions of relative average commodity prices to producers and consumers.

It is clear that the distortions of prices to producers and consumers of agricultural commodities produced in Australia, which are largely the result of non-tariff interventions in trade, are important.

There is scope for much more research on non-tariff instruments in Australia although the unavailability or secrecy of much of the information of import prices and domestic prices severely handicaps this area of research. There are at least three avenues that should be pursued

(i) more detailed studies of particular instruments;
(ii) the calculation of the implicit effective and nominal rates for commodities significantly affected by one or more non-tariff instruments;
(iii) the calculation of effective and nominal rates of implicit protection for selected commodities over a period of several years. These should include the commodities studied under (ii).

Studies under (ii) should indicate the ways in which non-tariff instruments conflict with or reinforce the protection given by substantive tariffs. It should also show how the decisions of the SAA and the Department of Customs and Excise through by-law decisions and other administrative changes alter the rates of protection decided by the Tariff Board. Studies under (iii) should show the extent of the variability of the protection to individual commodities over time which arises where there are non-tariff instruments. The implicit price changes to consumers should also be calculated.

[34] The implicit price change to consumers is defined for an export commodity as $(p_d/p_e) - 1$. When this is compared with the definition of the price to producers for an export commodity, as given in the Appendix the two factors which may offset each other are evident.

Some Difficulties in Interpreting Implicit Rates of Protection

Estimates of implicit rates of protection are sometimes used as measures or indicators of the production or consumption effects of non-tariff instruments. It is clear that they are not sufficient for this purpose. The change in production induced by any price change depends on the elasticity of supply as well as the proportionate change in the price to the producers, in all situations. There are two major complications which suggest that we should also be careful of interpreting an implicit rate of protection as the correct price change for predicting the change in production. First, there is the problem of the 'equivalence' of an explicit tariff and an implicit tariff. In this section, for convenience of language, I revert to the use of the term 'implicit tariff', meaning the price change to producers. Second, general equilibrium effects may be important. Parallel problems exist for the consumption effects but these will not be illustrated.

Tariffs used to predict production effects should be effective tariffs rather than nominal tariffs. The discussion of equivalence below is in terms of nominal rates but the arguments apply *a fortiori* to effective rates which allow for the possibility of non-equivalence between explicit tariffs and implicit tariffs on inputs as well as outputs.

An explicit tariff and an implicit tariff corresponding to some non-tariff instrument may be said to be equivalent when the explicit tariff used as an alternative to the non-tariff instrument and set at the level equal to the implicit tariff results in the same change in production as the non-tariff instrument. The equivalence between an explicit and an implicit tariff has usually been examined in terms of whether they have the same effect on imports rather than on domestic production as in the definition above. The effect on imports is relevant if one is concerned with the effect of instruments on the exports of the rest of the world whereas the effect on domestic production is the relevant effect if one is interested, as we are, in the effect on the structure of domestic production. This distinction matters because any two instruments may be equivalent in one sense but not in the other.[35]

This question of equivalence has been examined by international trade economists for the case of import quotas but the same question should also be posed for all non-tariff instruments. It may apply to non-tariff instruments affecting exports as well as those affecting imports. It is obviously a basic question when looking at both tariffs and non-tariff instruments in a general analysis of the structure of protection and

---

[35] Tariffs and non-tariff instruments may also differ in terms of their effects on public revenue and import prices. Some non-tariff instruments, such as dumping and support value duties, have the undesirable effect, compared to an *ad valorem* tariff that encourages the same level of production, of increasing the cost in foreign exchange which is paid for imports of the commodities.

production or when considering substituting tariffs for non-tariff instruments. It is a question separate from the difference between tariffs and most non-tariff instruments in terms of the greater frequency of change of the latter which was observed in the previous section.[36] Non-equivalence means that the implicit tariff which may apply at any one time and an equal explicit tariff have different effects on production. However, the questions of equivalence and relative variability of two instruments should not be separated completely since the greater variability of one instrument may directly affect production because of the greater uncertainty as to the level of protection which may apply in the future.

An import quota and an explicit tariff which is equal to the implicit tariff of the import quota are equivalent under certain market conditions. Necessary conditions for equivalence to hold are that there be perfect competition among domestic producers and among quota-holders and foreign suppliers, and that there be no constraints on domestic production such as production quotas and no price controls. Non-equivalence has been proven when any one of these conditions does not hold.[37] Of these conditions, that relating to perfect competition among domestic producers is probably the most important in Australia because many commodities are produced by only one or a few producers in Australia although there are production controls on wheat and dairy products which are subject to other non-tariff instruments.

When there is a monopoly or some other form of imperfect competition involving the ability to fix prices in the domestic industry, the choice between an explicit tariff and an implicit tariff may make an important difference to domestic production. If imports of the commodity competing with the local supply are restricted only by an *ad valorem* tariff, the local supplier(s) can raise the price of the domestically-produced commodity only to the level of the landed price of the import plus the tariff.[38] However, a quota restricting imports to a fixed quantity removes the one source of competition for the local producer(s). The use of a quota in lieu of a tariff converts a competitive market into an imperfectly competitive market, perhaps a monopoly of a single producer or a price-fixing arrangement among a small number of producers. With a quota and an imperfectly competitive domestic market, the implicit tariff will be much higher than the explicit tariff which induces the same

[36] Tariff and non-tariff instruments may also differ in other respects, such as the kind of legislative authority required, or the open or hidden nature of the instrument. Another difference is that explicit tariffs are subject to customs drawbacks in certain circumstances whereas the price increases due to non-tariff restrictions on imports are not.

[37] Non-equivalence in the presence of imperfect competition in any of the three groups has been shown by Bhagwati, 'On the Equivalence of Tariffs and Quotas', and in the presence of production controls by Bhagwati and Desai, *India: Planning for Industrialisation*, chapter 17.

[38] This assumes, for simplicity, that the domestic and the imported commodities are perfect substitutes.

effect on domestic production compared to the situation with free trade in the commodity because the local producer(s) will take advantage of their ability to raise prices.[39] In addition, a quota, unlike a tariff, may cause a decrease in domestic production.

The same possibilities of non-equivalence arise in the case of import prohibitions due to embargoes, quarantine regulations or other reasons on the one hand and prohibitive tariffs on the other. For example, if there is a single domestic producer, an import prohibition gives him a pure monopoly and he will set his price at the profit-maximising level. This will result in an implicit tariff, and a level of production that may be greater or less than that with free trade in this commodity. If the level of domestic production is greater than that with free trade, it is clear that there will be some tariff that would encourage the same increase in domestic production but this tariff would set a maximum to the domestic price that will be below the corresponding pure monopoly price. A prohibitive *tariff* which is less than the implicit tariff of an import prohibition is preferable because it will result in a lower domestic price and a greater domestic production than the import prohibition.

The presence of either imperfect competition, or production controls, or price controls will also cause non-equivalence in some other non-tariff instruments or combinations of instruments. As an example, consider the case of a combination of an import prohibition and a production subsidy in the presence of pure domestic monopoly.[40] This is the same as the case of import prohibition considered above except that the subsidy shifts downward the marginal cost of the monopolist. This combination (plus other non-tariff instruments) applies to dairying, for example, in Australia. The effect of the subsidy is to lower the domestic price and increase domestic production but non-equivalence of this combination to a tariff still holds.

There are other instruments which are equivalent to more than one *ad valorem* tariff. Consider, for example, the device of offset purchasing. This device ties the implicit tariff rate of the imported commodity to the implicit nominal rate of protection for the commodity produced under the offset arrangement.

There is another distinct reason why non-equivalence may occur even in the absence of imperfect competition, production or price controls. In some quite realistic situations there may not exist a tariff which will induce the same increase in domestic production as does the non-tariff instrument. Consider the case of an *ad valorem* production subsidy alone, as in Figure 10.1. S_d and S'_d respectively are the domestic

---

[39] This can be seen from the models developed by Bhagwati, 'On the Equivalence of Tariffs and Quotas', or W. M. Corden, *The Theory of Protection* (Oxford, 1971), chapter 9.

[40] With a subsidy, but no import prohibition, equivalence holds. Without an import prohibition (or quota) the local supplier cannot act as a monopolist.

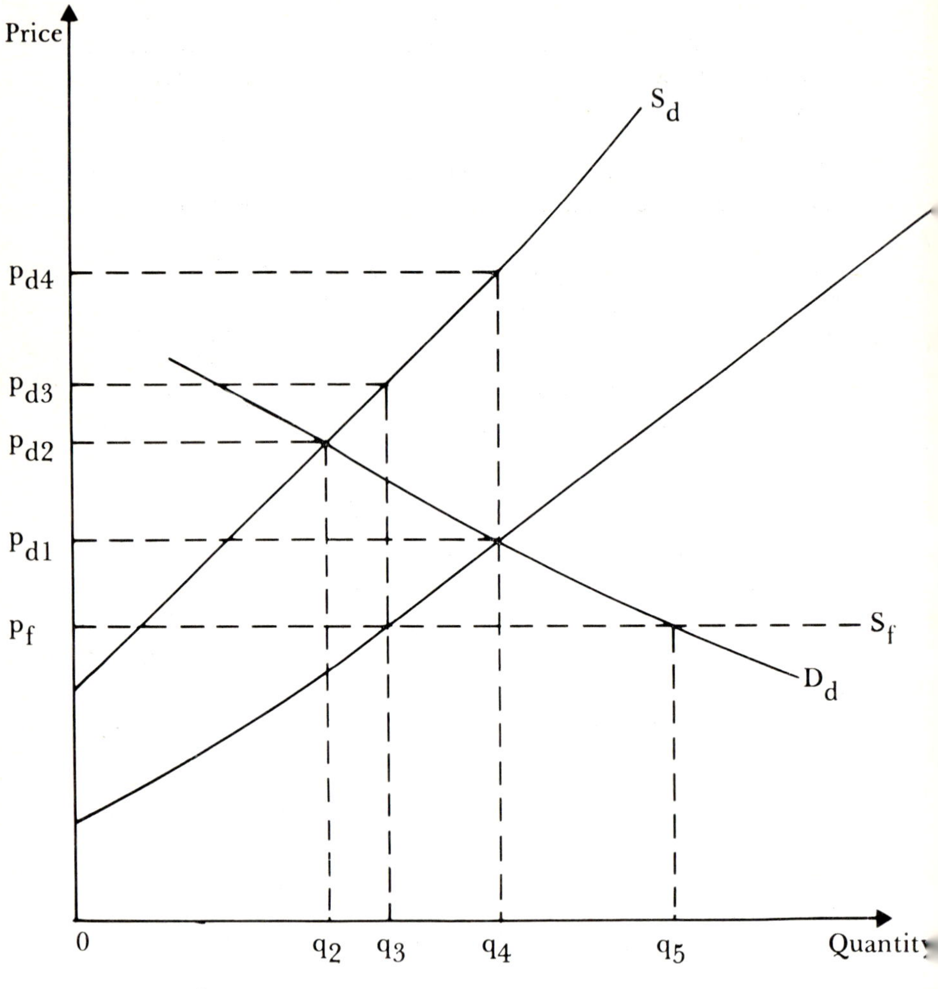

Fig. 10.1 A non-equivalent production subsidy and tariff.

supply curves without and with the production subsidy. D_d is the domestic demand curve for the commodity and S_f is the supply price of imports of the commodity from the rest of the world. With the production subsidy and no tariff domestic production is q_3. The implicit protection, defined as the percentage increase in the price received by the producer, is $(p_{d3}-p_f)/p_f$, with p_{d3} the price received by the producer. Without a production subsidy the maximum price that the producers may receive is p_{d2} and this requires a prohibitive tariff. Hence the maximum domestic production that can be achieved with a tariff as the only instrument is q_2. This is less than that achieved with the subsidy. Note that the greater production with the subsidy also allows imports of (q_5-q_3) because the price to consumers is less than the price received by the producers. If the subsidy is combined with a prohibitive tariff equal to (p_{d1}-p_f)/p_f or greater, which is less than the tariff required to prohibit imports in the absence of the subsidy, the producer price will rise further to p_{d4} and production to q_4.

It is clear that non-equivalence may occur frequently and we should therefore not regard the implicit tariffs for non-tariff instruments in general as having the same production effects as equal *ad valorem* tariffs. When multiple non-tariff instruments occur, as noted in the examples on pp. 137-40, the relationships are so complex that nothing short of a detailed econometric model can reliably estimate the joint effects of these combinations on production of the commodities concerned.

One extreme result of non-equivalence is that some non-tariff instruments may convert a commodity that would be an import commodity in the absence of these instruments into an export commodity, or vice versa. A simple example of reversal is provided by the production subsidy of a commodity which is, in the absence of this assistance, an imported commodity. If the production subsidy is sufficiently large, the fall in the market price of the commodity will enable producers to export the commodity. This may apply even if the subsidy is not paid on exports. On p. 98 we noted that Australian subsidies based on production are paid only on goods used in Australia. Other taxes-subsidies may effect a reversal of trade. It should be noted that the fact that a commodity benefiting from some form of assistance and presently exported is also protected from import competition, such as butter in Australia, does not itself prove the commodity would be an importable under free trade. The assistance increases the domestic price and hence the attractiveness of the domestic market to foreign suppliers.

The second major reason why the partial equilibrium estimates of implicit rates do not give a satisfactorily complete indication of the distortions is that they ignore some general equilibrium effects of the pattern of distortions on the whole economy. These may be unimportant when we consider changes in only one instrument but if all the distortions were removed the relative prices of many goods would change in some ways which are not apparent from the individual measures of each distortion. The most important general equilibrium effect of removing all distortions, which is the hypothetical situation that should be used to measure the extent of all distortions, would probably be the effect on the exchange rate.[41] With no distortions the exchange rate must be adjusted to balance the demand and supply of foreign exchange.

---

[41] If some non-tariff instruments were reduced as a condition of Australia's participation in multilateral reductions in these instruments, one would need also to assess the simultaneous effects on the industries benefiting from greater access to overseas markets.

Tariff and non-tariff protection of import-competing commodities reduces the demand for imports, and therefore the demand for foreign exchange, at the existing exchange rate while the subsidies on exports or export production serve to increase the supply of foreign exchange. It seems likely that the removal of distortions of both export and import trade would necessitate a small devaluation of the Australian dollar.

Under the usual assumption that the prices which Australia must pay for imports and the prices our exporters receive are given on the world markets and not affected by the small volume of Australian trade in relation to these markets, the effect of a change in the exchange rate on the calculation of effective rates of protection is to change all nominal tariffs by the same proportion. It is still possible for the exchange rate adjustment to alter the relative levels and rankings of effective rates of protection for different Australian industries because the adjustment will change the prices of non-traded commodities but in practice the rankings are largely preserved.[42] A more important effect of making this adjustment is to show that a zero or low nominal tariff or implicit rate of protection with the existing exchange rate may in fact indicate a substantial negative rate of protection in the economy when allowance is made for the distorted value of the exchange rate itself. Some instruments which appear at the existing exchange rate to encourage domestic production and reduce imports may actually discourage domestic production and encourage imports. Customs drawbacks may provide an example. On the other hand, the price of some inputs would increase with the adjustment. The zero duty after drawback is intended to neutralise the effect of tariffs on inputs and is permitted by GATT. However, if there were no distortions and a devaluation this has the same effect on a user as a positive tariff equal to the devaluation proportion if the existing exchange rate is maintained. Similarly, the entry of goods under by-law duty-free (and low tariffs) while other importables face high tariffs is really a subsidy to users rather than a tariff and generally results in the over-importing of these goods.

There is a second general equilibrium problem with the interpretation of rates of effective protection. The rankings of rates of effective protection are not sufficient to determine the direction in which the output and the use of resources by each industry are pulled. One industry with a higher rate of effective protection than another may contract while the other expands from the zero-distortion situation. The effective rates of protection are indicators of the differential incentives to producers to change their production of commodities. Knowledge of how production net of inputs changes when the relative price to producers of two

[42] This occurs, for example, in Evans's model of protection in Australia; Evans, *A General Equilibrium Analysis of Protection*, pp. 136-9.

activities changes by a given amount is also required before we can predict the direction of change of output.[43]

This point is esoteric but, nevertheless, vitally important as a simple example shows. It is apparent that in the case of land-intensive production of agricultural commodities or 'industries' it is not the ranking of the effective protection of one commodity over all industries in the economy which is important in determining whether the output of this commodity expands or contracts. Rather, it is the effective protection of this commodity compared to that for other commodities to which the same land and farm resources could be easily switched, which determines resource use and outputs. Both the fall in the price to consumers and the consequential increase in demand and the fall in the price to producers and consequential decrease in production following free trade in each commodity would reduce the exports of these commodities which are currently exported and increase imports of the imported commodities. However, the ending of the differential levels of protection and assistance to producers if trade in all the commodities were freed together would change the relative returns to investments in farming different commodities. The consequential switch of farmers from one commodity to another offering higher returns makes it difficult to predict even which commodities would be exported and which imported.

Although the complications of non-equivalence and general equilibrium make it more difficult to predict the effects which measured distortions have on the production of the commodities concerned, the evidence of the previous section is sufficient to show that non-tariff instruments do create serious distortions in the Australian economy. Further research should be done into the hitherto neglected area of non-tariff instruments as suggested in the previous section but we should not wait for further or more refined estimates of the implicit rates of protection. We can proceed immediately to work out policies which will reduce some of the more serious distortions induced by non-tariff and tariff instruments. The following four chapters consider multilateral and unilateral policies to reduce the costs of the distortions of Australian trade.

---

[43] That is, knowledge of the shape of the net transformation surface. Even this proposition does not hold strictly when the intermediate input coefficients are not fixed; see W. J. Ethier, 'General Equilibrium Theory and the Concept of Effective Protection', in H. G. Grubel and H. G. Johnson (eds.), *Effective Tariff Protection* (GATT, Geneva, 1971).

The partial elasticities of the net transformation surface are the analogues of the elasticities of supply in partial equilibrium.

11 Australian Participation in Multilateral Reduction in Non-Tariff Distortions

Prospects for a reduction in non-tariff distortions of Australian trade through participation in multilateral reduction in non-tariff distortions clearly depend on, first, the possibilities of any multilateral reduction occurring and, second, Australian willingness to participate and offer any reductions in its non-tariff distortions. The first factor is the more important since the reductions which Australia can offer are not likely to affect significantly any large-scale reductions involving many countries.

The Prospects of a Multilateral Negotiation of Non-Tariff Distortions

Non-tariff distortions of international trade have always been important in some countries and some areas of commodity trade. We noted in the Introduction the failure of the GATT to prevent the rapid growth of non-tariff distortions among its member countries. It is only in the last ten years or so that serious interest in multilateral reductions in these distortions has arisen and there are now several international organisations engaged in multilateral discussions of various non-tariff trade-distorting measures.

In February 1972 the United States and Japan, and the United States and the EEC announced their intentions of engaging in a new round of multilateral negotiations starting in 1973. According to these announcements the coming round of negotiations, to be held by the GATT, will include not only a continuation of tariff reductions from the Kennedy Round of GATT negotiations, but also non-tariff barriers and the liberalisation of trade in agricultural products. The GATT has also been active in another way. In November 1967 the members of GATT decided to investigate the non-tariff situation in a new way. Instead of asking members to supply information about their own practices, they were asked to supply information on non-tariff interferences which their own traders had encountered in other countries. This resulted in the list of some 800 non-tariff devices compiled in 1969. This list was first reduced to thirty and then to three in 1971: standards and their enforcement; quantitative restrictions and licensing; and customs valuation. A draft guideline on standards was completed by an expert working group in January 1972 and some working texts on valuation for customs have been referred to member countries.[1]

The OECD has become active in the area of non-tariff instruments in international trade. In 1972 the OECD recommended two methods of exchanging information on the operation of export credit and export credit guarantee systems relating to credit. The decision relates only to the exchange of information concerning credit on terms exceeding five years in duration.[2] The OECD's major work on non-tariff devices has been in the area of government purchasing. In 1962 the members of the OECD decided to investigate the possibility of reaching an international agreement on government purchasing practices. This followed a US decision to increase the margin of preference allowable under the Buy American Act. A draft convention was drawn up by a working party in 1967 on the basic principle that these purchases should not discriminate against foreign sources. This has subsequently been revised. However, these negotiations have apparently stalled on some fundamental issues including the necessity of public tender, the publication of details of tenders, and the scope of exceptions and derogations permitted by escape clauses.[3]

Regional trading groups, notably the EEC and EFTA, have been working towards harmonising the practices of their members concerning some areas of non-tariff distortions. In the area of standards the International Organisation for Standardisation and other international organisations have been working towards agreement on common standards for member countries.

The scope of the multilateral negotiations that will eventuate is very unclear at the time of writing this chapter (August 1972). This is partly the result of the uncertain progress being made in the organisations listed in previous paragraphs and the relations among these parallel movements. It is also partly a result of the change in the international trade order. This has been based in the post-World War II period on the GATT most-favoured nation principle but is now changing with the expansion of the EEC and counter-proposals by the US, Japan and

[1] GATT activities since 1967 concerning non-tariff instruments are reviewed briefly by Curzon and Curzon, *Global Assault*.
[2] Australia has agreed to the first system requiring members to exchange information on credit terms but has not yet agreed to the second part requiring members, when planning to guarantee a commercial credit of more than five years duration, to inform other participants and not to take any action before these participants have offered comments.
[3] The OECD work on government purchasing is reviewed by Curzon and Curzon, *Global Assault*, pp. 23-7.

other countries for North Atlantic Free Trade Agreements or other new trading arrangements. But it seems certain that one or more of the recent initiatives will bring forth significant negotiations in the near future.

It has long been claimed that progress in reducing non-tariff distortions will be more difficult than reductions of tariffs which have been achieved under the direction of the GATT. The large number of non-tariff devices, the diversity among countries in the form and importance of different devices, the hidden nature and scope for administrative discretion, and the extreme difficulty of measuring the effects of these instruments, all make them less tractable than tariffs to international comparison and multilateral negotiation.

The difficulties of achieving multilateral reductions in non-tariff distortions were illustrated by negotiations in GATT during and since the Kennedy Round. In the early stages of the Kennedy Round it was decided that the negotiations 'shall deal not only with tariffs but also with non-tariff barriers' and one of the four principal sub-committees of the Trade Negotiations Committee dealt with non-tariff barriers and a second with agricultural problems.[4] An early attempt to devise general standards governing non-tariff barriers was abandoned as negotiations proceeded in favour of the barrier-by-barrier approach that the GATT has followed since in the area of non-tariff instruments. In the end the only agreements reached among the contracting parties were the Anti-Dumping Code and the package deal in which the United States agreed to abolish the American Selling Price (ASP) method of valuation which it used for benzenoid chemicals and a few other commodities in return for tariff reductions in chemicals and the abolition of the road taxes in some European countries which discriminated against the higher horsepower vehicles from the United States. The latter agreement has lapsed because of the refusal of the US Congress to pass the legislation abolishing the ASP. As a result of the small progress made in the area of non-tariff barriers at the Kennedy Round the contracting parties decided to learn more of the nature and extent of non-tariff barriers. This led to an exchange of information concerning the barriers encountered by traders of each country and the list of 800 but, as noted above, subsequently the list of barriers being examined by GATT has been reduced to three groups and progress on these three groups has been small.

The form which multilateral negotiations may take is as unclear as the commodity coverage. Although other organisations are involved in work on non-tariff distortions it seems that GATT will play a major and perhaps the dominant role. However, the rules that may emerge may

---

[4] The treatment of non-tariff barriers in the Kennedy Round is reviewed by Craig Mathews, 'Non-Tariff Import Barriers and the Kennedy Round', *Common Market Law Review*, 1965, pp. 403-18.

differ from those that have been applied to the negotiation of tariff reductions. It has been suggested that there is a greater likelihood of effectively reducing some of these distortions if the GATT principle of unconditional MFN treatment were abandoned. Conditional MFN treatment would restrict the benefit of any reduction negotiated between two members of the Agreement only to those other countries making reductions.[5] There is also uncertainty as to whether the measures should be handled by the 'barrier-to-barrier' approach that GATT and the OECD have followed to date. This could lead to Codes of Conduct or agreements for separate areas such as customs valuation procedures, government purchasing policies and quantitative restrictions. One alternative is that several disparate groups of trade-distorting measures be negotiated simultaneously. There is a possibility that these non-tariff reductions could be tied to an Adjustment Assistance Code which requires countries to introduce adjustment assistance and then to reduce other non-tariff measures.[6] These and various other alternatives cannot be considered further here.[7]

It is clear that Australian preparations for negotiations should include a re-examination of its own non-tariff policy instruments which distort trade and the reductions it might make in the event of multilateral negotiations. The extent of these changes will determine the extent of Australian benefits from the negotiations which are conditional on a *quid pro quo*.

Australia's Likely Attitude to Multilateral Negotiations

One long-standing aspect of the Australian measures is that Australia has generally attempted to abide by those GATT Articles which concern non-tariff distortion and has pressed strongly in GATT for a reduction in export subsidies, import levies, quotas and other non-tariff barriers which restrict world trade in temperate agricultural products. However, Australia has not always followed GATT recommendations as we have noted earlier and Australia has not signed the Anti-Dumping Code. Nor has Australia signed the GATT Declaration giving effect to the provisions of Article 16(4), which concerns export subsidies. Probably the Australian non-tariff barriers which are most doubtful in terms of the Articles of GATT are its own export subsidies.

---

[5] The EEC and Japan have applied the GATT Anti-Dumping Code conditionally and the GATT and OECD negotiations on industrial standards are proceeding on this basis.

[6] This has been proposed by Curzon and Curzon, *Global Assault*, chapter 3.

[7] Various possible strategies for negotiating non-tariff measures, their advantages and disadvantages, are to be discussed in the report of the London Conference, Johnson and Metzger (eds.), *International Negotiations*. Some of the issues are also discussed by H. B. Malmgren, 'Negotiating Nontariff Barriers: The Harmonization of National Economic Policies', in *US Foreign Economic Policy for the 1970's: A New Approach to New Realities* (National Planning Association, Washington, 1971), pp. 79-109.

There are two other factors which suggest that any Australian Government would consider favourably any proposal for a multilateral negotiation of non-tariff instruments. First, Australia is one of the countries whose export of temperate agricultural products such as meat, dairy products and fruit are severely restricted by a variety of non-tariff barriers in the major markets for these commodities in the EEC and the US and Japan. Moreover, the entry of the United Kingdom into the EEC seems likely to reduce sharply access to the traditional market for butter, canned fruit and sugar and some other Australian agricultural exports. The value of Australian exports would probably increase more from a multilateral negotiation which achieved significant reductions in the non-tariff barriers for these agricultural products than the increase in imports from any concessions which Australia could make. The second favourable factor is that the Australian currency is presently one of the hardest and Australian bargaining would not be seriously constrained by concern for the effects of the negotiations on her balance of payments, even if it appeared that the negotiations might have a net adverse effect.

The negotiability of particular non-tariff distortions to international trade is largely a matter of surmise because the position of the Australian Government will no doubt depend on the scope and in particular the commodity coverage of any multilateral negotiations and because the government has not declared any general policy on non-tariff distortions to international trade. We may, however, obtain some pointers to the likely attitudes of Australian negotiators in the event of any multilateral negotiations or general agreements by examining the nature of the regulations, or Acts or Agreements under which trade is distorted, the policy objectives, recent changes to the non-tariff restrictions and the constraints on the government's actions.

Table 11.1 indicates that the Australian Government has considerable freedom to reduce some non-tariff distortions without legislative action if it wishes. The term administrative action is used loosely. In all cases any substantial change in the restrictions would certainly occur only after careful consideration of the change by Cabinet and in some cases, consultations with the industries affected and perhaps a reference to the Tariff Board. There is a sub-group of restrictions where the authorising legislation allows considerable change in the restriction by administrative action alone but other features of the restriction or the ending of the restriction would require legislation. This applies, for example, to direct regulation of imports by means of import licensing. In this case, the actual licences and the terms of the licences issued are controlled by statutory regulations which can be varied without legislation but the Tariff Board Act is also important because a section of this Act permits the Tariff Board to recommend to the government the use of quantitative restrictions for the commodities that are included in a reference to the Board for inquiry. In fact, all three cases of import licensing currently in effect were imposed after earlier Tariff Board inquiries.

Column 2 of Table 11.1 shows that a number of the non-tariff restrictions derive their legal authority from provisions of the Customs Act (as in the cases of prohibited imports, drawback, value for duty and manufacturing in licensed warehouses) or the Customs Tariff (as in the cases of the tariff preference quotas for selected imports from the developing countries, by-laws and support value duties). Changes in the Customs Tariff require an Act of Parliament.

There are no constitutional difficulties in the way of changing the non-tariff instruments studied in this book when legislation is required, with the exception of the export incentives grants, adjustment assistance which involves the State Governments and voluntary industrial standards. As a result of the transfer of the pay-roll tax itself from the Commonwealth Government to the State Governments in 1971, the future of the scheme after that time is very much in doubt. There is a qualification that the government has given an undertaking in some cases that the existing measures will not be changed for specified periods of time. For example, the bounties on exports of processed milk products and the production of butter, cheese and other butterfat products are determined by enabling Acts but both bounties are a part of the stabilisation scheme agreed to by the Commonwealth Government and the dairying industry in 1972. By contrast, some other countries with a Federal structure or different form of government face considerable constitutional difficulties. In particular the division of power in the US between the Executive and Congress has prevented the ratification of the abolition of ASP negotiated in the Kennedy Round and will hamper the US in future negotiations of non-tariff instruments. These problems are discussed at length in the US Study in the London Program which is to be published by the Brookings Institution.

With no constitutional constraints on the government, the negotiability of non-tariff barriers in Australia depends on the attitudes of the party with a majority in Parliament and the political constraints on its actions. Unfortunately, there are few indications of the present government's general attitude to non-tariff barriers. At the time the Tariff Board Act was amended in 1962 to allow the Tariff Board to recommend quantitative restrictions, the government stated the important principle that the 'Customs Tariff is the normal and accepted instrument for protection of Australian industry' and that the provision for quantitative restrictions would be used 'only as a last resort'. It has reiterated this view several times subsequently but the statement clearly does not encompass prohibited imports, value for duty, government purchasing policies, quarantine and some other non-tariff restrictions. No general

Table 11.1 Classification of non-tariff instruments in Australia

	Intention (type)	Regulation, Act or Agreement under which trade is restricted	Action required to change trade restriction
Import licensing and import-restricting tariff quotas	I	Customs (Import Licensing) Regulations under *Customs Act* and *Tariff Board Act*	Administrative action/Act of Parliament
Prohibited and restricted imports	I and III	Customs (Prohibited Imports) Regulations under *Customs Act*	Administrative action
Voluntary agreements	I	Butter: An agreement between New Zealand Dairy Board and Australian Dairy Produce Board Lamb: An arrangement between New Zealand and Australian Meat Boards Selected imports from Japan: Voluntary agreements under the 1963 Trade Agreement with Japan	Agreement between New Zealand Dairy Board and Australian Dairy Produce Board Agreement between New Zealand and Australian Meat Boards Discussion with Japanese Government and business representatives
Import-expanding tariff quotas	IV	Pork meat and cheddar cheese: New Zealand–Australia Free Trade Agreement Developing Country Tariff preference quotas: Second Schedule of the *Customs Tariff* (Act)	Negotiation with New Zealand Government Act of Parliament
Tariff classification	III	*Customs Act*	Administrative action
Value for duty	III	*Customs Act*	Act of Parliament
Complex structure of the Tariff	II	*Customs Tariff*: Schedules	Act of Parliament
By-law imports	IV and I	Second Schedule of the *Customs Tariff*	Administrative action
Manufacturing in licensed warehouses	IV and I	Customs Regulations under *Customs Act*	Administrative action
Temporary protection	I	Temporary protection is imposed after an inquiry by a Special Advisory Authority under *Tariff Board Act*	Administrative action/Act of Parliament

Australian Participation

Topic		Act/Regulation	Administrative action/Act of Parliament
Dumping and countervailing duties	I	*Customs Tariff (Dumping and Subsidies) Act*	Act of Parliament
Support value duties	I	Fourth Schedule of the *Customs Tariff*	Act of Parliament
Purchasing policies of the Commonwealth Government	II	Treasury Regulations under *Audit Act*	Administrative action
Discriminatory sales taxes	II	*Sales Tax (Exemptions and Classifications) Act*	Act of Parliament
Processed milk products bounty	I	*Processed Milk Products Bounty Act*. This Act fulfils an Agreement with the Commonwealth Government under the Five Year Plan in the *Dairying Industry Act 1967*	Act of Parliament. It would also require negotiation with the Australian Dairy Industry Council. The present Five Year Stabilisation scheme for the dairy industry is due to be extended in 1972
Export incentive grants	I	*Pay-Roll Tax Assessment Act*	Act of Parliament
Customs drawback	I	Provision in the *Customs Act*	Administrative action
By-laws for export	I	Second Schedule of the *Customs Tariff*	Administrative action
Export credit and credit guarantees	I	*Export Payments Insurance Corporation Act*	Act of Parliament
Subsidies to producers	I	Authorising Acts for each bounty or subsidy except in the case of the shipbuilding subsidy which is under the *Supply and Development Act*	Act of Parliament. Under the present Acts the bounties and subsidies are payable until specified dates in the future
Adjustment assistance	III	Dairy industry: *Marginal Dairy Farms Reconstruction Act* Rural reconstruction: *State Grants (Rural Reconstruction) Act 1971*	Act of Parliament. The Commonwealth has agreed to pay $25 million over the four years 1970-73 The Commonwealth has agreed to pay $100 million over the four years 1970-73
Trademarks	III	*Trade Marks Act*	Act of Parliament
Copyrights	III	*Copyright Act*	Act of Parliament
Goods descriptions	III	Commerce (Imports) Regulations under *Commerce (Trade Descriptions) Act*	Administrative action
Quarantine	III	Regulations under *Quarantine Act*	Administrative action

policy has ever been publicly stated for a number of these non-tariff instruments; for example, value of duty.

To gauge the likely views of the Australian Government to multilateral negotiation of non-tariff barriers which would involve Australia in making some concessions we must consider the policy objectives for particular measures and recent trends in the use of these measures. The second column of Table 11.1 classifies non-tariff distortions according to the intent of the trade-distorting instrument. The four types applied to Australian imports in the table are:[8]

Type I   measures intended to protect domestic industries from import competition or to assist domestic industries in competing on export markets.

Type II   measures which are intended primarily to aid non-trade-restriction objectives but which are periodically and intentionally used to restrict trade.

Type III measures which are intended and used exclusively to aid non-trade-restricting objectives but which have the unintentional effect of restricting trade.

Type IV   measures which have the effect of increasing imports.

Measures which increase imports are not objectionable to our trading partners. The case of tariff quotas is quite straightforward. However, by-laws, and to a much lesser extent manufacturing in licensed warehouses, have a double-edged effect in increasing imports of the commodities entering at concessional rates of duty but increasing the effective protection available to the producers using these commodities as inputs. The last aspect and the administrative discretion given to the administering department by these provisions are of concern to other countries but the more important aspect is the effects these have on the pattern of production in Australia. This is considered in the next chapter as a question of the desirability of unilateral change.

There are a number of Type III measures with unintentional protective effects which arise because imports are restricted or prohibited to protect public morals (for example, censorship under the prohibited and restricted imports), public health (for example, prohibitions on certain imports of pharmaceuticals), plant and animal life (quarantine regulations), national trademarks and copyrights and similar objectives. The use of regulations in all these instances is recognised in the GATT. Where the regulations appear unnecessarily strict they may be changed, though Australia, like all other countries, would wish to retain the final decision in these matters.

[8] These four types are an extension of the three used by Ingo Walter, 'Non-Tariff Barriers and the Free Trade Area Option'. *Banca Nazionale Del Lavoro Quarterly Review*, March 1969, pp. 16-45.

Another feature of the use of non-tariff restrictions in Australia is the small use of Type II restrictions which are one of the main methods by which some developed countries covertly and on a substantial scale restrict imports. There are few complaints that Australia has deliberately used health or technical and safety regulations, or customs valuation or tariff classification to restrict trade or impose higher duties to protect Australian producers. There are complaints, many of them justifiable, that the large number of classifications in the Australian Tariff and the difficulty of determining whether a good will be allowed entry at concessional rates under by-laws and other features of the complex structure of the Australian Tariff make it difficult for importers and exporters in other countries alike to know what duty will be imposed on some exports to Australia. The purchasing policies of the Commonwealth Government have been used to protect the Australian industries but the extent of protection is not known.

There are two general groups of Type I measures whose objective is to protect or assist particular producers. Both groups will be difficult to change and the Australian Government will probably resist attempts to negotiate reductions in the levels of these instruments through any multilateral negotiations. The first group consists of the various measures which restrict imports by quantitative regulation (import licensing, some prohibited and restricted imports, voluntary agreements), temporary protection, dumping and support value duties. The use of each of these instruments is restricted to a small group of commodities. The most difficult aspect of most of these measures is that they are concentrated in troublesome areas of protection where existing producers are continually seeking protection from growing imports; areas such as textiles, shipbuilding and some chemicals. I attach great importance to the possibility of reducing protection in these areas by the provision of adjustment assistance and such adjustment assistance may be an integral part of a multilateral negotiation, as some have proposed,[9] but it is more likely that the Australian Government would adopt the simpler and politically safer policy of resisting change in these areas.

The second group of deliberately protective or assisting measures are the various forms of production and export subsidies. There are considerable political constraints on the present government to the negotiation of these measures.

Liberal-Country Party coalitions have been in government without interruption for 22 years. The more numerous Liberal Party members of Parliament depend on the Country Party members for the majority in the House of Representatives and this has placed the Country Party in a strong position to protect the interests of its rural constituents. The present leader of the Country Party, like his predecessor, is both Deputy

---

[9] See, for example, Curzon and Curzon, *Global Assault*, chapter 3.

Prime Minister and Minister for Trade and Industry. It is the Department of Trade and Industry which is primarily responsible for general trade policy and for Australian trade negotiations with other countries. The political power of the Country Party enhances the interest of the Australian Government in a world-wide reduction of non-tariff barriers for agricultural commodities but it also means that the Australian Government is most reluctant to make any concessions concerning the subsidies and other assistance to agricultural producers unless the balance of change for these commodities alone is clearly to Australia's advantage. The strong stand of the present Australian Government in this respect is made even more certain by its recent actions. We noted on p. 130 that the one area of non-tariff distortions in Australia which had been increased in the last three years was the area of assistance to farmers.

Undoubtedly, the main determinant of any Australian Government's willingness to negotiate non-tariff trade-distorting instruments is the prospect in the negotiations for a freeing of world trade in the country's exports of temperate agricultural products. These exports are presently severely restricted by non-tariff barriers in the major markets of the EEC, the US and Japan and may soon be largely excluded from the United Kingdom. Australia will be looking to the negotiations to redress what it considers the unfair balance of past tariff negotiations in favour of manufacturing products and is unlikely to be seriously interested in these negotiations unless they hold the prospect of some significant reductions in the non-tariff barriers for her agricultural exports.

This raises a vital point which the Australian Government will probably have to face at some stage of future negotiations. It seems likely that negotiations under GATT, or other negotiations, will either restrict severely the agricultural commodities to be included in negotiations or give priority to the reduction of non-tariff distortions affecting world trade in manufactures. There are several indications of this. Despite good intentions, the only major agreement in the Kennedy Round concerning agricultural commodities was the International Grains Agreement. As another example, the Report of the OECD's High Level Study Group released in September 1972 reached agreement on the procedures to reduce industrial protection but implied that agriculture is fundamentally different from industry and that we must wait many years before distortions to trade in agricultural products can be substantially reduced. Similarly, at an early stage of the London Program it was agreed by the major countries to exclude agricultural products.

While the high levels of government protection, the greater outward immobility of resources used in the agricultural sector and the associated problems of income redistribution make the problems of non-tariff distortions of trade in agricultural commodities more difficult than some of the problems concerning non-agricultural trade, these events reflect more fundamentally the greater concern of the major European and North American countries and Japan with the distortions of trade in manufactures. Even in the US and Canada distortions of their trade due to measures affecting their agricultural commodities are a smaller part of their total concern with non-tariff distortions than in Australia.

While other countries' non-tariff restrictions on imports of primary products certainly restrict present and future Australian exports and production of some major farm products, this aspect of non-tariff distortions is not the only major aspect that should concern Australian negotiators. The other important aspect of non-tariff distortions is the harm some of them do to the value of real output in the Australian economy. Several of the measures substantially distort the pattern of production in the manufacturing sector and we have pointed out the economic costs of these measures in preceding chapters. Moreover, even if overseas markets for meat, dairy products and other farm products are opened by the removal of non-tariff restrictions in the major potential markets, there will still be a need for major reconstruction in the farm sector. The present plight of some farm producers should not jeopardise Australian participation in a multilateral negotiation that could substantially improve the allocation of resources throughout the Australian economy.[10]

---

[10] Since this chapter was written the author has considered some other aspects of the approaches Australia should adopt in the GATT negotiations which are now due to start in September 1973; 'Australia's Trade Position and Policies', a paper to be delivered to the Australian Institute of International Affairs' Conference on Australia's Foreign Relations, The Economic Issues, in Sydney, 9-11 June 1973.

12 Possibilities of Unilateral Changes in Non-Tariff Distortions

The high costs of some non-tariff instruments indicate that Australia would gain from a unilateral reduction in some non-tariff restrictions on imports.

The suggestion of unilateral action, however, poses a dilemma. While unilateral action would bring benefits to the economy it would also reduce Australia's 'bargaining coin' at the multilateral negotiating table if serious multilateral negotiations do eventuate. The consideration of unilateral change to Australian non-tariff distortions before or during international negotiations of non-tariff distortions must therefore trade-off the potential benefits from unilateral action and the loss of bargaining strength.

On the other hand, the reductions in non-tariff distortions of trade which Australia can offer are not likely to have a major effect on the outcome of the 1973 GATT negotiations or other trade negotiations. We should therefore proceed with a unilateral review of non-tariff distortions. The greatest need for unilateral action in Australia will arise if the multilateral negotiations or reductions in non-tariff barriers do not come about, at least for some years. In any event Australia should immediately review some of the non-tariff distortions. Such a review will become more important as the Tariff Board's Tariff Review progresses.

The Problem of Piecemeal Policy-Making

When we consider the presence of taxes, tariffs, subsidies and other restrictions on the production or sale of many commodities, the problem of improving the allocation of resources and pattern of consumption becomes very complex. These problems are much more complex than the usual textbook case in which there is only one distortion with perfectly free production and trade elsewhere in the economy. In a *distortion-ridden* economy the usual presumption that permitting freer trade in one or a small sub-set of commodities will improve the welfare of the economy no longer holds.

The most appealing reform policy would be that the Commonwealth Government undertake a systematic review and reform of protection and assistance to all commodities, import-competing and export and other commodities alike, and due to tariff and non-tariff instruments alike. Despite its appeal, such a proposal is both impracticable in terms of the magnitude of the task and no doubt unacceptable politically. For both reasons any reform must be piecemeal; that is, it must proceed to minimise the effects of distortions in the economy by changing the instruments which have been approved for review in the light of other instruments and associated distortions which cannot be changed at the same time. We are therefore inevitably concerned with problems of *piecemeal policy-making*.[1]

The basic problem of piecemeal reform of an economy with many distortions is that reducing some non-tariff distortion in a way which appears to bring the relative prices to some producers or consumers more into line may create or aggravate divergences between other relative prices. When considering the protection of one or a small number of commodities in isolation we should consider the effects the change in this protection will have on three other groups of commodities: (a) commodities in other industries which are substitutes or complements in consumption for the commodities under consideration; (b) commodities which compete with the commodities under consideration for scarce primary resources; and (c) other commodities which use as inputs the commodities under consideration. The first two sets of commodities group together horizontal relationships of gross substitution and complementarity in production and consumption. The last recognises the vertical input-output relationships. In using these three groups of commodities to analyse the effects of particular instruments or their removal, it will sometimes be useful to distinguish within these three groups between the relationships among importables and the relationships between the importables under consideration and the group of exportables. The latter set of relationships between importables and exportables may be particularly important because some of the greatest

---

[1] The author has considered the problem of piecemeal protection policy as a problem in the theory of the second-best in a paper, 'Optimal Intervention in a Distortion-Ridden Open Economy', *Economic Record* (forthcoming). See also T. J. Bertrand and J. Vanek, 'The Theory of Tariffs, Taxes, and Subsidies: Some Aspects of the Second Best', *American Economic Review*, December 1971, pp. 925-31. In another paper I have applied these basic ideas to suggest some guidelines for tariff reform within the Australian Tariff Board's sequence of industry tariff reviews; 'Problems and Criteria in Setting Tariffs' in H. W. Arndt and A. H. Boxer (eds.), *The Australian Economy: A Second Volume of Readings* (Cheshire Publishing Ltd, Melbourne, 1972).

distortions of relative prices to producers and also consumers are the distortions of the prices of importables relative to the prices of exportables which arise from some non-tariff restrictions on imports.

It should be noted that instances of the costs of all three divergences above have been recognised in Australia and have formed part of existing non-tariff barriers, though the general principle and the full significance of these divergences has not been appreciated. There are several minor examples of the desirability of giving equal levels of nominal protection to commodities which are close substitutes in consumption. The occasional use of substitute notices (p. 54) and the extension of import licensing to cover polypropylene as well as polyethylene products (p. 14) and the lists of chemical substitutes paying the same duties exemplify the same principle.[2] As an example of the third divergence, the case for granting assistance to exporters in order to offset the burden of tariffs on important materials inputs has been recognised in the granting of several bounties and subsidies (p. 94) and the practice of giving drawbacks of customs duties or by-laws for exports (pp. 119-20). An example of recognising the remaining kind of divergence is given by the 'front-runner' policy applied by the Department of Customs and Excise to the cancellation of a by-law when a material or component becomes available from an Australian supplier (see p. 48). It has not been recognised that this policy is an attempt to maintain, upon a change in by-law status of a material or component used by one manufacturer, the effective protection available to this producer vis-à-vis the effective protection available to other producers of competing goods. However, we shall see that none of these policies are correct when we take other distortions into account.

These same inter-commodity relationships in production and consumption, together with an understanding of the nature and extent of the distortions, determine what piecemeal policies are best. We shall now consider several examples of existing distortions induced by non-tariff instruments and propose changes which are based on a recognition of the particular problems of piecemeal reform in a distortion-ridden world.

Some Examples

Example 1. By-Law Imports

The first example we shall consider is that of the important by-law system. This illustrates the importance of both vertical input-output relationships and horizontal relationships among substitutes. It was noted on p. 49 that, from the point of view of the economy as a

---

[2] There are similar provisions for substitutes in the collection of excise duties.

whole, the main deficiencies of the by-law system stem not from the exercise of discretion given to the Department of Customs and Excise but from the principles which underlie the granting of by-laws. The basic principle that has underlain all by-laws since their inception is that a domestic manufacturer should not have to bear the burden of higher costs due to tariffs when the tariffs are levied on goods not produced in Australia. It was recognised that this raised the effective rates of protection for user industry but the implications of this practice for the *pattern* of effective protection, which really determines the allocation of resources by producers, were not realised. (The same principle underlies many of the sales tax exemptions, notably those for 'aids for manufacture' and hence it has a wider application than the by-law system.)

On pp. 145-8 we found that the by-law system has a major effect on the pattern of effective protection for Australian industries. It has served mainly to increase substantially the rates of effective protection for a few industries using as major inputs goods imported under by-law. It also leads to sudden and substantial changes in the protection available for individual commodities within industries.

The by-law system could be improved. The Tariff Board has pressed for a reduction in the high rates of anticipatory protection afforded by 'dragnet' and other items in the Tariff and proposes to examine these in its review of chapter 84 of the Tariff. The reduction of the high substantive rates of tariffs on capital goods that may be considered for by-law entry would have the beneficial effect of reducing the increases in protection for local producers of the capital goods upon the cancellation of a by-law. It may also reduce the applications for by-law entry, since the rates of concession implied by the by-law (the differences between the substantive tariffs on normal imports and the rates on by-law imports) would be reduced.

A second possible change is that the interpretation of 'reasonably available' local goods could be narrowed to include only goods which the buyer considers to be available on delivery and other terms comparable to those of imported goods. This would increase by-law imports and remove the high level of protection given to some producers of capital goods. In addition, the high rates of substantive duty available to Australian producers who satisfied the narrower criterion of availability should be reviewed, as proposed by the Tariff Board.

It should be clear, however, that these changes are inferior to a systematic review of all tariffs which includes the incorporation of the existing by-law system into the substantive rates of duty in the Customs Tariff. It is possible to achieve the same effect on the Australian production of a commodity which follows from a given by-law on an input together with a tariff on the commodity produced by a change in the substantive tariff on the commodity.[3] Tinkering with the system as discussed above will not solve the basic problems. For example, the change in the interpretation of 'reasonably available' discussed above would reduce the problem of high rates of anticipatory protection but it would only do so at the cost of aggravating the problem of high rates of effective protection for other commodities by extending low rates of duty on important inputs admitted under by-law. It is typical of a piecemeal change in policy that it has a beneficial effect on the economy in one respect and an adverse effect in some other respect.

If the present by-law system is retained serious distortions will remain in the economy. The system leads to the over-production of commodities enjoying high rates of effective protection partly because of by-law entry of imported inputs, unless these rates are reviewed by the Tariff Board whenever there is a significant change in by-laws. It leads to the over-consumption of those materials or capital equipment whose costs are reduced by by-law admission relative to the costs of other materials and labour. It also leads to a different and probably more varied pattern of nominal tariffs on the final import-competing goods produced than would a system of nominal tariffs without by-law concessions that yields the same pattern of effective protection.[4] It increases the costs of administering the tariff in both the public and private sectors. Moreover, each departmental decision which affects by-laws imports also affects the rate of effective protection of commodities in the production of which the by-law commodity is used as an input. To neutralise these changes on using industries would require continual investigation and changes in the nominal tariffs protecting the commodities concerned by the Tariff Board.

If serious distortions of prices and production in the import-competing sector are to be greatly reduced, the by-law system in its present form must be abolished. It is founded on a misconception: namely the view that the increased costs which high rates of duty on capital inputs cause to a producer are necessarily harmful to the economy. For the economy, ignoring problems of adjustment, the important consideration is the rate of effective protection in alternative uses for the resources which the producer uses. The criterion for changing tariffs on capital inputs should be in terms of improving the allocation of resources among commodities. This can only be done if the tariff-fixing is confined to one body and this body is not constrained by the present idea of by-law admission for non-competitive imports.

[3] One can demonstrate this equivalence theorem. An exception arises if the tariff required on the commodity is prohibitive.
[4] This point was made by R. H. Snape, 'Options for External Economic Policy', *Economic Papers*, no. 41, September 1972. This result increases the distortions in relative prices to consumers among importables but the nominal tariffs on produced importables and thus the prices of these commodities relative to non-importables are less distorted with by-laws.

Example 2. Customs Drawbacks and By-Laws for Exports

The traditional argument for drawbacks is that an exporter who can compete on world markets should not have to pay a higher price for imported materials because a tariff is imposed to protect a domestic manufacturer.[5] This partial equilibrium argument may not be valid in an economy ridden with taxes and subsidies. Whether duty-free entry for materials used by an exporter reduces the distortion in the price to the producer depends on the effective subsidy paid to the exporter through other subsidies and export concessions compared to the rates of effective subsidies received by other exporters and the effective protection import-competing producers receive. Moreover, the drawback may distort relative inputs prices. When, as in Australia, high levels of effective protection mean that the removal of tariffs may necessitate a devaluation of the country's currency, tariffs on imported materials which are used in the manufacture of goods subsequently exported should not be lowered below the notional tariff that corresponds to the shadow price of foreign exchange. Yet, the drawback may be desirable if non-tariff taxes and subsidies in the economy discriminate against the producer. (In such a case it may be optimal to impose a lower tariff on the inputs but the best policy will depend on which other instruments are variable. For example, if permissible a uniform subsidy on all inputs, including primary inputs, is equivalent to the desired production subsidy in this case.) In other cases zero duty on inputs results in over-exporting and it is equivalent to a tax on the Australian producer of inputs which are substitutable for the imported inputs. Moreover, we may note that there is no remission of duty paid on machinery and capital equipment used in the manufacture of exported goods. There is no difference between the higher cost of manufacture due to tariffs on materials and the higher costs due to tariffs on machinery and capital equipment, with appropriate adjustments for the output of goods from the machinery or equipment which are not exported and the working life of the capital good. Finally, drawback is not allowed for the same input when the output is sold domestically rather than exported, thus creating a new distortion in the use of the input.

Example 3. Government Purchasing Policies

Similar issues are raised by government purchases. It was noted on p. 70 that all Commonwealth Government purchasing authorities are supposed to apply a notional tariff to all tenders involving imported goods which is equal to the duty that would be paid if the goods were

---

[5] In looking for a quotation, I was astounded to find an excellent statement of this case for drawback in Adam Smith's *The Wealth of Nations*, chapter IX, 'Of Drawbacks'.

not imported by the government. With the present Customs Tariff, this results in widely varying levels of protection to local suppliers in the area of government purchasing, assuming the rule of notional duty pricing is practised. If no notional duties were applied, then the nominal rate of protection for all goods sold to the Commonwealth Government would be zero since government imports from both General and Preferential sources enter duty-free.

The issue must be approached from the point of view of the structure of protection which is best for the nation. The plausible argument that actual or potential sales of goods to the government should receive the same levels of protection as sales of the same goods to the private sector, which gives rise to the notional duty pricing rule, is not in fact a sound argument when there are widely varying levels of protection throughout the economy which distort the patterns of resource allocation and consumption. Essentially what happens if the notional pricing rule is followed is that the rule removes any possibility of divergence between rates of protection for a commodity when sold to the public sector or private sector but it extends the wide variation among effective rates of protection through the Tariff and the distortions this causes into the area of the government purchases. Whether this notional duty improves or worsens the allocation of resources through the economy has to be decided. And, conversely, whether the optimal policy is the removal or some other variation of the notional duty has to be decided.

The existence of separate rates for government imports provides an opportunity to practise a piecemeal reform of part of the pattern of protection. It may be objected that the government should not alter in this way the rates of duty which have been reached after a Tariff Board public inquiry and recommendation. However, the Customs Tariff itself does exempt goods imported by or for the Commonwealth Government from duty and, therefore government is free to determine rates as with other by-law rates. In the long term a reference should be sent to the Tariff Board to advise on government purchasing. Meanwhile the government should fix rates on government imports to reduce distortions.

Almost all of the goods which the Commonwealth Government produces are not competitive with any goods produced by the private sector although there are some exceptions such as aircraft production. (Goods imported by government owned Corporations such as Trans-Australia Airlines are dutiable.) This is certainly true of the whole areas of Public Service and defence production. Hence we do not generally need to consider the effects of government production on privately-produced substitutes.[6] Moreover, few government-produced

---

[6] A special case for a made-to-measure tariff on government imports may arise if the domestic industry is subject to decreasing unit cost and private demand at the existing tariff on private imports is not sufficient to encourage local production.

goods or services are significant direct inputs into the production of other goods or services in the private sector and therefore we do not need to be concerned with this source of divergences in the area of government purchases and production. We cannot say in general whether the government sector draws resources away from more or less efficient areas of private production. Thus we need be concerned mainly with the efficiency of government production of goods and services.[7]

These factors suggest that government purchases should be subject to uniform rates of duty. Should the rate be zero or some positive rate? Should it be the average of the rates applied to private imports after the Tariff Board's Review? The best policy would seem, in the case of government imports, the simple rule of a uniform *ad valorem* duty which reflects roughly the present cost in terms of foreign exchange of these imports, with other distortions still present.[8] This is the tariff that, taken together with the present exchange rate, would be equivalent to the free exchange rate that would equate the demand and supply of foreign exchange. With present macroeconomic budget and monetary policies and protection this tariff would be low and probably negative, that is it would be an import subsidy. (This recommendation is modified later on p. 209 when we consider adjustments to other distortions are also feasible.) There would still be some under-production and over-production in the economy (and corresponding over-consumption and under-consumption in the private sector) because some tariffs levied on private imports of these goods are lower or higher than the optimum rates.

If a uniform *ad valorem* rate applied to government imports, it would probably be advisable actually to levy the duty on government imports to ensure that the rate is enforced. The uniform duty would need to be supplemented in order to avoid different rates of protection applied by individual government purchasing authorities by means of supposed non-price features of tenders. The obvious means of correcting this potential abuse is to specify and enforce the present principle of the 'lowest price consistent with satisfactory quality', indicating more precisely the acceptable grounds on which a more expensive Australian tender or bid may be accepted. These should only include such factors as quality or performance differences of some kind, superior delivery

---

[7] This is an instance of the importance of separability of sectors. For the purposes of this piecemeal policy change, it is assumed that tax rates and total government expenditure is fixed but the policy change may change the allocation of the budget between domestic and imported goods and also perhaps among the goods and services provided. If the change also leads to a significant change in government expenditure and taxes collected, these changes would need to be considered.

[8] The rule above is analogous to the shadow pricing rule for domestically-supplied inputs in a closed economy which has been proposed by J. E. Stiglitz and P. Dasgupta 'Differential Taxation, Public Goods and Economic Efficiency', *Review of Economic Studies*, 1971, p. 161.

or maintenance terms. Objectives such as encouraging production in some areas to reduce unemployment are much better served through fiscal, monetary and other general unemployment policies or other appropriate policies. The pursuit of 'lowest price' would be greatly assisted if basic features at least of all tenders received were made public along the lines of the United States practice referred to on p. 71 and the system were made less secret.

Example 4. Tariff versus Subsidy

Assume that taxes and subsidies to other commodities are given and that in this distortion-ridden economy it is desirable to increase the production of a particular commodity by some means. There is a standard argument in economic literature that it is preferable to increase the production of an importable commodity by a subsidy on production rather than a tariff.[9] This often-cited rule is derived from a situation in which there is free trade in the economy, that is there are no distortions, and the commodity is a final commodity, and world prices are fixed. In this case a subsidy avoids the consumption loss of a tariff.

In a distortion-ridden economy the rule need not apply for a final commodity. Consider that we wish to increase production of a commodity. A subsidy will be preferable to a tariff as a means of encouraging production of the final commodity only when the distorted prices to *consumers* of other commodities to which it is a close substitute are higher than they would be in a distortion-free economy. In this event a subsidy or a tariff would improve the price to the producer, but a subsidy will compensate for the under-consumption of its substitutes whereas a tariff would have the additional and harmful effect of raising and distorting the prices of this group of commodities to consumers. If the commodity has close complements whose relative price is distorted upwards a tariff is preferable.

The choice between a subsidy and a tariff is complicated by a second factor. In Australia most of the production subsidies have been paid on intermediate inputs and not final commodities; the exceptions are butter and cheese and books. On p. 94 we noted the common view that subsidies are preferable to tariffs to protect capital goods and raw materials because they do not lead to increased costs of production in the user industries. This is an interesting early appreciation of the

---

[9] See, for example, W. M. Corden, 'Tariffs, Subsidies and the Terms of Trade', *Economica*, August 1957. This aspect of distortions has been reviewed by J. N. Bhagwati in an important paper, 'The Generalized Theory of Distortions and Welfare' in J. N. Bhagwati *et al.* (eds), *Trade, Balance of Payments and Growth* (North Holland Publishing Co., Amsterdam, 1971), pp. 69-90.
This example differs from the previous three in that the 'distortion' arises because of an additional objective of policy; it is 'instrumental' rather than 'autonomous' in Bhagwati's terminology.

different effects tariffs and subsidies have on the effective protection of the user industries,[10] but it is another instance of the failure to recognise it is the relative effective protection which determines production. A subsidy on an input will be generally preferable to a tariff if the commodity in which it is used is an importable receiving a low rate of effective protection or an exportable (provided it does not receive other subsidies which already compensate it for the direct and indirect effects of tariff protection for the import-competing commodities).[11] These guidelines are rather different from the arguments that have been advanced in favour of subsidies.

These examples of non-tariff distortions show that it is possible to devise some rules to guide piecemeal changes to the pattern of protection. But they also show that the relationships of substitutability and complementarity in both production and consumption that must be considered and the rules that must be followed in each case are very complex when we assume that there are distortions elsewhere in the economy in the light of which we devised the best possible piecemeal changes in each area. On pp. 192-4 I consider some rules that are more practicable.

The Tariff Review is a Piecemeal Policy

It has not been sufficiently realised that the 'systematic and comprehensive' review being undertaken by the Tariff Board,[12] or the Tariff Review as it has become known, is also a piecemeal review, albeit a review of much greater scope and complexity than those considered above. It exemplifies more clearly some of the difficulties of piecemeal review. Moreover, consideration of the proposed changes to tariffs is of direct relevance to the possibilities of piecemeal changes to non-tariff-induced distortions because, as noted, both tariff and non-tariff instruments jointly determine the extent of distortions of trade. The non-tariff-induced distortions must be considered in the framework of the proposed changes to tariffs.

[10] When the bounty on sulphuric acid was substituted for the previous duty in 1923 the reason given was that the duty represented 'a tax on the raw material used in the production of an essential commodity'; Tariff Board, *Report and Recommendation on Fertilizers*, 5 December 1929.

[11] The result is complicated by the fact that other commodities may use the same input and, by the effects of the subsidy on the relative price of the final goods to consumers or investors. If the latter are important, we should also look at relative nominal tariff rates. More generally one should consider the effective taxation of the commodity, including the differential levels of commodity, excise and other taxes and subsidies on the commodity.

[12] The evolution of this proposal and its main features can be traced in the Board's *Annual Report* for each of the years from 1966-67 to 1969-70. This proposal has now been accepted by the government and in May 1971 the Board received the first set of industry references covering the important machinery and related goods area.

While its new procedure will enable the Board to look systematically at all the main commodities produced in an import-competing industry under the review and to examine the tariffs on most importable manufactures eventually, neither of which it is able to do under the present system of *ad hoc* references, the review is still limited in several important respects. First, the review will be confined to 'those manufacturing industries which are highly protected by Australian standards'[13] that is, only some of the import-competing manufacturing industries. Some highly protected industries such as automobile assembly and shipbuilding are excluded. The former is due for independent review in 1974 and the latter was reviewed in 1972 but the rates of protection are still very high in this industry. Second, for those commodities included in the production of these industries, the Board will consider only protection of the domestic producers vis-à-vis foreign producers. Third, even within this manufacturing sub-sector, there are a large number of instruments which directly affect the level of protection of different import-competing commodities to which the Tariff Board is not free to recommend changes; for example, government purchasing policy concerning government imports, discriminatory sales tax exemptions and quarantine regulations. It is not clear whether the Board intends in the Review to consider changes to para-tariff features such as manufacturing in bond and, most important, the by-law system. Fourth, the Board is to review one industry at a time. Fifth, the Board seeks to restrict the effective rates of protection generally within a range 25 to 50 per cent.

The main implications of the first exclusion of export industries and import-competing primary commodities is apparent. Distortions within these sectors of the economy due to changes in the relative prices among these commodities may not be removed by the Tariff Review. The prices to consumers and producers of these commodities relative to the prices of import-competing manufactures are also an important part of the distortions induced by the protection and assistance to both the import-competing manufacturing sector and the export and primary sectors. In this regard the minimum average level of 25 per cent which is set down in the Board's point of reference is important.

The implications of the second and third limitations are evident but those of the last two are less obvious and have not been widely appreciated in Australia. The last two are now considered in turn.

In reviewing the protection for all commodities in any one industry,

---

[13] The restriction of the Review to 'highly protected' industries only was first announced in the guide to the Review procedures, *The Tariff Review* (Tariff Board, Canberra, September 1972), p. 3. Previously the Board planned to begin with industries enjoying the highest levels of protection: *Annual Report for 1969-70*, para 44.

the Board may improve the allocation of resources *within* the industry by changes in the relative rates of protection afforded the individual commodities of the industry. But in doing so the Board may unwittingly worsen the allocation of resources through new divergences between the levels of protection given to the commodities of the industry under review on the one hand and those given to closely related commodities of other industries on the other. These new divergences could be divergences among any of the three sets of related commodities which were listed earlier in this chapter. We have already seen examples of how piecemeal changes to non-tariff distortions can create new divergences. The Tariff Board has appreciated the importance of the relationships between commodities in production which arise because some importable commodities are used in the production of other importable commodities.[14] When some of the commodities of one industry whose tariffs and protection are reviewed are used as important inputs by another industry, any changes in the tariffs of the first industry will clearly alter the effective protection received by the input-using industry. If the latter industry has already been reviewed the revised tariffs on its inputs may give too little or too much protection to the industry at a higher stage of production. In order to minimise this problem, the Review should start with those industries which are important as suppliers of intermediate inputs to other industries.

The first two industries which are now under review, 'Machinery' and 'Manufactures of Metal' are industries which supply important inputs to other industries as well as being industries with high levels of effective protection. Subsequent reviews may significantly alter the pattern of protection already decided in earlier revisions of other input-using industries but the order of review announced by the Board[15] together with the limited total coverage of the Tariff Review indicate that this may not be a serious problem. There are other divergences between commodities which are substitutes or complements in consumption and between the commodities under review and exportable commodities which compete with the industries under review for scarce resources which arise when the input-output relationships are minimised. These problems of new divergences are inherent in the nature of the piecemeal approach and cannot be eliminated.

There are also serious deficiences inherent in the Board's proposed points of reference of 25 and 50 per cent. Many economists and groups such as the Vernon Committee have suggested that there should be a single uniform *ad valorem* tariff in Australia in place of the existing

[14] Tariff Board, *Annual Report for 1969-70*, para 43. See also Gruen and Evans, 'Tariff Policies', p. 38.
[15] *The Tariff Review*, p. 2.

spread of tariffs.¹⁶ This view is based on the assumption that the present exchange rate is overvalued compared to what it would have to be if there were no restrictions on imports and no incentives to export industries. The uniform *ad valorem* tariff is suggested as an alternative to a currency revaluation that would give all import-competing commodities the same level of protection. It is this argument that lies behind the Tariff Board's proposed narrowing of the rates of protection but strictly speaking it implies a single uniform *ad valorem* tariff rate for all commodities at any time and, moreover, a rate that varies over time to equate the demand and supply of foreign exchange.¹⁷

There is another serious aspect of the points of reference. Some tariff rates are constrained to zero for several reasons—those bound under GATT agreements, or under the New Zealand-Australia Free Trade Agreement and other trade Agreements, or under the preferences offered to the developing countries, and some *de facto* rates applied to government purchasing decisions. With the *average* levels of effective protection for industries constrained generally to a minimum of 25 per cent,¹⁸ the result must be that the effective rates of protection for many commodities within these industries must be zero, and others less than 25 per cent and, therefore well below those rates for other commodities. Considerable differences in the rates of effective protection for importables within the import-competing sector will, it seems, remain after the systematic review of the Tariff by the Board.

Finally, we should note that there is a limitation of a different kind in the Tariff Board's procedure. The Board may only recommend changes in protection. It is the legislation of the government which actually determines the rates of protection. In a recent address the Minister for Trade and Industry stated: 'I don't exclude the possibility that some changes in the structure and operating performance of industry sectors may need to be made from time to time. But I venture to suggest that no Government would take any action which might involve major disruption of large areas of secondary industry, or threaten the employment situation'. Moreover, he stated 'I don't mean to convey by these remarks that tariffs are by any means the only way in which industrial development in Australia is to be helped. New policies, new modes of assistance, will need to be evolved to sustain and encourage sound development of

---

¹⁶ The argument is reviewed by W. M. Corden, 'Australian Economic Policy Discussions in the Post-War Period: A Survey', *American Economic Review*, June 1968, Supplement, pp. 100, 108. The Vernon Committee's views are stated in the *Report of the Committee of Economic Enquiry*, vol. I, paras 14:15-14:19.

¹⁷ Actually, with distortions present in the export sector because of the overvalued currency and differential export subsidies, the uniform rate is not the optimal policy since the tariff rates can partially compensate for the efforts of these distortions on export and other industries: see Lloyd, 'Problems and Criteria in Setting Tariffs'.

¹⁸ However, it is not clear that the Board will use a minimum rate of 25 per cent effective protection.

manufacturing industry, and to assist it to adapt to change', and 'I would also like to emphasise that the Government is no way bound to accept the Tariff Board's recommendations . . . At the same time, the Government has emphasised repeatedly that in making tariff decisions, it is frequently necessary to take account also of a wide range of non-economic considerations'.[19] These comments suggest that the effects of the Tariff Board's review may be more limited than the Board intends unless there is a change in government policy.

Thus the Tariff Board's proposed systematic review will not end all the divergences within the import-competing manufacturing sector and it may not even reduce divergences between the rates of protection of this sector overall on the one hand and on the other hand the sectors producing exportables and non-traded goods and services.

One way of increasing the benefits of the Board's Tariff Review is to devise criteria which attempt to take into account the divergences between the import-competing commodities and other commodities but such a policy may complicate the Board's task and make it more difficult to eliminate eventually some of the distortions.[20] There is also a serious danger that many people are pinning too much hope on the Board's Review, believing that it will end the serious distortions in the economy due to the protection of import-competing commodities.

For these reasons I would have definitely preferred an across-the-board cut in all tariff rates *plus* those equivalent tariffs implied by import licensing, content plans and other devices in place of the present Review. An even better policy would be an immediate reduction in all high rates of nominal and effective protection, rather than the present approach.[21] These reforms are very much simpler and could, therefore, be carried out immediately. Their most important feature is that they would increase welfare because they reduce distortions. The Board's procedure differs from this in two ways apart from the length of the Review. First, it does not apply to all import-competing industries. Second, we cannot be sure that the Board will recommend or the government will accept recommendations for significant lowering of protection.

It should be clear that these criticisms of the Board are criticisms

---

[19] Address at the opening of Australian Tube Mills Plant, 5 June 1972.
[20] See 'Problems and Criteria in Setting Tariffs' for an attempt by the author to develop guidelines for an industry-by-industry review of protection.
[21] The proposition that an across-the-board cut in tariffs must increase welfare is an application of the theorem that an equi-proportional reduction in distortions must increase welfare; E. Foster and H. Sonnenschein, 'Price Distortion and Economic Welfare', *Econometrica*, March 1970, p. 290.

Strictly speaking this theorem requires constant opportunity costs and a reduction in distortions involving exportable goods as well as all importables. The first of these requirements is satisfied with international trade if we assume that Australia can trade any amount of its exports and imports at fixed world prices. This assumption is commonly made in Australia and is probably approximately true.

that its Review does not go far enough in terms of its commodity coverage and likely changes in the degrees of distortion for these commodities. They are quite different from and do not support the criticisms of others who have opposed the Board's systematic review.

These criticisms of the Board's procedure are relevant to the discussions below of possible ways of reforming the non-tariff-induced distortions of Australian import and export trade.

What Piecemeal Reductions in Distortions Should We Have?

The above discussion of piecemeal changes in individual areas raises a number of vital questions. What areas of protection or assistance should we consider? In what order should we take them? What instruments should we change?

To begin with we should reiterate that distortions due to non-tariffs barriers to imports or assistance to other producers must be considered along with tariff-induced distortions for any commodity since both the tariff-induced and the non-tariff-induced distortions *jointly* determine the changes in production and consumption. This is especially important in the Australian context as we have noted that in many 'trouble areas' of production there are a number of both tariff and non-tariff forms of protection or assistance which assist producers of the same commodities. A distortion may not be removed or minimised by changing one instrument, say either a protective tariff or a subsidy or a quantitative restriction, if other instruments remain and may be changed in a way which neutralises the first change.

The *first principle* that can be enunciated for piecemeal policy-making is that the broader the scope of a review of distortions, the greater the possibility of reducing the loss of national output and welfare from the distortions. The aim of reform or review should be to remove all serious distortions in the economy and this can only be accomplished by removing altogether those present practices and forms of assistance which give rise to the distortions.

Any proposal to change non-tariff-induced distortions should be considered in the context of the scope and methods that are to be used by the Board in its Tariff Review. As many non-tariff instruments apply to commodities not included in the Tariff Review the review of non-tariff instruments should supplement rather than be incorporated in the Tariff Review.

The *second principle* is that policies that result in the greatest distortions of relative prices to producers and consumers should definitely be reduced.[22] This change will reduce the divergences and the distortions

---

[22] This is actually an application of one of the findings that have emerged from formal economic models of the theory of the second best; R. G. Lipsey and K. Lancaster, 'The General Theory of the Second Best', *Review of Economic*

that take the economy away from the highest attainable position of production and consumption. Thus the highest rates of effective protection should be reduced. If the nominal tariffs (or tariff equivalents) which affect consumption are not so high relatively as the prices to producers it may be desirable to achieve this change by raising the tariffs on its inputs. It does not necessarily follow, however, that the lowest rates of effective protection of importables should be raised. This is so because these prices may not be high relative to the prices of other exportable and non-importable commodities and one cannot, therefore, immediately know in which direction they should be changed. One application of this principle is that it may be better for the Tariff Board to recommend a lowering of all high rates of protection than for it to recommend a lowering of all high rates and a raising of all low rates.

A *third principle* can be enunciated on the assumption that the ultimate objective of reform is to remove all serious distortions in the economy. This principle is that it is desirable to remove completely the source of distortions which have a substantial effect in the economy, such as by-laws. This policy could involve some conflict between short-term gains and long-term gains. It may be that given the present changes under consideration it is not desirable in the short term to remove a particular distortion but in the longer term with more changes under consideration it is desirable to remove the distortion. If such a distortion is not removed quickly we may have a pattern of distortions that changes continually but does not improve.

In particular, we have seen that some of the present non-tariff distortions arose, and some quite justifiably, in response to the penalties to some producers and the distortions created by high tariffs on importables. For example, high tariffs created the need for by-laws, and the creation of by-laws then created the need for by-law preferences in order to protect existing UK preferences for normal imports. Drawbacks and other export subsidies were also a compensation for the high levels of some tariffs. Unfortunately these new complications do not cancel all effects of the original distortion and they increase the complexity of the pattern of distortions. It is clearly necessary to remove the source of these distortions, in this case to cut high rates of tariffs, if the complex pattern of distortions is to be reduced. Once this has been done the distortions which followed as an attempt to compensate for the prior policy, in the case above the by-laws and export subsidies, are no longer justified and can be removed. In addition to leading more speedily to a reduction in distortions and the number of distorting policy instruments, this sequence of reviews should reduce the adjustments in the economy

---

Studies', 1958-59, p. 25; M. McManus, 'Comments on the General Theory of the Second Best', *Review of Economic Studies*, June 1959, p. 219; Bertrand and Vanek, 'The Theory of Tariffs, Taxes and Subsidies', pp. 925-31.

and the need for adjustment assistance. For example, export industries whose export subsidies are removed are compensated, in part at least, by the reduced protection of importables which supply them with inputs or compete with them for labour and other resources.

There is a related *fourth principle*. Simple and obvious approximate rules may be much better in the long run than more complex rules which try to take into account some other current distortions and in the process themselves add to the complexity of the pattern of instruments and distortions. Attempts such as those on pp. 180-7 which try subtly to correct for distortions elsewhere in the economy may be too subtle as they may make it more difficult to see and achieve further desirable reforms and, if they are not implemented correctly, they will introduce new distortions. The present Tariff Review is an illustration of the dangers. It is based on the idea of a uniform tariff as a second-best substitute for free trade plus devaluation but its limited coverage and the wide range of tariff rates which it permits may mean the final structure of relative prices is far from free trade. Another aspect of this principle is that the larger the area of policy-making which is being re-examined the more likely it is that removing all the differential taxes, subsidies and tariffs which affect production and consumption of these commodities will move the pattern of consumption close to the best attainable pattern.

A *fifth principle* is that instruments which are hidden, such as discretion in fixing duties or making government purchases, are undesirable because the levels of protection which result are unknown and variable.

13 The Role of Adjustment Assistance

The absence of adjustment assistance for manufacturing industries is one of the least satisfactory features of the Australian system of protection. This applies to protection by means of both tariff and non-tariff restrictions alike. The provision of adjustment assistance for import-competing manufactures would represent a major change in protection philosophy in Australia. However, there are now several precedents abroad and the interest in adjustment assistance as a way of increasing the liberalisation of world trade and raising domestic incomes is increasing very rapidly.[1] Two of the earliest schemes to provide assistance on a broad basis to industries adversely affected by reduced protection were the various Funds of the EEC and the adjustment provisions of the US 1962 Trade Expansion Act which prepared the US for the Kennedy Round of Tariff negotiations. The Canada-US Automotive Agreement of 1965 contained provisions for adjustment assistance. Several European countries have established public corporations for industrial reorganisation; for example the UK Industrial Reorganisation Corporation. There have also been several schemes for particular industries adversely affected by increased international trade, notably the cotton industry.[2]

Until 1972 there had not been any public discussion of adjustment assistance for industries affected by reduced protection in Australia, either by the Commonwealth Government or business representatives, as far as I am aware. At the time of the announcement by the Minister

[1] The most detailed study to date of adjustment assistance is that by Roy A. Mathews, *Industrial Viability in a Free Trade Economy: A Program of Adjustment Policies for Canada* (University of Toronto Press, Toronto, 1971).
Curzon and Curzon, *Global Assault*, chapter 3, propose an international Adjustment Assistance Code drawing the line between proper and improper forms of assistance and forming the basis of future trade negotiations. While their intention is laudable there is a danger that a narrow interpretation of the proper forms of adjustment assistance would increase the reluctance of countries to make the concessions their Code is designed to foster.

[2] See United Nations Conference on Trade and Development, Adjustment Assistance Measures, TD/B/C.2/86, 20 November 1969.

for Trade and Industry that the government would amend the Tariff Board Act to allow the Tariff Board to complete its systematic review of the Tariff in six years the Chairman of the Tariff Board intimated the Board's recommendations could include suggestions concerning adjustment assistance. He stated that work being done by the Board's own staff and specialist consultants would allow the Board to

> be in a better position to gauge the re-allocative effects of its recommendations which cause sudden changes with unduly disruptive effects . . . It will be able also to identify cases where complementary action by the Government is necessary, where retraining or relocation of employees displaced as a result of implementing its recommendations may be needed.[3]

In commenting on the Minister's announcement of the expansion of the Tariff Board, the ALP spokesman on Trade and Secondary Industry, Dr Cairns, outlined in the House the Labor Party's view that it would not allow an industry to be closed down where it was needed for employment in a particular area, that it would not accept recommendations from the Board for tariff revisions unless disemployment benefits were made to the disemployed, and that it would consider compensation to owners, in certain circumstances, if industry had to be closed or curtailed to meet the needs of public policy.[4] In July, the Prime Minister has stated the government view that firms will not be expected to adjust overnight and that the government favoured a 'gradual process of change'. In a few tariff revision reports the Tariff Board has recommended a phasing of duty or subsidy reductions to give the industry concerned more time to adjust.[5] This is probably the only form of assistance the Board can recommend at present. Other non-tariff restrictions on imports, notably quantitative restrictions on textiles and temporary protection, have been used to delay the time when import competition will force adjustment, sometimes for several years.

Although the public interest in adjustment assistance may have been aroused, the difficult problems of delimiting the areas where adjustment assistance is justifiable and also of devising effective programs have not been debated at all. In this chapter I shall be concerned with possible assistance to aid the adjustment of exporters, as well as those competing with imports, to changes in government policies and programs. (The same case for adjustment assistance would apply to free trade areas or other policies reducing protection.) They involve the same essential issue—how to encourage the movement of resources from those areas of the economy in which their marginal social productivity is low to

[3] *Canberra Times*, 13 April 1972.
[4] *CPD*, H. of R., 1972, p. 1611.
[5] For example, reports on *Knitted Shirts and Outergarments*, 29 April 1971 and *Shipbuilding*, 25 June 1971.

the areas in which it would be higher. However, the case for adjustment assistance must be carefully argued. It is easy to fall into loose, logically false arguments in support of adjustment assistance. Moreover, the kinds of assistance must be carefully circumscribed if they are to be effective,[6] and not cost hundreds of millions of dollars annually which would be in excess of the total budget for adjustment assistance that is politically feasible.

The purpose of adjustment assistance is to aid the movement of resources to areas of production in which they have the highest marginal productivity for the economy and thereby to increase the real incomes of consumers. Much of the discussion of reducing protection in Australia is producer-oriented, attaching a zero weight to the conflicting interests of consumers. (As another example of producer-orientation in our trade policies recall the discussion of dumping.) Adjustment assistance is a means of moving, in carefully specified circumstances, part of the short-term cost of adjustment to the general taxpayer and thereby increasing the permanent benefits from the movement of resources to more productive employment. Only the broad aspects of a desirable program of adjustment assistance can be considered here.

Acceptable Arguments for Adjustment Assistance and Their Limited Scope

There are three possible arguments in support of adjustment assistance.

The first argument is derived from the efficiency of national resource allocation. If adjustment to change in market or production conditions by the company or employees adversely affected is hindered by the presence of impediments to movements in resources, resource allocation may be improved by the provision of adjustment assistance. Such impediments could arise in a number of ways—for example, deficiencies in information of future market prospects or alternative employments, prices received by producers in the affected industries higher than the value of the product to the economy because of monopoly or price support schemes. All of these impediments reduce the outward movement of resources from contracting industries or firms. Assistance is called for only if the source of the impediment cannot be removed directly and if the resource costs of supplying the information or overcoming the other impediments are less than the gain in national output

---

[6] The experience to date in many countries has not been very promising. The US adjustment assistance program has not been very effective; see M. D. Fooks, 'Trade Adjustment Assistance', *United States International Economic Policy in an Interdependent World*, Report of the Commission on International Trade and Investment Policy (Washington, DC, 1971), vol. I, pp. 343-66. See also Mathews, *Industrial Viability* for criticisms of the Canadian, UK and other programs. On pp. 128-9 above we noted the difficulties encountered in devising effective adjustment assistance to Australian rural producers.

from the resource reallocation. It should be noted that this argument applies more generally than only to situations where the need to readjust follows some change in government policy. It applies to all changes in market demand and supply conditions where these impediments to change are present. For this reason it calls for rather different policies as noted below.

The second argument is an equity rather than an efficiency argument. Some economists have suggested there is a moral obligation to assist any employer or employee who established production facilities or took a job under the reasonable expectation that the existing protection against import substitutes or subsidies to producers of exportables would continue. Changes in profits or employment due to shifts in the demand for products or the introduction of new competitors are a risk that should ordinarily be borne by the producers.[7] In the case of a substantial change *without warning* in *government* taxes or other policies affecting particular commodities, some consider the government and, hence the taxpayers, should bear part of the cost of adjustment.

This argument must be very carefully delimited. In the first place it may apply only to cases where there is a change in some government policy or program which reduces the level of protection or assistance previously available. It does not provide grounds for adjustment assistance in any situation where a producer receives some government protection or assistance and does not make an adequate profit to continue with this level of protection or assistance.[8] There are also many instances where government protection or assistance is given and investment and employment decisions are taken in the knowledge that this assistance is promised only for a specified time, or it is known this assistance may be reduced or eliminated. Bounties are examples of assistance which is authorised for a fixed period at the end of which the bounty must be reviewed. Decisions taken in an industry which knows its tariff protection is coming up for review are in the second category. Adjustment assistance can only be contemplated on equity grounds in situations in which past investment and employment decisions were made where some government protection or assistance was promised or there was a reasonable presumption it would continue beyond the present, and such assistance is now revoked.

Even in the situation of an unforeseen change in government policy adjustment assistance may not be warranted. Obviously no government can be obliged to compensate those adversely affected by any change in

[7] There may be a case for government intervention in some form if there are costs or benefits to the economy which are external to the producers in a contracting industry but this is a special case of the different problem of externalities.
[8] There may be a case for adjustment assistance due to shifts in the demand and supply functions on either of the other two grounds but this will not be considered here.

its policies. We could take the view that all government actions are known to be reversible and therefore are a risk to be accepted by private business and employees, like the risks of changes in market demand or supply. This seems a harsh view. Any judgment is a value judgment. I believe that adjustment assistance should be available when a government reneges on a definite promise of financial assistance or protection and this promise has led companies and their employees to make major decisions. In other cases of an uncommitted but also unforeseen change in government policy, adjustment assistance should not be provided unless it satisfies at least the following criteria:[9] it should encourage producers to move resources into higher marginal productivity lines of production or plants; the company or its employees is harmed significantly and demonstrably by the change in policy; it is short-term assistance, not permanent support. The second criterion should not be applied so strictly that little adjustment is provided, as such an interpretation would increase the opposition to change in policies. This was exemplified by the US adjustment assistance provisions.

In respect of the third criterion the present government policy of 'gradual change' is too gradual. For example, in the May 1972 statement on shipbuilding the government stated it was extending the phased reduction of bounties recommended by the Tariff Board so that the subsidy of 45 per cent will continue until December 1975, the subsidy at 35 per cent to December 1970 instead of December 1968. The costs of these 'interim' measures may be very substantial over eight years. The tariff quotas on textiles and chains introduced in 1972 prolong protection without encouraging adjustment.

The third argument is perhaps the most important. The absence of adjustment assistance has heightened the opposition to tariff reform and a lowering of non-tariff barriers. Much of the opposition to the proposals made since 1967 by the Tariff Board to review systematically the Australian Tariff, beginning with the industries receiving higher average levels of effective protection, has come from these highly protected industries. These industries are not persuaded that such changes should be accepted because they are in the interests of the economy as a whole. Similarly, the availability of adjustment assistance should overcome some of the opposition to proposals in this study to reduce protection given by some non-tariff barriers. The provision of adjustment assistance should permit a greater reduction in both tariff and non-tariff barriers to imports. It should also reduce references to the Tariff Board or Special

---

[9] If the value judgment that adjustment assistance should be available in these circumstances is accepted, it implies that when a government introduces an unforeseen subsidy or other financial assistance or protection to encourage new production and this fortuitously raises the income received by existing producers, some part of the windfall gains should be paid back to the government and used perhaps to finance windfall losses.

Advisory Authority for tariff revisions, quantitative restrictions or dumping duties, because these are the only forms of assistance to industries facing increased import competition at present.

An adjustment assistance program should apply to all industries and their employees. This is essential if the program is to achieve the purpose of moving resources from areas of production with lower productivity to areas of higher productivity. We should avoid programs restricted to particular industries, partly because this restriction would mean that resources were maintained in other industries with low productivity and partly because the possibility of the adjustment assistance turning into disguised long-term subsidies is probably greater if it is selective.

Strategies to Reduce the Need for Adjustment Assistance

The need for some adjustment assistance in the event of a major reduction or change in the protection of Australian industries from import competition is unavoidable. However, there are two features of manufacturing production in Australia which reduce the costs of labour adjustment. The concentration of manufacturing employment in a few cities, principally in Sydney and Melbourne, reduces the need for intra-city movement when adjustment cannot be confined to individual plants. Secondly, the small size of most Australian plants, the very factor responsible for high unit costs of production on some commodities, means that changes in industrial production can be made without releasing large supplies of labour on to local labour markets.

There are several strategies which can reduce the amount of adjustment required in the location and employment of existing enterprises and, therefore, the amount of adjustment assistance that is desirable.

One of the most important policies will be the maintenance of full employment.[10] Substantial unemployment increases the demand for adjustment assistance in two ways. It will lower the total domestic sales of some commodities for which the share of the domestic producers is already adversely affected by increased import competition. It also increases the difficulty of finding new employment for those displaced by the change in protection policies.

The need for adjustment assistance may also be reduced by careful choice of the sequence of changes in the levels of protection or assistance to Australian producers. Some of the present non-tariff distortions arose in response to other prior non-tariff or tariff distortions. When distortions offset each other partially the effects of their simultaneous reduction will also offset each other partially. For example, export industries whose export subsidies are removed would be partially com-

---

[10] The maintenance of high levels of employment was certainly one of the reasons why the adjustments in the EEC went so smoothly.

pensated by the simultaneous reduction in protection of importables which supply them with inputs or compete with them for labour and other resources. Elsewhere we have noted several examples of offsetting distortions.

There would be a similar beneficial effect if the reduction in the non-tariff distortions of Australia were to occur as part of a global reduction in non-tariff and perhaps also tariff distortions to other countries. This may occur under the GATT plan for a multilateral reduction in trade barriers beginning in 1973. In the event of multilateral changes some Australian producers would have greater market opportunities in other countries lowering their barriers to imports at the same time as the Australian domestic markets were contracted by lowering protection in Australia. The opportunities for a mutual worldwide rearrangement of production and trade patterns are perhaps greatest for Australia in the area of trade in agricultural products. Since this is also one of the areas of production in which there is a great resistance to change, this possibility is important.

Another important strategy is the prevention of new areas of inefficient or marginally efficient production emerging under high levels of protection or assistance. The farm adjustment assistance programs have been more costly and less successful in some areas because subsidies and other forms of financial assistance have encouraged marginal farmers to stay in the production of products with declining sales and in some cases have encouraged new producers to enter the market at the same time as adjustment assistance programs have been designed to assist producers to adjust to changing market circumstances. Certainly we should cease encouraging the production of new products or the increased production of products presently produced in areas of production where we may need to offer adjustment assistance in some form in the foreseeable future. Many of the problems and obstacles to reduced protection in the areas of fertiliser production, plastics and chemicals, and textiles, concern enterprises which were set up or greatly expanded in the last ten years in response to excessively high levels of protection.

Forms of Assistance

The strategies outlined above should greatly reduce but will not eliminate the necessity for adjustment by some producers. Those cases which satisfy the criteria outlined earlier should then be eligible for some form of assistance. The forms of assistance may vary. In the first place not all adjustment assistance involves financial payments or subsidies by the Commonwealth (or State) Government. Indeed it will generally be desirable to use a non-financial form of adjustment assistance where possible so that the government financial adjustment assistance can be used where the economic problems of adjustment still persist. The most obvious non-financial form of adjustment assistance is the progressive phasing of changes to tariff or non-tariff distortions of international trade. For example, high substantive tariff rates could be lowered and low by-law rates could be raised, where desirable, in several steps according to a fixed timetable. Import prohibitions and import licences could be relaxed by several planned extensions of quotas or licences.

The question of the most efficient form of financial assistance is a difficult one.[11] It will depend first on the reasons for which the assistance is provided. If it is due to a market impediment, the precise nature of the impediment will also suggest the appropriate form of assistance. For example, if employees are reluctant to move because they do not know of alternative job possibilities or there is no available means of acquiring the skills for available jobs or they cannot obtain the finance to undertake retraining, then the best policies are to provide employment services or retraining courses or finance for participation in such courses, as the case may be.

If the equity argument applies the choice is more difficult. The most important criterion is that the assistance be temporary and designed to move the company or its employees into the production of other commodities. Above all, it must be recognised that no company or employee has the 'right' to demand government assistance simply because the company or its employees require this assistance to stay in the present business or occupation. There should be no 'existence principle' in the area of adjustment assistance. The interests of consumers must predominate in the long run. It must also be borne in mind that 'assistance in adjustment to economic change is intended to increase flexibility and mobility, not as compensation for injury'.[12] There should be no payments made as compensation to capital owners or employees. Mathews has argued that some compensation payments to the worst-affected companies and employees may be necessary 'in the pragmatic terms of what will make a move to free trade acceptable to the [Canadian] public'.[13] Such payments are less likely to expedite the movement of resources than payments which are tied to labour retraining, plant re-equipment and the like.

The case for assisting employees seems stronger than that for assisting the owners of the capital invested. Some provisions of company taxation, such as those enabling companies to carry forward current losses into the future earning periods and investment allowances, mean that the

---

[11] Several forms of possible assistance to both firms and employees and the experience of Canada, the United States and the United Kingdom in operating various kinds of adjustment assistance programs are examined by Mathews, *Industrial Viability*.
[12] Otto R. Reischer, quoted in Mathews, *Industrial Viability*, p. 12.
[13] *Industrial Viability*, p. 71.

Commonwealth Government already bears much of the losses incurred by companies. The similar provisions in personal income taxation, such as those relating to moving expenses of income taxpayers, are less important and less widely used. However, the distinction between assistance to employee and employer is not rigid. Assistance to an employee may enable a company to continue producing some commodities that it might otherwise have ceased to produce and, similarly, assistance to employers may obviate the necessity of some companies reducing their workforce.

In providing assistance to employees there are numerous choices among different kinds of retraining programs, relocation grants and other assistance. There is a choice as to whether the government should establish its own programs or whether it should subsidise private businesses to establish or operate such programs. There is also a choice between providing a subsidy in the form of a non-repayable grant or a loan on 'soft' subsidised terms. These choices are difficult. These choices and the institutions that will be required to implement them will require detailed investigation.

14 Conclusions and Recommendations

There are two basic sources of the costs to the economy which should be distinguished. These are

(i) differential levels of protection for importables and assistance to exportable commodities which distort prices to consumers and producers, and
(ii) inferior instruments being used to achieve a given level of protection or an objective other than protection.

On the side of imports, the policy of successive Australian Governments since the signing of the Ottawa Agreement in 1932 has been to assist only domestic industries which are 'economic and efficient'. Unfortunately, this term has been greatly abused. In some references to the Tariff Board the government has given special directions which include the direction that the government considers an industry under review to be economic and efficient. In advising the government on levels of protection for commodities under other references with no special directions the Tariff Board has attempted to interpret this vague guideline of 'economic and efficient'. It has stated that in setting the recommended levels of protection it considers a number of aspects including the effects on consumer prices, the costs to user industries, the use of local resources, the possibilities of exports, infant industry and defence considerations, and the need to set a level of protection for an 'economic and efficient' industry which is sufficient to enable the industry to earn a 'reasonable' return on funds employed.[1] The Board has used these criteria in determining the levels of bounties and quantitative restrictions as well as tariffs. The notional duty procedure has carried

---

[1] The most comprehensive outline of the criteria followed by the Tariff Board was given in its *Annual Report for 1958-59* (Canberra, 1960). In the 1960s and especially since the introduction of the concept of effective protection the Board's view has changed.

the tariff rates so determined for private imports over to government imports. These multiple criteria of the Board and independent action by governments, government departments and other authorities, have led to protection for domestic production of commodities which are certainly not produced efficiently compared to the cheapest source of supply in world markets. It is these cheapest sources which determine comparative advantage or efficiency.

Given the level of protection of an industry or group of commodities, there are still many alternative instruments of protection. Some forms of tariff such as support value duties and content plans have the undesirable features that the implied levels of nominal protection are not apparent and are subject to change with changes in the landed costs of imports or domestic demand or other variables. As another illustration of the costs of choosing an instrument which is inferior to another available, consider the decision to aid a group of domestic producers by means of subsidies. A production subsidy may, in some circumstances, have the advantage over a tariff that it does not distort prices to consumers or users. The government has endeavoured to aid many Australian producers, especially farmers, by subsidising particular inputs such as fertiliser. Such input subsidies aid the producers but in doing so distort the relative prices of inputs and raise the costs of production to the economy by encouraging the overuse of the subsidised input.[2]

The system of protection and the Customs Tariff has been asked to do too much in the way of achieving objectives other than protection. The tariff or other forms of protection can only protect Australian production from imported commodities. They are not effective instruments for achieving many of the purposes for which they are being used or have been suggested. For example, many in Australia, and even the Tariff Board,[3] argue that there may be higher or lower tariffs on particular commodities if the production of these commodities gives rise to certain externalities. Most externalities which arise in production depend not on the particular commodity produced but on the particular process used or a particular input and it is the process or the particular input, as the case may be, generating the externality which should be subsidised.[4] For example, to achieve the objective of decentralisation, protection of importable commodities is clearly a very inefficient instru-

[2] In the fertiliser example there are the added complications that we should be moving marginal farmers off their farms, not encouraging them to continue production and compete with efficient farmers, and that some fertilisers pollute neighbouring water supplies. We should be taxing these fertilisers and aiding the farmers by means of adjustment assistance.

[3] For example, *Annual Report for 1969-70*, paras 29, 32.

[4] This is the same principle of choosing the appropriate instrument but the opposite case to that in the previous paragraph. In that case, it was desired to increase *production* and for this objective subsidies on particular *inputs* are inefficient.

ment since it only discriminates in favour of domestic production whereas we require some policy that discriminates among domestic producers in favour of those in the particular area which it is considered desirable to develop.[5] Similarly, it is much better to stimulate skills and research activities which are considered desirable by means of direct subsidies to these skills or research activities rather than protecting the importable industries in which they may occur. Protection of a commodity by means of a tariff or production subsidy increases the payments to other factors as well which are used in the production of the protected commodities. Moreover, the same skills may also be used and therefore could also be developed in exportable commodities. As yet another example we have suggested that cuts in the level of protection rather than higher tariffs or import licensing may encourage greater realisation of economies of scale. These examples and the general point concerning the unsuitability of instruments of protection to achieve these objectives are well known to economists but they continue to be ignored by politicians and many public servants despite their obviousness.[6]

Recommendations

Major changes should be made to the use and the levels of non-tariff instruments in Australia. Australia should prepare for and participate in multilateral negotiations as discussed in chapter 11. The following recommendations concern possible unilateral changes.

We shall consider non-tariff distortions of imports first. I recommend the abolition of the following non-tariff instruments of protection—by-law system for private imports, manufacturing in bond, import-restricting tariff quotas, sales tax exemptions which discriminate in favour of (or against) domestic suppliers, voluntary quantitative restrictions, support value duties, protective import prohibitions and import licensing. The objections to these instruments have been given in previous sections but the main points will be recapitulated.

The by-law system should be abolished because it distorts the pattern of effective protection and because it will be much more difficult to reform the distortions of the import-competing sector and to maintain any chosen pattern of effective protection if by-laws remain. An exception might be made in the case of by-laws for export but even here, as noted below, a simple uniform subsidy on exports, or better an overall reduction in protection of importables, is the preferred policy. Special by-laws for diplomats, international organisations, etc. should be con-

[5] The Tariff Board recognised this in its report on *Knitted Shirts and Outergarments*, p. 21.
[6] A particularly clear development of these points is given by Bhagwati, *The Theory and Practice of Commercial Policy* and also in his paper, 'Generalized Theory of Distortions'.

Conclusions and Recommendations 207

tinued. The manufacturing in bond system is based on the fallacious notion that imports which are not incorporated in the final product should be exempt from duty. The sales tax exemptions are a hidden form of protection. Voluntary quantitative restrictions, import-restricting tariff quotas and protective import prohibitions on imports such as those which restrict imports of some primary commodities are objectionable because the restrictiveness of these instruments is not widely known, because they are equivalent to relatively high, and in some cases prohibitive tariffs, and because the restrictiveness of these instruments increases as the demand for imports or local costs increase.

For similar reasons support value duties and import licensing should be ended completely. They were both based on false economic arguments in the first place as observed on pp. 66-7 and pp. 17-18. The argument used in support of restrictions of second-hand and disposal machinery and equipment by import licensing resembles the traditional argument against the 'unfair' practice of dumping. In both cases a distinction should be drawn on the one hand between second-hand or 'dumped' goods which are likely to remain freely available at very cheap prices, and are therefore a cheap way for the economy to acquire such goods, and on the other hand predatory dumping. Similarly, the argument that Australian industries in which there are economies of scale of plant size should be protected from import competition, thus allowing the domestic manufacturers to increase their output and lower unit costs, which has been employed to justify import licensing (in the case of aluminium products), as well as dumping actions and the introduction of support value duties on selected chemicals, is generally false.

Of course, these forms of protection could not be abolished without some other adjustments. In cases of all commodities currently protected by these forms of protection the same protective effect at any time can be achieved by *ad valorem* tariffs.[7] The levels of protection given by *ad valorem* tariffs are not hidden and are easily regulated. *Ad valorem* tariffs have the further desirable feature that they are constant and, therefore, certain.

Where these non-tariff instruments of protection apply to commodities being considered in the Tariff Review these changes should be incorporated in the recommendations of this Review. In addition, as many non-tariff instruments apply to commodities not included in the Tariff Review, the government should send a reference to the Tariff Board asking the Board to review the protection given to all commodities currently affected by all of these instruments and to recommend the rates of *ad valorem* duties in place of instruments.

[7] With the exceptions of those commodities for which non-tariff instruments have raised the price received by the producers above the level that even a prohibitive tariff can achieve. See pp. 162-3. Any distortion which is greater than that of a prohibitive tariff is almost certainly undesirable.

There will be strong pressures on the Department of Trade and Industry by vested interests not to change some tariffs and para-tariffs features such as the by-law system and import licensing. Moreover, it may be difficult to change the levels of effective protection going to the motor vehicle and parts, petroleum and dairy products industries, which have been in the past protected by special package plans for five years or other fixed periods and largely protected by methods other than *ad valorem* tariffs such as the content plans for motor vehicles and subsidy and marketing controls for the dairy products industry. The government has already announced that the manufacture of motor vehicles and components will be referred to the Tariff Board in 1974 and the chemical industry in 1975. Whether the Board will use the same criteria in recommending tariffs for motor vehicles and components as used in the industries included in the Review, and whether the government which receives them will treat them in the same way is not clear.

If the levels of protection currently due to both tariff and non-tariff instruments were reduced producers of these commodities and their employees should definitely be eligible for the adjustment assistance measures outlined in chapter 13. This assistance is a crucial part of these recommendations. Many of the uses and problems of non-tariff instruments of protection are traceable to a reluctance to adjust to changes in the international competitiveness of these Australian producers and an appeal to the government to use non-tariff instruments to stem the more competitive imports. The long-run costs to other sections of the economy of such policies are great.

In addition to the instruments that should be abolished, there are a number of important instruments which affect the levels of protection and lie outside the usual scope of Tariff Board activities. These should be reviewed by the government. They include temporary protection, government purchasing policies, the principles of anti-dumping action, and value for duty.

Temporary protection should be returned to the Tariff Board. This would reduce the conflict due to the different evaluations of the Board and Special Advisory Authority and the continual see-saw of references between the Board and the SAA. It would also be advantageous to the economy to have public hearings for temporary protection. The need for temporary protection in some cases and the different criteria which the Tariff Board would have to use for temporary protection would continue as at present. This change, together with the incorporation of by-laws into the substantive rates of duty, would reduce the present treble system of tariff-fixing by the Tariff Board, the Department of Customs and Excise and the SAA to a simpler more consistent one of the Tariff Board making recommendations on tariffs to the government.

For government imports, the best policy from a long-term point of view in which the economy converges to a situation with few distortions is that the present system of notional duty be ended and no actual or notional duties to be applied to government imports. The tendering and purchasing procedures of individual government purchasing authorities should also be tightened to ensure that the principle of 'lowest price' is followed, with due allowance under explicitly-stated criteria for non-price characteristics of possible purchases. Basic features of *all* tenders for a government purchase should also be made public. An exception for *ex post* publicity and for tendering should be made for all purchases below some dollar value. The present limit of $1,000 for the estimated value of supplies below which tenders need not be called is too low. In the current OECD debate on government purchasing procedures suggestions for a minimum threshold below which contracts would not be subject to the provisions of an agreement have ranged from $50,000-$100,000. It is much more important to avoid significant preferences to local suppliers in large or repeated government purchases than to prescribe detailed procedures for small purchases.

Australia should make the minor changes to anti-dumping actions necessary to conform to the GATT Anti-Dumping Code.

Amendments to the value for duty practices in Australia were considered in chapter 3.

The quarantine regulations and prohibited import regulations which are intended for objectives other than protection should be examined to see that they do not have any unnecessary trade-restricting effects.

For *agricultural* commodities the possibilities of change are basically different in one important respect. There is no overall body which is responsible for or capable of making a public inquiry into the levels of assistance to producers of different agricultural commodities in Australia. Yet, there are great differences among the agricultural commodities in terms of the rates of protection producers currently receive under a diversity of forms of protection and financial assistance and the distortions to consumer prices. Without entering into the area of political predictions it can be stated that there is some hope for a systematic review of assistance to rural industries. In May 1972 the Liberal Party presented to the government its recommendations for a Rural Industries Board to co-ordinate and rationalise all policy for rural industries, to be serviced at least initially by the Bureau of Agricultural Economics. It would hold public inquiries and operate much along the lines of the Tariff Board. The Labor Party is also in favour of a review of all protection by a Protections Board.

The main obstacle to a general review of protection of import-competing and exportable agricultural commodities is the opposition of the Country Party, the Liberal Party's coalition partner. It is staunchly opposed to a Rural Industries Board which would conduct a systematic review of policies affecting agricultural commodities. Indeed, because of the Country Party's role in the present government, the area of policies which protect domestic agricultural producers against imports and subsidise agricultural producers is probably the area of non-tariff distortions which will be most difficult politically to reform. This is unfortunate since this study has shown that agriculture is one of the sectors of the economy, along with such manufacturing industries as shipbuilding, textiles and chemicals, which benefits most from a wide range of non-tariff instruments. We have noted that subsidies to producers, export subsidies and adjustment assistance go principally to agricultural producers. It is not so well recognised that many agricultural commodities in Australia are substantially protected from imports by numerous non-tariff instruments: prohibited imports, voluntary quantitative restrictions, quarantine regulations. (Moreover, agricultural producers receive many taxation concessions and it is notable that all agricultural commodities are free of sales tax and wine is the only agricultural commodity which is excisable. These distortions, which are not directly related to trade flow, lie outside the scope of this study but they also affect the overall level of protection and assistance going to different producers.)

All forms of protection, subsidies and assistance to agricultural producers should be reviewed systematically. Protection by means of voluntary and statutory quantitative restrictions and prohibitions is undesirable for the same reasons as quantitative restrictions on manufacturing. The absence of a systematic review of agricultural programs and their differential effects on different agricultural producers will become more serious as the Tariff Board Review proceeds and, hopefully, eliminates some of the serious inter-commodity distortions among producers of importable manufacturing commodities.

We need also to consider exports of manufactures. Exports of manufactures excluding processed primary products were 19 per cent of total exports in 1970-71 and have been increasing more rapidly than other exports as a group. Almost all manufacturing industries are substantial exports. Even industries such as 'Machinery' and 'Manufactures of Metal' which are the first up for review in the Tariff Board's timetable are substantial exporters. Almost one-half of the total export subsidies (48·6 per cent) under the former pay-roll tax rebate for increased exports in 1967-68, the latest year for which statistics are available, went to producers in the category 'Metals, metals manufacture and machinery' which is roughly coterminous with the two Tariff Board industries.

The optimal pattern of specialisation within the manufacturing sector is too broad a subject to be examined here but some points can be made briefly. First, it is likely that the major inefficiencies in production in the Australian economy occur within industries or more generally within the broad sectors of the economy. Distorted prices to producers encourage resources to move into the production of the wrong commodities. Resource mobility in response to changes in the prices to producers may be greater within industries where the production of different commodities still requires much the same managerial and labour skills and kind of machinery than the mobility of resources between industries or sectors. Lowering protection in manufacturing industries may have the effect of forcing some firms to produce a more narrow range of commodities but at the same time of increasing the quantities of the commodities it continues to produce. It may also lead them to increase their exports as prices of these goods are lowered because of the reduced protection and the resources released from no longer producing other commodities can be employed in increasing the production of these commodities.[8] Where economies of scale due to plant size or to the length of production runs and series are important in Australian manufacturing industries the gain from a more rational allocation of resources among producers of different commodities will be enhanced.

The assistance available to all exporters under a number of separate schemes should be reviewed together. This poses a problem. It is clearly desirable to simplify and co-ordinate the level of assistance given to exporters of agricultural and manufactured and mineral commodities alike. It was also suggested that it would be advantageous if all forms of protection of importables and of assistance to exportables produced in the agricultural sector were reviewed together. These suggestions imply that all agricultural importables and all exportable commodities be reviewed simultaneously. But such a task would be even larger than the Tariff Board's present task and is not manageable. Because agriculture commodities are affected by so many different tariff and non-tariff distortions and the level of these varies greatly among the commodities produced by this sector, it is necessary to consider these together and then to examine the level of subsidies that should be paid to exporters of manufacturing commodities.

The only valid argument for export subsidies is that the present exchange rate is undervalued compared to what it would be if import-competing commodities were not protected. Therefore, exporters receive less in terms of Australian currency for goods sold in foreign markets than they would if there were no protection which distorted the prices in favour of the producers of import-competing commodities. This argument has been used repeatedly in Australia.[9] We should note,

[8] Some models which are relevant to this question can be found in Pursell and Snape, 'Economies of Scale', and Lloyd, *New Zealand Manufacturing Production*, chapter IV.
[9] See for example, Corden, 'Australian Economic Policy', pp. 106-7; the *Report of the Committee of Economic Enquiry*, vol. I, paras 14, 19. Recently,

however, that it applies an *ad valorem* subsidy which is uniform, paid only on actual exports (and not on the total production of exportable commodities) and is the only form of assistance to exporters. In all respects the present system of *ad hoc* subsidies and bounties to the producers and exporters of various commodities deviates substantially from that which can be justified.

It is not likely that the present pattern of assistance to export producers in Australia could be rationalised in this way. There is no machinery for such a review and the political pressure for greater subsidy for some commodities could probably not be resisted. There is another and better strategy. If the serious distortions among producers of exportable commodities and between these producers and other producers are to be greately reduced, it will be necessary to reduce the level of protection for import-competing commodities which is used to justify assistance to these producers. The export subsidies are an example of non-tariff distortions which have arisen to try to correct the effects of some prior distortion in the economy and illustrate the advantages of eliminating or reducing the prior distortion as a means of reducing the whole pattern of distortions over attempts to offset earlier distortions. A reduction in both the level of protection and export subsidies may require a small devaluation of the exchange rate, in order to maintain the balance of demand and supply of foreign exchange. Reduced protection of importables and a devaluation of the Australian dollar would assist agricultural producers. As an alternative to more subsidies this policy has the decided advantages that it will encourage efficient producers of the agricultural commodities for which there are overseas markets and it will encourage exports of manufactures too. It would be a definite step towards a reduction in all distortions of trade in the economy.

Desirable changes in adjustment assistance were discussed briefly in chapter 13.

If, for political or other reasons, the government desires to assist particular producers or finds unpalatable recommendations such as those in this chapter to reduce existing assistance to particular producers, it should still not use instruments which distort consumer prices or the prices of inputs The instruments that I have suggested should be abolished all cause avoidable economic losses. If certain producers must be favoured we can at least minimise the loss of real income to the economy.

---

the Wool Board used a variation of this argument in a report on 'Secondary Industry Protection and the Wool Industry'.

On the other hand this argument for free trade with a fixed exchange rate also implies an equal uniform *ad valorem* tariff on all imports. The zero duty on imports of many agricultural inputs through customs drawbacks, by-laws and the use of subsidies to producers are in effect hidden subsidies to the agricultural producers, as noted on p. 164.

Postscript   Election of a Labor Government

Since the text was completed in the third quarter of 1972, the Australian Labor Party won a majority of seats in the House of Representatives in the Australian elections of 2 December 1972 and the Whitlam Ministry has taken office. The return of a Labor Government after 23 years of unbroken government by the Liberal-Country Party Coalition will undoubtedly mean important changes in the next three years in the field of non-tariff distortions of Australian trade. In the four months since taking office, many decisions that will affect non-tariff distortions have already been taken. However, the direction of change in policies is still not clear in most cases. A brief interpretation of the main changes is given below.

The Labor Party gave few indications before the election of its policies towards non-tariff instruments. Because of their complex, overlapping, and often hidden and discretionary nature, non-tariff instruments of government intervention in import and export trade are not normally a popular subject of public discussion. However, some indications of the direction of changes to come can be gleaned from the statements during the election campaign.[1]

Labor Party policies requiring non-tariff interventions to Australia's international trade will be strongly influenced by the general economic objectives of the new government. One macro-economic objective on which the Labor Party will put greater emphasis is that of full employment. If this policy is interpreted to mean that even temporary unemployment between jobs is unacceptable, it could lead the government

[1] The principal source used is the official platform speech of the ALP delivered by Mr Whitlam, then Leader of the Opposition and now Prime Minister; 'Australian Labor Party Policy Speech—1972', 13 November 1972. See also *Towards A New Australia*, edited by John McLaren, Cheshire, 1972. This book is a collection of essays by the principal ALP spokesmen put out for the election by the Victorian Fabian Society. Where no other source is given, references are to reports in the daily press, mainly the *Australian Financial Review*.

to oppose proposals to reduce protection to some Australian manufacturers. (Recall some of the earlier statements by Dr Cairns, now Minister for Trade and Secondary Industry, quoted in chapter 3, on the necessity to provide alternative employment for any employee who might be 'disemployed' as a result of tariff changes recommended by the Tariff Board.) On the other hand, a state of full employment does itself facilitate the movement of labour from jobs for which the demand is decreasing. Similarly, the Labor Party's declared interest in consumer protection might have the novel result that the interests of consumers as well as those of producers are weighed in deciding upon a change in the level of protection to import-competing producers. 'A Labor Government will not hesitate to use its powers as a customer, and through tariffs, subsidies and contracts to prevent unjustified price rises.'[2] The power which the Tariff Board has had under the Tariff Board Act to investigate whether manufacturers are taking advantage of protection to charge unnecessarily high prices was used only once by the previous Coalition Government.

The Labor Party promise to establish a machinery for economic planning should have important implications for non-tariff instruments since these are one of the major causes of distorted prices and the resulting inefficient allocation of resources, but there was little indication before the election of the scope and powers of the economic planning machinery which the Labor Party may have in mind. Dr Cairns, now Minister for Trade and Secondary Industry, had stated that 'provision for the development and maintenance of the [secondary] industry . . . would extend beyond tariffs or subsidy and would include such things as loans to carry over seasonal and other terminating disadvantages and assistance in exporting such as long-term credit, shipping and insurance which would have meaning and reality'.[3] The last Commonwealth Conference of the ALP in June 1971, wrote into the ALP Platform under the heading 'Economic Planning' the intention to 'Protect Australian industries, where necessary, by tariffs, import control, and/or subsidies to safeguard Australian living standards and to develop Australian resources'.[4] My study has indicated that new non-tariff forms of assistance must be very carefully constructed if they are not to reduce economic welfare.

Another general objective of Labor Party policy which has an important bearing on one non-tariff distortion is the policy of 'open government'. In chapter 5 we noted that there is no way at present in Australia of knowing the extent of preferences given to local suppliers over foreign suppliers in the awarding of contracts for government purchases. *Ex post*

---

[2] 'Australian Labor Party Policy Speech—1972', p. 7.
[3] *Towards A New Australia*, p. 91.
[4] Quoted by Mr Hurford, in ibid, p. 56.

publicity in government tendering does not preclude substantial preferences, as the coexistence of this publicity and the Buy American Act in the US demonstrates, but it does at least reveal their extent. Since the new government has promised[5] to introduce a Freedom of Information Act along the lines if US legislation it is to be hoped that it will allow access *ex post* to the basic price and quality information for all tenders for government purchases as in the US.

After the government took office the first indication of the shape of policies was the reorganisation of Commonwealth Government Departments and Ministries which were announced in December 1972 and January 1973. The separation of the former Department of Trade and Industry into a new Department of Secondary Industry and Department of Overseas Trade was expected but the transferral of the administration of the Tariff Board Act, except to the extent to which it is administered by the Minister for Customs and Excise, from the Minister for Trade and Industry to the Prime Minister was not expected. This has generally been interpreted to mean a strengthening in the position of the Tariff Board. The independence of the Board has been questioned publicly by the Chairman of the Board in his dispute during the election campaign period with the former Minister for Trade and Industry over the delay in sending the reference concerning colour television to the Board. This administrative change may in the long term make important changes in the method of sending and reviewing references to the Tariff Board.

A lesser known Senator, Senator Wreidt, has been appointed as Minister for Primary Industry instead of either of the members of the House, Dr Patterson and Mr Grassby, who had spoken out loudly for the rural interests when the Labor Party was in opposition. This appointment and the decision to revalue the Australian dollar, are widely regarded as a defeat for the members within the Party with rural interests. The Country Party, which as the unabashed lobby for rural producers in Parliament has always known how to protect its electoral interests, quickly interpreted these events as clear evidence that Mr Whitlam had 'written off' primary industry.[6]

Another change in departmental responsibilities which has potentially important implications for distortions of trade concerns shipbuilding. It was decided in December that responsibility for administering the Supply and Development Act, under which the Shipbuilding Board and the subsidies to Australian shipbuilders have operated, would be transferred from the former Department of Shipping and Transport to the new Department of Secondary Industry but in March it was transferred back to the new Department of Transport. The control of imports of

[5] 'Australian Labor Party Policy Speech—1972', p. 29.
[6] Statement by Mr Anthony, leader of the Country Party, reported in *Australian Financial Review*, 20 December 1972.

ships under the prohibited imports regulations remained with the new Department of Transport.

Several Ministers in the new government have now made a large number of decisions relating to non-tariff instruments and announcements that other instruments are under review. Brief comment is made on each important change.

The revaluation of the Australian dollar is the most important decision affecting international trade taken to date by the Labor Government. On 23 December 1972 it was announced that the Australian dollar had been unilaterally revalued by 7·05 per cent. This decision was taken by the Prime Minister, Deputy Prime Minister and the Treasurer alone, before the Ministry was formed. On 14 February 1973 the US announced that it was devaluing the dollar against gold by 10 per cent and some other countries soon followed suit. Despite pressure from exporters the government stuck with the exchange rate fixed in December. This entailed a further appreciation of 10 per cent against the US dollar and some other currencies but, as the yen appreciated vis-à-vis the Australian dollar, the trade-weighted exchange rate was little changed from that fixed in December. Almost all economists applauded these decisions to revalue, although a few argued that it would have been better to wait and see what effect the new government's restrictions on capital inflow and other trade policies have on the balance of payments.

After the revaluation decisions the Labor Government has steadfastly resisted strong pressures for substantial revaluation compensation such as that granted by the previous government after the 1967 devaluation of pound sterling. In December the government announced that it would consider sympathetically the case for assistance to 'some rural industries which are facing difficulties and problems of adjustment to changed circumstances [and] may find it particularly difficult to bear the consequences of the exchange rate appreciation'.[7] In January an interdepartmental committee was established to consider the payment of revaluation compensation to exporters adversely affected by the December revaluation. The Treasurer indicated that compensation would not be paid to mining companies but in February the Minister for Minerals and Energy did officially press upon the Japanese Government the view that there should be a review of the export prices in mineral contracts between Australian exporting and Japanese importing companies which had been denominated in US dollars. On 6 February the Minister for Primary Industry announced that, following the recommendations of the Committee, the government would pay assistance to Australian farm exporters only under stringent conditions. The conditions were that the problems of adjustment were already being faced

---

[7] From the text of the statement by the Prime Minister, reproduced in the *Canberra Times*, 26 December 1972, p. 12.

at the time of revaluation and that the industry would experience particular difficulty in bearing the consequences of the revaluation. Producers of export apples and pears and canning peaches, pears and apricots are the only rural producers to meet these conditions to date. They are eligible for a welfare grant of up to $1,500 per farm, depending on the volume of fruit produced plus a grant of $1,000 to farmers growing predominantly export apples and pears and $500 to farmers predominantly growing canning fruits in cases of extreme financial difficulty. This is emergency adjustment assistance to these producers rather than compensation for the revaluation decision and it is expected that this assistance may not exceed $3 million. After the appreciation of the Australian dollar vis-à-vis the US dollar, pound sterling and some other currencies in February it was announced that the same conditions would apply to rural export industries adversely affected by this currency change. On 10 March the Minister for Overseas Trade announced that revaluation compensation would be paid to manufacturing exporters on condition that the applicant demonstrate that hardship had resulted from a reduction in export prices as a result of the revaluation and that he had taken out forward exchange cover where it was available. There is to be no assistance for export sales made after 31 December 1973 and the payment per applicant is not to exceed $100,000. This assistance appears to be greater in relation to the value of exports adversely affected than that paid to rural producers.

The Labor Government insistence that payments be in the form of strictly temporary adjustment assistance rather than compensation for a decision by government is a marked improvement over previous policies. The government must retain the right to make decisions relating to the par value of the currency. The risks of exchange rate change are merely another risk of market change, provided the government does not prevent exporters from obtaining forward exchange cover as happened with the dairy and wheat producers in 1967.

The same hardening in attitudes towards subsidies for rural producers is evident in other decisions. In March the Labor Party Parliamentary Caucus voted to accept a Cabinet recommendation that the interest rate on rural debt reconstruction loans should be increased from 4 per cent to 5 per cent. The object of this proposal was to increase the percentage of loans for farm build-up rather than debt reconstruction and thereby to encourage greater long-term adjustment in the agriculture sector. However, the actual change in policy announced by the Minister for Primary Industry after a meeting with the State Government Ministers for Agriculture is less certain to increase adjustment. The interest rate on loans for debt reconstruction is to continue at 4 per cent but the States have agreed not to approve debt reconstruction applications amounting to over 50 per cent of the total to the State without the agreement of the Commonwealth Government. Other subsidies to rural producers are to be reviewed critically, especially those where the bulk of the payments have in the past gone to the larger and richer farmers. However, we should remember that the assistance rural producers, and especially producers of dairy products, wheat and sugar, receive from direct government subsidies is less than that they receive from consumers through two-price schemes and import restrictions which permit prices on the domestic markets to be considerably greater than world prices (see chapter 10). The renegotiation of the wheat stabilisation agreement will provide an important test of whether the new government is as critical of these transfers of real income from consumers as it is of the transfers which necessitate expenditure by the Federal Government. One hopeful sign is that in February the Australian Agricultural Council, which consists of Commonwealth and State Ministers, did increase the national quota for production of table margarine from 6,000 tons to 22,000 tons.

Whereas the changes concerning agriculture appear likely to reduce distortions of international trade, the new government has made a number of changes relating to trade or production of manufactures which appear likely to continue or to increase distortions of this trade.

One of the first important decisions concerned the export incentive grant scheme and market development allowance. The Treasurer took the position that these schemes should be ended on 30 June 1973 when the present authority for them expires. The Minister for Overseas Trade took the contrary position that they should be expanded to encourage business confidence and to compensate manufacturers for the revaluation of the Australian dollar. An interdepartmental committee was set up to resolve these differences. After receiving the report of the former committee the Economic Committee of the Federal Cabinet made a compromise recommendation that the export incentives be continued on the present bases for one more year to June 1974. These incentives will be reviewed again in the meantime.

The Australian broadcasting industry seems likely to be pressed to increase again the proportion of Australian-produced material shown on television. This is the declared policy of the government. The Minister for the Media is considering a number of alternative policies.

The Minister for Science announced in March a new policy of reserving patent licences held by the CSIRO for Australian-owned companies only. This is intended to aid the new government's objective of increasing Australian ownership of industries in Australia. The pursuit of this objective is also one of the motivating factors behind announced changes in government purchasing policies.

Although government purchasing policies under the new government are far from clear there has been a series of announcements by

Ministers. On 19 December 1972 the Prime Minister announced 'that government contracts should be awarded to Australian companies in cases where an Australian and an overseas-controlled firm submit tenders which meet specifications and are equal in price and continuity of supply'. He also announced that government contracts with oil companies will be switched to Ampol and H. C. Sleigh, both of which are Australian owned oil companies principally, at the end of 1973, provided their tenders are considered equal to others. On 20 February 1973 the Minister for Labour, Mr Cameron, announced that his department is preparing a labour code for all contractors wishing to tender for government purchases, that this labour code would include such things as the extra week's leave given to Commonwealth Public Servants and that first priority in government tendering would be given to tenderers who complied with the labour code. The Minister of Works has already issued a directive to his Department stating that in awarding contracts, consideration should be given to the relationship of the contractor with the 'Trade Union Movement'.[8]

Discrimination among tenders from Australian based companies on the basis of the company's domestic or overseas ownership is new in Australia. It would discriminate against subsidiaries of foreign companies producing in Australia as well as against foreign suppliers. It conflicts with the previous government's policy of the lowest price consistent with satisfactory quality. The Prime Minister's announcement does not enable us to determine the real extent of preferences that may result. The announcement relates only to 'other things being equal' comparisons. If two tenders are really equal in price and other characteristics the choice between them is of little economic consequence. But the tenders are rarely equal in price and other important supply characteristics. Will some preference be granted to 'Australian companies' in situations in which the tenders are not equal? The announcement by the Prime Minister was made during the month of rule by the Prime Minister and Deputy Prime Minister alone and before the formation of the ministry. Decisions taken during this period were supposed to be of considerable national importance. This announcement may herald a movement towards a restrictive 'Buy Australian' policy in government purchases, at a time when the OECD and other countries are working towards the reduction in discrimination in government purchases.

The announcement concerning government contracts for oil products purchases honours a pledge during the election to switch government purchases of oil products to Australian-owned and controlled companies where the price, availability and accessibility of supplies are as

---

[8] For a discussion of the proposed labour code and new directive see *CPD*, 8 March 1973, pp. 362-76.

good as those of other companies.[9] This decision stemmed from the Labor Party view that the petrol strike in July 1972 had been prolonged by collaboration between the foreign-owned oil companies and the previous government.

The use of government purchasing as an instrument to achieve objectives other than the least cost provision of government goods and services illustrates the costs of using an inappropriate policy instrument which was noted in the text in relation to past uses of other non-tariff instruments. There are some administrative reasons why this government purchasing is a poor instrument to enforce a labour code (or to increase Australian ownership). It is difficult with more than 20 purchasing authorities as in Australia to enforce and audit such regulations. Buying departments have selfish interests in continuing to buy from the cheapest source, unless they are compensated by an addition to their budget. More basically, the choice of instruments is bad because it is ineffective and imposes avoidable economic costs. The labour code can only influence those employers contracting directly for government purchases. It would be more effective if the objective were applied to all employers, those who do not contract with the government as well as those who do, and to use the established arbitration wage fixing machinery to settle contract issues between employer and employee. There are costs imposed on the rest of the community because taxpayers who ultimately finance these purchases receive less services in return or they pay more for the same services when the government purchasing authority forgoes the cheapest source of supply for goods which it purchases.

The Minister for Transport has announced a policy of reserving 40 per cent of Australian commodity trade for Australian shipping lines in both the bulk and liner trade. This implements a recommendation of the Santiago meeting of UNCTAD in 1972 that each country is entitled to carry 40 per cent of its own trade, with an additional 40 per cent being carried by its trading partners and the remaining 20 per cent by carriers of third countries. However, this recommendation was intended for the developing countries. If carried out its effect will be to increase needlessly the costs of transporting our commodity exports and imports. This in turn will either require massive subsidies or it will reduce the profitability of our export productions and increase the protection received from transport margins for our import-competing manufacturers. Moreover, it will tend to reduce the efficiency of Australian manufacturing industries where there are economies of scale from larger volumes or longer runs because of the higher domestic prices.

Other policies concerning non-tariff instruments are known to be under review. These include customs by-laws, motor vehicle content

[9] 'Australian Labor Party Policy Speech—1972', p. 24.

plans and shipbuilding subsidies. In February the Minister for Overseas Trade and Secondary Industry announced that an important and far-reaching review of the system of customs by-laws would be undertaken by an interdepartmental committee with representatives from the Departments of Secondary Industry, Overseas Trade, Customs and Excise and Treasury. Any major change in the by-law system will have a substantial effect on the levels and pattern of effective protection. This by-law review is closely related to the question of content plans for the motor vehicle industry since by-law admission of components not produced in Australia is a vital part of the protection for these producers. The applications by Nissan and Toyota to enter the 85 per cent local content program have precipitated an examination of these programs but it still is not possible to judge from statements by the Minister for Secondary Industry whether there will be any major change in these programs. In March the Minister for Overseas Trade and Secondary Industry and the Minister for Transport made a joint announcement that there would be 'an urgent comprehensive review of the levels and modes of assistance accorded the Australian shipbuilding industry . . . to provide assistance which would assure the continuing development of a rationalised and efficient shipbuilding industry in Australia'. This review is to be done by the departments, not the Tariff Board. The issues of shipbuilding policy came to a head with the threatened closure of the Brisbane shipyard of Evans Deakin Industries Ltd. The government took several measures to forestall this event including the waiving of the conditions on the granting of a subsidy in order to enable the shipyard to secure an order for an oil rig. Although these measures did not prevent the closure of the yard, they showed the extent to which the government was prepared to go, in one industry at least, to prevent the close-down of an inefficient plant. The reason for these actions was the desire to prevent the lay-off of workers in the yard.

Superimposed on the decisions or pending decisions relating to particular non-tariff instruments are a number of new but more general policies which are certain to have important implications for some non-tariff restrictions of trade. Several of these have emanated from the Department of Secondary Industry. In February the Minister for Secondary Industry outlined the government's proposals to develop industry planning groups across the whole range of industry, both secondary and primary. The first of these is the Textile and Apparel Industry Advisory Panel. While it is intended that these panels will involve all sections of the community in industry planning, including the unions and consumer representatives, the first indications from the development of the Textile and Apparel Industry Advisory Panel are not encouraging. It appears that the panel will be overwhelmingly producer-dominated and, therefore, producer-oriented. The heads of major textile companies alone may constitute a majority of the membership and the union representatives can be expected to be equally protectionist. Quantitative restrictions are to be examined but, to judge from ministerial statements, the main questions that will be examined are whether the restraints should be negotiated by the government or the industry and whether they should be bilateral or global. The Minister has also announced that an 'import watch' on sensitive items of Australian textile and apparel production will be instituted within the Department of Secondary Industry itself.

A unit to develop assistance for small manufacturers is to be set up within the Department of Secondary Industry. The Australian Industries Development Corporation is to be expanded to make it 'the major instrument for the Australian ownership of Australian economic enterprise'. Both of these organisations could be used to improve the efficiency of plants and to rationalise the structure of Australian industries but equally they could be used to increase assistance to Australian producers and protect the *status quo*. On the export side of commodity trade the energy policy which is being prepared for the Minister for Minerals and Energy and the decision by the government in January to extend export controls to cover all Australian minerals will have important, but as yet unknown, effects on mineral production and exports.

There are two other new bodies which are important throughout the field of trade policy. In February the Prime Minister announced that the government was going ahead with its plan to appoint a Protection Commission which will advise the government on assistance for both primary and secondary industry. This plan was advanced earlier in the election campaign but was not included in the policies listed in the Prime Minister's Speech on 13 November 1972. When established, this body could provide overall co-ordination of non-tariff and tariff policies affecting different industries. This co-ordination is badly needed with the increased proliferation of departments, interdepartmental committees and organisations. At this time it is not known whether the responsibilities of the Commission will cover all industries and all instruments of protection and assistance, as in my opinion it must if it is to be effective, or whether there will be important exclusions. The second body with some authority over subsidy forms of assistance is the special task force headed by Dr Coombs, former governor of the Reserve Bank, which is to scrutinise the expenditures of the previous government before the next Budget in August 1973.

The key to whether Labor policies are going to be oriented towards improved efficiency and lower consumer prices or to the protection of existing production lies in the attitude of the new government to industry adjustment and adjustment assistance. This attitude has not been formulated yet. During the election campaign the ALP committed itself to the principle of retraining labour whose skills are no longer in demand and stated 'there shall be no limitations on appropriate training and retraining'.[10] In March the Minister for Labour announced that yet another interdepartmental committee has been formed to draw up a proposal for an integrated approach to structural change in the economy. One hopeful sign is the stated intention to switch the policy emphasis in the Department of Labour from measures to increase employment to measures to increase the efficiency of the work force. But it remains to be seen whether this manpower policy can be integrated with the industry panels and other policies in a way which will expedite structural change in the industries which will be vulnerable to increased competition if their protection is reduced.

Taking an overall view one sees several contradictions in the Labor Party's statements and actions which have yet to be resolved. On the one hand, their stated support for the Tariff Review, the need to adjust to technological change and the need for rural reconstruction, and the supporting action to strengthen the position of the Tariff Board and reduce the influence of the Ministers in favour of rural support programs, all point towards a reduction in non-tariff and tariff-induced distortions of trade. On the other hand, the strong streak of economic nationalism, especially the view that Australia should own and control the development of its national resources, the commitment to full employment including employment between jobs and the division of responsibilities between so many departments, boards, commissions, panels and interdepartmental committees may obstruct progress towards the objective of a more efficient allocation of resources.

Some of the contradictions and uncertainties of policies are understandable in a government that is returned to power after 23 years and has an urgent desire to change many of the policies of the outgoing government. Some divisions in Cabinet over issues such as export incentives and rural adjustment reflect real differences in the philosophy of individual Ministers and the composition of their electorates. Other actions such as the zig-zag policy towards the shipbuilding industry seem partly the result of undue haste.

The Labor Government is more interventionist than its predecessor but it remains to be seen whether it will co-ordinate its interventions better. Part of the difficulty lies in the multiplicity of objectives but part also lies in the failure to realise the interrelationships between instruments affecting the same industries and between industries. There are disturbing indications that the new government is using the wrong instruments to achieve its chosen objectives and that it may be prone to use non-tariff instruments restricting trade, such as content plans,

---

[10] 'Australian Labor Party Policy Speech—1972', p. 25.

import or export prohibitions and other administrative controls, in preference to tariffs and subsidies which give an open and measurable degree of incentive to producers. Despite some reforms it is unlikely that the problem of widely varying non-tariff distortions of trade which led me to undertake this study will diminish rapidly.

18 April 1973

Appendix Notes on the Estimates of Price Changes in Tables 10.2, 10.3 and 10.4

Measurement of the implicit rate of protection for a commodity involves the comparison of actual prices realised from sales of the commodity with estimates of the prices that would apply in a postulated situation of competitive pricing on the domestic market. The percentage changes in average implicit prices to producers given in Table 10.3 were obtained from the following expressions. For an export commodity:

$$\Delta \bar{p}/\bar{p} = [(\bar{p}_d a + \bar{p}_e b + s_d + s_e)/\bar{p}_e - 1] \, 100$$

and for a non-export commodity:

$$\Delta \bar{p}/\bar{p} = [(\bar{p}_d + s_d)/\bar{p}_i - 1] \, 100$$

Where

$\bar{p}_d$ = average price realised from sales of produce on domestic markets.
$\bar{p}_e$ = average price realised from sales of produce on export markets.
$\bar{p}_i$ = estimated import parity price of equivalent commodity.
s_d = subsidy per unit of production paid on sales on domestic markets.
s_e = subsidy per unit of production paid on sales on export markets.
a = quantity sold on domestic markets/quantity sold on domestic and export markets.
b = quantity sold on export markets/quantity sold on domestic and export markets.

It can readily be seen that these definitions of the change in the average price received by producers are equivalent in principle to the measure of the 'level of protection' which Stuart Harris obtained by dividing total actual returns for the commodity by total sales valued at the export or import parity.[1] His measures may be converted into percentage changes simply by subtracting 100. The percentage change form is customary in international trade studies and is directly comparable with percentage changes in prices due to tariffs.

[1] Harris, 'Some Measures of the Levels of Protection', Column I of Table III for export commodities and Column I of Table IV for non-export commodities.

226 Appendix

The total price change for a commodity can be decomposed into the price change due to the payment of subsidies directly to the producers and the price change due to higher prices on the domestic market because of tariff and non-tariff protection from import competition. The decompositions for an export and a non-export commodity are respectively

$$\Delta \bar{p}/\bar{p} = [(s_d + s_e)/\bar{p}_e] 100 + [(\bar{p}_d a + \bar{p}_e b)/\bar{p}_e - 1] 100$$

and

$$\Delta \bar{p}/\bar{p} = [s_d/\bar{p}_i] 100 + [\bar{p}_d/\bar{p}_i - 1] 100$$

The estimates of the first terms of these expressions which show the price changes due to direct subsidy payments for the selection of agricultural commodities considered in this study are reported in Table 10.2.

The percentage changes in implicit prices to consumers given in Table 10.4 were obtained by dropping the terms in the above expressions for direct subsidy payments to producers and sales to overseas consumers. Thus, for export commodities we use the expression:

$$\Delta \bar{p}/\bar{p} = [\bar{p}_d/p_e - 1] 100$$

and for non-export commodities:

$$\Delta \bar{p}/\bar{p} = [\bar{p}_d/p_i - 1] 100$$

The following notes specify the prices used in the estimations and the primary data sources for each commodity. The domestic prices used are those realised for sales in principal markets and export parity prices are those realised for export sales f.o.b. main ports unless otherwise specified. Where more than one domestic market exists for a commodity the average price has been obtained by weighting these prices according to market shares based on quantities sold.

BUTTER

p_d weighted average of prices realised for sales on interstate and intrastate markets including sales for manufacturing purposes.

Source: annual sales and values of butter taken into account for equalisation purposes, 'Annual Report of Directors', Commonwealth Dairy Produce Equalisation Committee Ltd, various issues.

p_e average price realised for sales on overseas markets.

Source: ibid.

Subsidy   includes bounty paid on production and devaluation compensation for years 1966-67 to 1970-71.

Source: ibid.

Note: the implicit rates of protection for butter given in Table 10.3 represent the changes in implicit prices received by manufacturers.

Appendix

CHEESE

p_d — weighted average of prices realised for sales on interstate and intrastate markets.

Source: annual sales and values taken into account for equalisation purposes, 'Annual Report of Directors', Commonwealth Dairy Produce Equalisation Committee Ltd, various issues.

p_e — average price realised for sales on overseas markets.

Source: ibid.

Subsidy — includes bounty paid on production and devaluation compensation paid for years 1966-67 to 1970-71.

Source: ibid.

Note: The implicit rates of protection for cheese given in Table 10.3 represent the changes in implicit prices received by manufacturers.

WHEAT

p_d — average price realised for sales on domestic markets.

Source: Australian Wheat Board Gazette—various issues and information provided by the Wheat Board.

p_e — average price realised for sales on export markets (includes devaluation compensation).

Source: ibid.

s_e — government contributions to Australian Wheat Industry Stabilisation Fund (excludes devaluation compensation).

Source: ibid.

Note: devaluation compensation included in export price for wheat and excluded from subsidy estimates on grounds that prior to sterling devaluation, the AWB was not permitted to take out forward exchange cover. The implicit rates of protection for wheat given in Table 10.3 represent the change in implicit prices received by producers, net receipts for terminal.

SUGAR

p_d — average net price per ton paid to mills for raw Queensland sugar intended for Australian consumption (net of Sugar Board charges).

Source: *Queensland Year Book*.

p_e — average net price per ton paid to mills for raw Queensland sugar sold on export markets.

Source: ibid.

Subsidy — includes devaluation compensation paid 1966-67 to 1970-71.

Note: the implicit rate of protection represents the change in implicit prices received by Queensland sugar mills.

228 *Appendix*

Eggs

p_d average price realised for sales on domestic markets (includes sales of egg pulp—converted to egg shell equivalents but excludes backyard production).
Source: Annual Report *Australian Egg Board*—various issues.
p_e average price realised for sales on export markets (includes sales of egg pulp converted to egg shell equivalents).
Source: ibid.
Subsidy includes devaluation compensation 1966-67 to 1970-71.

Dried Vine Fruits

p_d weighted average f.o.b. prices realised for sales of currants, sultanas and raisins on domestic market.
Source: Australian Dried Fruits Association.
p_e weighted average f.o.b. price realised for sales of currants, sultanas and raisins on export markets.
Source: Australian Dried Fruits Association.
Subsidy includes devaluation compensation paid 1966-67 to 1970-71.

Barley

p_d average price for (ports) realised on domestic sales by the Australian Barley Board.
Source: 'Annual Report', Australian Barley Board, various issues.
p_e average price realised from sales on export markets.
Source: ibid.
Note: the Australian Barley Board accounts for approximately one-third of barley produced in Australia.

Rice

p_d millers price to wholesaler f.o.r. (Sydney).
Source: 'Annual Chairman's Report', Rice Market Board of NSW, various issues.
p_e average f.o.b. price realised on sales on export markets.
Source: 'Overseas Trade Bulletin', CBCS.
Note: implicit rates of protection represents change in implicit prices received by millers.

Cotton

p_d average returns to growers—cents per pound.
Source: 'Cotton Growing in Australia 1963', BAE (1953-54 to 1962-63). 'The Market Outlook for Raw Cotton', BAE, QRAE, July 1969. 1963-64 to date.

p_i price f.o.b. Gulf Ports USA plus the cost of freight (import parity price nearest probable supplier).
Source: United States Department of Agriculture 'Cotton Situation' (1953-54 to 1963-64) World Cotton Statistics, International Cotton Advisory Committee (1964-65 to date).
Subsidy   Commonwealth bounty payments to growers paid 1953-54 to 1970-71.
Note: subsidy has since ended, last payment made 1971-72.

LINSEED

p_d net price for linseed free of impurities f.o.r. capital cities.
Source: L. W. McLennan, 'Linseed: A Statistical Analysis . . . 1947-48 to 1956-57' and Department of Primary Industry marketing division fortnightly bulletin, 'Vegetable Oilseeds Market News'.
p_i price f.o.b. Pacific Ports, Western Canada, plus the cost of freight.
Source: 'Canadian Production, Trade and Prices for Principal Agricultural Products, 1952-58', Canadian Department of Agriculture, also 'Grain Statistics Weekly' and 'Grain Trade of Canada', Canadian Bureau of Statistics.
Note: domestic price is price paid to grower for linseed remaining after impurities removed.

TOBACCO

p_d average auction price for dried leaf tobacco.
Source: Annual Report, Australian Tobacco Board, various issues.
p_i average import price f.o.b. plus freight.
Source: CBCS, 'Imports Cleared for Home Consumption', various issues.
Note: leaf is imported matured. Import price was therefore adjusted *upwards* by 6 per cent to allow for the greater quantity of leaf (i.e. less moisture) per ton, and to convert the import price to a basis comparable to the domestic price.

Table A.1 Australian imports, 1970-71, by kind, and average rates of duty ($ million f.o.b.)

IMPORTS AT SPECIFIED RATES OF DUTY	UK	Canada	NZ	All countries receiving Preferential Tariff	Declared Preference countries	USA	Japan	EEC	EFTA	All countries receiving General Tariff	All countries
Free												
For Commonwealth Govt	43·2	1·3	0·3	45·0	0·4	59·4	5·8	25·7	3·9	0·6	145·5
By-law imports	221·4	27·7	4·8	255·9	2·2	387·0	68·0	111·3	52·0	95·4	899·7
Other free	292·3	80·2	59·7	460·0	99·1	106·2	33·4	35·5	19·4	641·1	996·1
Outside packages	13·2	3·5	1·6	18·5	1·4	10·6	10·4	9·7	2·2	411·1	56·9
Total free	570·0	112·25	66·3	779·4	103·1	563·2	117·7	182·3	77·5	1,184·7	2,098·3
Dutiable by-law imports	0·6	0·3	0·0	0·9	1·4	122·2	61·9	70·8	23·5	282·2	284·6
Normal imports at *ad valorem* rates under 10%	18·8	2·4	1·1	22·8	1·6	118·1	87·2	87·9	30·4	363·2	399·9
Total	273·9	34·4	22·6	334·2	45·3	292·0	327·8	248·6	76·4	1,021·2	1,400·7
Normal imports other than *ad valorem* rates	37·5	16·7	6·2	61·1	28·0	58·8	58·4	33·9	18·7	217·5	306·7
TOTAL IMPORTS	882·0	163·8	95·1	1,175·6	177·8	1,036·1	565·7	535·6	196·1	2,705·6	4,103·8

AVERAGE RATES OF DUTY FOR SPECIFIED IMPORTS*†											
Average rate on all by-law imports	0·0	0·0	0·0	0·0	0·0	2·9	2·2	2·9	2·3	2·3	1·8
Average rate on all normal imports at *ad val.* rates	22·3	22·5	17·0	22·0	30·6	25·0	28·2	26·2	25·1	26·0	25·2
Average rate on all normal imports other than *ad val.*	70·6	12·4	9·6	47·9	42·9	35·8	29·1	43·1	15·0	37·5	41·1
AV. RATE ON TOTAL IMPORTS	9·9	6·0	4·7	8·7	14·6	10·0	20·2	15·9	12·1	13·6	12·3

Source: Adapted from the CBCS tables 'Customs Clearances at Specified Rates of Duty : Australia, 1970-71', and 'Customs Duty Collected at Specified Rates of Duty : Australia 1970-71', (Canberra, 15 December 1971).

Notes: * These are averages of the *ad valorem* rates (or equivalent *ad valorem* rates) on individual items, weighted by the share of total commodity import clearances. They were computed by dividing the duty collected by the value of imports cleared.

† No deductions have been made for drawbacks and refunds. These totalled $44 million in 1970-71. When the adjustment is made for drawbacks and refunds, the average rate of duty on all imports is 11·2 per cent rather than 12·3 per cent.

References

Anthony, J. D. Address by the Acting Prime Minister at the Opening of Australian Tube Mills Plant, Sunshine, Victoria, 5 June 1972.
Australian Industries Development Association. 'Government Purchasing Policies'. AIDA *Bulletin*, no. 214, November 1970.
— 'The Special Advisory Authority'. AIDA *Bulletin*, no. 231, June 1972.
Australian Financial Review, 6 August 1971.
— 'This Week . . . The Nation'. 8 November 1971.
Australian Labor Party. 'Australian Labor Party Policy Speech—1972'. Delivered by Gough Whitlam. Blacktown Civic Centre, 13 November 1972.
Australian Wool Board. 'Secondary Industry Protection and the Wool Industry'. Canberra, March 1972.
Baldwin, R. E. *Nontariff Distortions in International Trade*. The Brookings Institution, Washington, D.C., 1970.
Bellany, I. and Richardson, J. L. 'Australian Defence Procurement'. *Canberra Papers on Strategy and Defence*, no. 8, Australian National University Press, Canberra, 1970.
Bertrand, T. J. and Vanek, J. 'The Theory of Tariffs, Taxes and Subsidies: Some Aspects of the Second Best'. *American Economic Review*, vol. LXI (1971), pp. 925-31.
Bhagwati, J. N. 'More on the Equivalence of Tariffs and Quotas'. *American Economic Review*, vol. LVIII (1968), pp. 142-6.
— *The Theory and Practice of Commercial Policy: Departures from Unified Exchange Rates* (Princeton University International Finance Section Special Papers in International Economics, no. 8). Princeton, 1968.
— 'On the Equivalence of Tariffs and Quotas', in J. N. Bhagwati, *Trade, Tariffs and Growth*. Weidenfeld & Nicolson, London, 1969.
— 'The Generalized Theory of Distortions and Welfare', in J. N. Bhagwati *et al.* (eds), *Trade, Balance of Payments and Growth: Papers in International Economics in Honor of Charles P. Kindleberger*. Amsterdam, 1971.
— and Desai, P. *India: Planning for Industrialization*. Oxford University Press, London, 1970.
Brigden, J. B. *et al. The Australian Tariff: An Economic Enquiry*. Melbourne University Press, Melbourne, 1929.
Campbell, K. 'Rural Reconstruction'. *Current Affairs Bulletin*, vol. 48 (1971), pp. 67-78.
Canberra Times. 'Tariff Review to be Speeded Up' (By W. Bracken). 13 April 1972.
Candler, W. and Hampton, P. 'The Measurement of Industrial Protection in New Zealand'. *Australian Economic Papers*, vol. 5 (1966), pp. 47-58.

References 233

Committee for Economic Development of Australia. *Non-Tariff Distortion of Trade*, P Series no. 8. Melbourne, September 1969.
Commonwealth of Australia. Australian Banks Export Re-finance Corporation. Annual Reports, *CPP*, 1971-72 and 1972-73.
— Australian Dairy Produce Board. Forty-Sixth Annual Report for the Year Ending 30 June 1971. *CPP*, no. 97 of 1971.
— Budget Speeches, *CPP*, 1971-72 and 1972-73.
— Bureau of Agricultural Economics. *Debt Reconstruction and Farm Adjustment*. Canberra, 1971.
— Commissioner of Taxation. *Commonwealth Taxation Assessment, 1969-70*. Canberra, 1971.
— *Forty-Ninth Report of the Commissioner of Taxation 1969-70. CPP*, no. 140 of 1970.
— *Taxation Statistics 1969-70. CPP*, no. 48 of 1971.
— Commonwealth Bureau of Census and Statistics. 'Customs Clearances at Specified Rates of Duty: Australia, 1970-71'. Canberra, 15 December 1971.
— 'Customs Duty Collected at Specified Rates of Duty: Australia, 1970-71'. Canberra, 15 December 1971.
— *Commonwealth Gazette*. Canberra, 1970 to 1972.
— *Commonwealth Sales Tax*. Canberra, 1970.
— Department of Customs and Excise. *Annotated Customs Tariff*. 2 vols., as amended. Canberra, 1 January 1970.
— *Appraisement Circular*, no. 23 of 1971.
— *Consolidated Customs By-Law References*, as amended. Canberra, January 1971.
— *Facts About the Australian Dumping Law*. Canberra, January 1971.
— *Functions*. Canberra, undated.
— *Overseas Trade, 1970-71*. Bulletin no. 68, Canberra, 1972.
— *Review of Activities 1970-71*. Canberra, 1971.
— Department of Health. *Plant and Animal Quarantine: Notes for Importers*. Canberra, July 1968.
— Department of Trade and Industry. *The Australian System of Tariff Preferences for Developing Countries*, 3rd ed. Canberra, 1 July 1971.
— *History of Australia's Import Licensing Measures from December, 1939*. Canberra, 1959.
— Export Payments Insurance Corporation. *Annual Reports*. Canberra, 1957 to 1972.
— *National Accounting Estimates of Public Authority Receipts and Expenditure, August, 1971*. Issued by the Commonwealth Treasury as a Supplement to the Treasury Information Bulletin.
— *National Income and Expenditure. CPP*, no. 55 of 1971.
— *Parliamentary Debates*, House of Representatives, 1901 to 1972.
— *Parliamentary Debates*, Senate, 1901 to 1972.
— Parliamentary Joint Committee on Public Accounts. Forty-Second Report. *Treasury Regulation 52: Minutes of Evidence*. Canberra, 1959.
— Forty-Eighth Report. *Treasury Regulation 52: Minutes of Evidence*. Canberra, 1960.
— Seventy-Seventh Report. *Treasury Regulation 53: Minutes of Evidence*. Canberra, 1965.
— *Report of the Committee of Economic Enquiry* (Vernon Report). 2 vols., Canberra, 1965.
— *Report of the Dairy Industry Committee of Enquiry* (McCarthy Report). Canberra, 1960.
— *Reports of the Special Advisory Authorities* [Canberra]:
   Aluminium and Aluminium Alloy Waste and Scrap (13 November 1963). *CPP*, no. 2 of 1964-65-66.
   Industrial Radiographic Equipment (5 November 1970). *CPP*, no. 8 of 1971.

234 References

Commonwealth of Australia. *Reports of the Special Advisory Authorities* [Canberra]: (*Continued*).
Knitted Coats, Jumpers, Sweaters and the Like (8 December 1967). *CPP*, no. 15 of 1968.
Knitted Shirts (14 May 1969). *CPP*, no. 185 of 1969.
Penicillin and Streptomycin (27 July 1962). *CPP*, no. 14 of 1964-65-66.
Polyethylene Monofil and Rope (24 December 1965). *CPP*, no. 2666 of 1964-65-66.
Timber (27 June 1962). *CPP*, no. 70 of 1964-65-66.
— *Reports of the Tariff Board* [Canberra]:
Agricultural, Horticultural, Etc., Machinery (19 June 1970). *CPP*, no. 4 of 1971.
Aluminium Ingots, Etc. (3 April 1964). *CPP*, no. 22 of 1964-65-66.
Alumina, Unwrought Aluminium and Aluminium Products (10 March 1967). *CPP*, no. 75 of 1967.
Chain and Chains (Dumping and Subsidy Act). *CPP*, no. 83 of 1971.
Chemical Industry—Support Values Review (29 April 1968). *CPP*, no. 65 of 1968.
Collapsible Sun Lounges (Dumping and Subsidies Act) (14 December 1965). *CPP*, no. 292 of 1964-65-66.
Concluding Interim Report on the General Textile Reference (21 September 1967). *CPP*, no. 8 of 1968.
Continuous Man-Made Fibres (Interim Report) (2 March 1962). *CPP*, no. 33 of 1962-63.
Dimethyl Silicone Fluids (Dumping and Subsidies Act) (12 June 1969). *CPP*, no. 74 of 1969.
Earthmoving, Excavating and Materials Handling Machinery and Equipment (16 October 1967). *CPP*, no. 16 of 1968.
Ethyl Acetate (Dumping and Subsidies Act) (20 June 1968). *CPP*, no. 241 of 1968.
Fertilizers (5 December 1929). *CPP*, no. 23 of 1929-31.
Industrial Chemicals and Synthetic Resins (13 April 1966). *CPP*, no. 358 of 1964-65-66.
Knitted Shirts and Outergarments (29 April 1971). *CPP*, no. 124 of 1971.
Knitted Shirts (16 June 1967). *CPP*, no. 124 of 1967.
Metal Reinforced Rubber Belts or Belting (27 September 1967). *CPP*, no. 6 of 1968.
Penicillin and Streptomycin (27 July 1962). *CPP*, no. 72 of 1962-63.
Pigments and Colour Lakes (Dumping and Subsidies Act) (27 May 1968). *CPP*, no. 83 of 1968.
Pneumatic Rubber Tyres (Dumping and Subsidies Act) (8 March 1968). *CPP*, no. 25 of 1968.
Shipbuilding (4 October 1963). *CPP*, no. 35 of 1964-65-66.
Shipbuilding (25 June 1971). *CPP*, no. 95 of 1972.
Timber (6 September 1963). *CPP*, no. 13 of 1962-63.
Tractors, Engines and Other Parts (8 May 1967). *CPP*, no. 129 of 1967.
— Report of the Trade Practices Tribunal. *Frozen Vegetables and Other Matters* (6 August 1971).
— Tariff Board. Annual Reports, *CPP*, 1935-36 to 1971-72.
— *The Tariff Review*. Canberra, September 1972.
Corden, W. M. 'Tariffs, Subsidies and the Terms of Trade', *Economica*, vol. 24 (1957), pp. 135-42.
— 'Australian Economic Policy Discussion in the Post-War Period: A Survey'. *American Economic Review*, vol. LVIII (1968), no. 3, part 2 Supplement, pp. 88-138.
— *The Theory of Protection*. Oxford University Press, London, 1971.
Crawford, J. G. *Australian Trade Policy 1942-66*. Australian National University Press, Canberra, 1968.

Curzon, G. and Curzon, V. *Hidden Barriers to International Trade* (Thames Essay no. 1, Trade Policy Research Centre). London, 1970.
— and —. *Global Assault on Non-Tariff Trade Barriers* (Thames Essay no. 3, Trade Policy Research Centre). London, 1972.
Diamond, P. A. and Mitchell, F. 'Customs Valuation and Transport Choice'. *Journal of International Economics*, vol. 1 (1971), pp. 119-26.
Edwards, G. W. 'Rural Reconstruction: Theory and Principles'. (Address to Section 24 of ANZAAS, Brisbane, May 1971.)
Ethier, W. J. 'General Equilibrium Theory and the Concept of Effective Protection', in Grubel, H. G. and Johnson, H. G. (eds.), *Effective Tariff Protection*. Geneva, 1971.
Evans, H. D. *A General Equilibrium Analysis of Protection: Effects of Protection in Australia*. North Holland, Amsterdam, 1972.
Fooks, M. D. 'Trade Adjustment Assistance', in *United States International Economic Policy in an Interdependent World*. (Report of the Commission on International Trade and Investment Policy.) Washington, D.C., 1971.
Foster, E. and Sonnenschein, H. 'Price Distortion and Economic Welfare', *Econometrica*, vol. 38 (1970), pp. 281-97.
GATT. *Basic Instruments and Selected Documents*, vol. IV. Text of the General Agreement 1969. Geneva, 1969.
— *Basic Instruments and Selected Documents, Fifteenth Supplement*. Geneva, 1968.
Giersch, H. 'The Trade Optimum'. *International Economic Papers*, vol. 8 (1957), pp. 156-84.
Groenwegen, P. D. 'Defence Policy and Procurement'. (Seminar on Defence Policy and Procurement sponsored by Sydney University Extension Board and the Centre for Continuing Education at the Australian National University, at the Australian Academy of Science, 23 April 1971.)
Grubel, H. G. and Johnson, H. G. (eds.), *Effective Tariff Protection*, GATT, Geneva, 1971.
Gruen, F. H. and Evans, H. D. 'Tariff Policies and the Tariff Board'. *Australian Economic Review*, no. 14 (1971), pp. 37-42.
Harris, S. F. 'Some Measures of Levels of Protection in Australia's Rural Industries'. *Australian Journal of Agricultural Economics*, vol. 8 (1964), pp. 124-44.
Hindley, B. *Britain's Position on Non-tariff Protection*. (Thames Essay no. 4, Trade Policy Research Centre.) London, 1972.
International Chamber of Commerce. *Non-Tariff Obstacles to International Trade*. Paris, 1969.
Johnson, H. G. 'The Cost of Protection and the Scientific Tariff'. *Journal of Political Economy*, vol. 68 (1960), pp. 327-45.
— 'A Note on Tariff Valuation Bases, Economic Efficiency and the Effects of Preferences'. *Journal of Political Economy*, vol. 74 (1966), pp. 401-2.
— and Metzger, S. D. *International Negotiations on Non-Tariff Barriers*. Allen & Unwin, London, 1973.
Kojima, K. 'Nontariff Barriers to Japan's Trade'. *Hitotsubashi Journal of Economics*, vol. 13 (1972), pp. 1-39.
Kreider, C. 'Valuation for Customs'. *Quarterly Journal of Economics*, vol. 56 (1941), pp. 157-9.
Kreinen, M. 'More on the Equivalence of Tariffs and Quotas', *Kyklos*, vol. 23 (1970), pp. 75-8.
Lipsey, R. G. and Lancaster, K. 'The General Theory of the Second Best'. *Review of Economic Studies*, vol. 26 (1958-59), pp. 11-32.
Lloyd, P. J. *New Zealand Manufacturing Production and Trade with Australia* (Research Paper no. 17, New Zealand Institute of Economic Research). Wellington, 1971.
— 'The Value of Tariff Preferences for the Developing Countries: Australian Experience'. *Economic Record*, vol. 47 (1971), pp. 1-16.

— 'Problems and Criteria in Setting Tariffs' in Arndt, H. W. and Boxer, A. H. (eds.), *The Australian Economy: A Second Volume of Readings*. Cheshire Publishing Pty Ltd, Melbourne, 1972.
— 'Optimal Intervention in a Distortion-Ridden Economy'. *Economic Record* (forthcoming).
McClaren, J. (ed.). *Towards a New Australia*. Cheshire Publishing Pty Ltd, Melbourne, 1972.
McManus, M. 'Comments on the General Theory of Second Best'. *Review of Economic Studies*, vol. 26 (1958-59), pp. 209-24.
Malmgren, H. B. 'Negotiating Nontariff Barriers: the Harmonization of National Economic Policies', in National Planning Association, *US Foreign Economic Policy for the 1970's: A New Approach to New Realities*. Washington, D.C., 1971.
— *Trade Wars or Trade Negotiations? Non-tariff Barriers and Economic Peacekeeping*. Atlantic Council of the United States, Washington, D.C., 1970.
Mathews, C. 'Non-Tariff Import Barriers and the Kennedy Round'. *Common Market Law Review*, vol. 8 (1965), pp. 403-18.
Mathews, R. A. *Industrial Viability in a Free Trade Economy: A Program of Adjustment Policies for Canada*. University of Toronto Press, Toronto, 1971.
Melvin, J. R. 'Commodity Taxation as a Determinant of Trade'. *Canadian Journal of Economics*, vol. 3 (1970), pp. 62-78.
Middleton, R. N. 'Technical Specifications—A Case Study of Non-Tariff Barriers to Trade'. *European Free Trade Area Bulletin*, March 1971.
— 'Technical Specifications—A Case Study of Non-Tariff Barriers to Trade (2)'. *European Free Trade Area Bulletin*, June 1971.
Moffat, G. G. *Import Control and Industrialisation*, Melbourne University Press, Melbourne, 1970.
Organisation for Economic Co-operation and Development. *Government Purchasing in Europe, North America and Japan: Regulations and Procedures*. OECD, Paris, 1966.
Pursell, G. and Snape, R. H. 'Economies of Scale, Price Discrimination and Exporting'. *Journal of International Economics*, vol. 3 (1973), pp. 85-92.
Robinson, P. 'Defence and Australian Industry'. (Seminar on Defence Policy and Procurement sponsored by Sydney University Extension Board and the Centre for Continuing Education at the Australian National University, at the Australian Academy of Science, 23 April 1971.)
Smith, Adam. *An Inquiry into the Nature and Causes of the Wealth of Nations*. Edited by E. Cannan. The Modern Library, New York, 1937.
Smith, R. E. *Customs Valuation in the United States*. Chicago University Press, Chicago, 1948.
Snape, R. H. 'Options for External Economic Policy'. *Economic Papers*, no. 41, September 1972.
Stiglitz, J. E. and Dasgupta, P. 'Differential Taxation, Public Goods and Economic Efficiency'. *Review of Economic Studies*, vol. 38 (1971), pp. 151-74.
Throsby, C. D. (ed.). *Agricultural Policy*. Penguin Books, Sydney, 1972.
United Nations. *Incentives for Industrial Exports*. E.70 II, D.8. New York, 1970.
United Nations Conference on Trade and Development. *Adjustment Assistance Measures*, TD/B/C.2/86.
Viner, J. *Dumping: A Problem in International Trade*. Chicago University Press, Chicago, 1923.
Walter, I. 'Nontariff Barriers and the Free Trade Area Option'. *Banca Nazionale Del Lavoro Quarterly Review*, no. 88 (1969), pp. 16-45.
— and Chung, J. W. 'The Pattern of Non-Tariff Obstacles to International Market Access'. *Weltwirtschaftliches Archiv*, Bd 108 (1972), pp. 122-34.
Wilczynski, J. 'Dumping in Sino-Australian Trade'. *Economic Record*, vol. 42 (1966), pp. 397-415.
Wollaston, H. N. P. *Customs Law and Regulations*. Sydney, 1904.

Index

Across-the-board tariff cut, 191
Adjustment assistance:
  Australian Labor Party view, 196, 217-18;
  criticisms of, 128-9;
  debt reconstruction, 124n., 125, 128;
  desirable criteria, 199;
  economic arguments for, 127-8, 197-200;
  in EEC, 195;
  experience in other countries, 197n.;
  farm build-up, 125, 126, 128;
  farm rehabilitation, 125, 128;
  forms of, 201-3;
  importance of, 175, 208;
  labour retraining, 126;
  for manufacturers, lack of, 123-4, 195;
  and resource allocation, 197-8;
  for rural producers, 124-9, *see also* Marginal dairy farms reconstruction;
  strategies to reduce, 200-1;
  Tariff Board recommendations, 124, 196, 199;
  in UK, 195;
  in US, 195
Agricultural products:
  implicit price change to consumers, 156-8;
  implicit price change to producers, 149-55, 218;
  method of review, 209-10;
  not in London Program, 5
American Selling Price, 31n., 168, 171
Annotated Tariff, 35
Anti-Dumping Code, *see* GATT, Anti-Dumping Code
Australia-Canada Trade Agreement, 45, 57

AIDA, 54n., 76
Australian Banks' Export Re-Finance Corporation, 121
Australian Agricultural Council, 218
Australian Industries Development Corporation, 222
Australian Labor Party:
  attitude to rural subsidies, 217-18;
  contradictions in policies, 223;
  economic objectives, 213-14;
  election, 213;
  and 'open government', 214-15;
  policies towards non-tariff instruments, 213-14;
  reorganisation of government departments, 215;
  use of inappropriate policy instruments, 220
Australian Resources Development Bank, 121
Australian Shipbuilding Board, 139, 149
Australian Wool Board, 156n., 211n.
Australia's international reserves, 104, 112

Beef, 154-5
Bounties:
  defined, 93n., *see also* Subsidies
Border tax adjustments, 87n.
Brigden Committee Report, 93n., 94, 100
Brussels Agreement, 30, 30n., 31
Brussels Tariff Nomenclature, 28-9
Bureau of Agricultural Economics, vi, 124n., 125, 150, 209
Butter, *see* Dairy industry; Voluntary agreements with New Zealand
Buy American Act, 71n., 167, 215
'Buy Australian' policies, 76n., 219

237

238   Index

By-laws, *see* Customs by-laws; Excise by-laws
By-law imports:
  mainly capital goods, 131;
  statistics of, 37;
  see also Customs by-laws

Cairns, Dr J. F., 43n., 214
Cameron, C., 219
Chemical industry:
  composite tariff rates, 39;
  and dumping, 59;
  and importance of non-tariff instruments, 133;
  in other countries, 141;
  Tariff Board review of, 137-8;
  see also Support value duties
Codes of conduct, 169
Commerce (Trade Descriptions) Act, 83
Commodity agreements, 6
Complements, *see* Substitutes
Content plans:
  for bounties, 39n.;
  for excise duties on spirits, 39n.;
  for imports (brined cherries) 40, (coffee) 40, (motor vehicles) 40, 208, 220, (peanut oil) 40, (petroleum) *see* Indigenous crude oil absorption scheme;
  for sales tax exemptions, 39n.;
  for television, 39n., 218;
  for tractor bounty, 40, 101;
  undesirable features of, 205
Coombs, Dr H. C., 222
Cotton, 228
Countervailing duties, 64-5, 173
Country Party, 176, 210, 215; *see also* Liberal Party-Country Party Coalition
Copyright Act, 83
Crawford, Sir John, 2
Customs Act:
  abolitions of, 206;
  and by-laws, 43;
  and non-tariff restrictions, 171;
  and prohibited imports, 18, 79, 81;
  and quantitative restrictions, 13, 79;
  and value for duty, 29;
  by-law rates, 36, 37n., 42, 44;
  by-laws for exports, 6, 119-20, 130, 145, 183;
  criteria (reasonably available) 43, 45-6, 181, (suitably equivalent) 43, 45-6;
  determinations, 44;
  double-edged nature of, 47;
  First Schedule, 42n., 43;
  'front runner' policy, 48, 180;
  history of, 42;
  importance of, 5, 42, 132;
  limited period by-laws, 43;
  under New Zealand-Australia Free Trade Agreement, 43n.;
  not understood, 43n., 149, 133;
  and pattern of effective protection, 49, 181;
  purpose of, 42, 181;
  proposed changes to, 181-2;
  review of, 221;
  reference to Tariff Board, 49-50;
  Second Schedule, 42n., 43;
  shortfall by-laws, 46;
  standing by-laws, 42;
  see also By-law imports
Customs drawback, 119-20, 131, 183

Customs Tariff:
  Act, 10n.;
  complex structure of, 35-41 *passim*;
  'dragnet' items, 50, 148, 181;
  multi-column structure, 35, 37-9;
  and non-tariff instruments, 10n., 171;
  schedules, 35;
  see also Customs by-laws; Tariff preferences; Tariffs

Dairy industry:
  Australian Dairy Produce Board, 105;
  butter, *see* Subsidies, on production (butter and cheese);
  cheese, *see* Subsidies, on production (butter and cheese);
  Dairying Industry Act, 105, 106;
  devaluation compensation, 102, 107, 114-15, 116, 140;
  forms of assistance to, 139-40;
  import restrictions, 103, 140;
  processed milk products bounty, 105-7;
  prohibited imports, 20, 103;
  quarantine restrictions, *see* Quarantine regulations;
  raw milk, 93n.;
  stabilisation plan, 103, 105, 140, 171;
  two-price scheme, 103;
  see also Marginal dairy farms reconstruction scheme; Subsidies, on production (butter and cheese)
Dairy Industry Committee of Enquiry, 125n.
Department of Customs and Excise:
  assistance to the author, v;
  customs drawbacks, 119-20;
  and dumping, 57-9;

Department of Customs and Excise (continued):
  manufacturing in licensed warehouses, 52;
  tariff-fixing by administration, 41-53 *passim*, 134, 208
Department of Labour and National Service, 124n.
Department of Overseas Trade, 215
Department of Secondary Industry, 215, 221
Department of Shipping and Transport, 215
Department of Trade and Industry:
  assistance to the author, v;
  primage duties, 37;
  reorganisation of, 215
Department of Transport, 215, 216
Devaluation compensation:
  and GATT, 114-15;
  to manufacturers, 115-17;
  to primary producers, 114-15, 151
'Dragnet' items, *see* Customs Tariff, 'dragnet' items
Drawback, *see* Customs drawback
Dried vine fruits, 228
Dumping:
  definition of injury, 58;
  dumping duties, 42;
  freight dumping, 56;
  GATT view of, 55, 59, 63;
  history of, 55;
  intention of, 173;
  kinds of, 56;
  and measurement of protection, 150;
  normal dumping, 56;
  normal values, 56-7;
  not harmful, 60-4;
  procedures, 57-8;
  predatory, 18, 62-3, 207;
  sales dumping, 55, 56, 63;
  third-country dumping, 56, 57, 61;
  see also GATT, Anti-Dumping Code; Support value duties

'Economic and efficient' production, 204
Economies of scale, 61, 206, 207, 211
Edwards, G., vi
EEC: and non-tariff practices, 167; trade relations with US, 2; UK accession to, 22, 38n., 78, 170
Effective protection:
  effects of by-law system on, 49, 145-8;
  recognition of, 36n.;
  see also Tariff Board, calculation of effective rates

EFTA, 167
Eggs, 228
Excise by-laws, 42
Excise taxes, 90-1
Export incentive grants scheme, 107-12, 131, 132, 145, 210, 218
Export market development rebate, 117-19, 131
Export parity prices, 150, 151
Exports Payments Insurance Corporation, 121-3 *passim*
Export subsidies, *see* Subsidies, on exports

Fairhall, Sir Allen, 74
Foot-and-mouth disease, 82
Free trade exchange rate, 110, 164
Freedom of Information Act, 215
F 111s, 73

GATT:
  Anti-Dumping Code, 2, 59, 63, 64, 132, 168, 169, 209;
  Australian complaints to, 117n.;
  and Australia's export subsidies, 115-16, 120, 132;
  Articles relating to (countervailing duties) 1, (dumping) 1, 132, (export subsidies) 1, 115-16, (government purchasing) 1n., (private restrictive practices) 1n., (standards) 1n., (temporary quotas) 17, (value for duty) 31;
  barrier-to-barrier approach, 169;
  conditional MFN, 169;
  enforcement procedures, 1;
  Kennedy Round, 2, 168, 171, 176;
  list of 800 non-tariff devices, 2, 167;
  most-favoured-nation principle, 167, 168;
  Protocol of Provisional Application, 1;
  quantitative restrictions, 17;
  regulation of non-tariff trade interventions, 1;
  seventh round of negotiations, 2, 166;
  tariff rates bound, 190
General equilibrium analysis, 7, 136n., 163-5
Government purchasing policies:
  ALP policies, 218-20;
  defence purchases, 72-5;
  Department of Supply procedures, 70;
  ex ante publicity, 71;
  ex post publicity, 71, 209, 215-16;
  international negotiation of, 71, 167, 209;

Government purchasing policies (continued):
'lowest price' principle, 70;
list of potential suppliers, 71;
non-price characteristics; 74, 77;
notional duty, 70, 75, 77-8, 183-4, 209;
OECD, 71;
offset orders (civil aircraft) 74n., (computers) 74n., (defence) 74, 76;
in other countries, 71;
PMG policy, 77;
proposed changes to, 185-6, 209;
secrecy concerning, 68, 71;
and tariff preferences, 78;
tendering procedures, 69-70;
Treasury Directions, 70;
Treasury Regulations, 69, 75-6;
see also State Governments, purchasing policies
Grassby, A., 215
Gregory, R. G., vi

Harris, Dr S. F., 152, 225
Hartke-Burke Bill, 2
Holt, Rt Hon H., 112

Imperfect competition, 160
implicit rate of protection, *see* Implicit price changes to producers
Implicit price changes to consumers:
of agricultural commodities, 156-8;
definition of, 142, 226;
problems of measuring, 143-4
Implicit price changes to producers:
of agricultural commodities, 149-55, 218;
decomposition of, 226;
definition of, 142, 225;
manufacturing and agriculture compared, 154-5;
problems of measuring, 143-4;
in shipbuilding industry, 148-9
Implicit tariffs, 142, 159-63; *see also* Implicit price changes to consumers; Implicit price change to producers
Import licensing:
abolition of, 206;
history of, 2-3;
intention, 172;
Japan-Australia Trade Agreement, 11;
and temporary protection, 12-16 *passim*;
and textile industry, *see* Textile industry;
see also Special Advisory Authority

Import parity prices, 150, 151
Import quotas:
by-law imports, 25n.;
equivalent to explicit tariff, 159-60;
non-equivalent to explicit tariff, 160-3
Indigenous crude oil absorption scheme, 40, 90
International Organisation for Standardisation, 167
Intra-industry substitution, 112

Japan-Australia Trade Agreement, 11, 53; *see also* Voluntary agreements, with Japan

Lamb, *see* Voluntary agreements, with New Zealand
Liberal Party-Country Party Coalition, 12, 175
Linseed, 229
London Program:
countries in, 2n.;
excluded agricultural products, 5;
focus, 8;
origin of, 2;
scope of, 4-5, 134, 171

Manufacturing in licensed warehouses, 6, 51-3, 130, 131, 133, 145, 172
Marginal Dairy Farms Agreement Act, 126
Marginal dairy farms reconstruction scheme, 125, 126
Melville, Sir Leslie, vi
Minister for Labour, 219
Minister for Science, 218
Minister for Shipping, 101, 139
Minister for Transport, 220
Minister of Works, 219
Multilateral negotiation, *see* Non-tariff distortions, multilateral negotiations of

Narcotics Drug Act, 19n.
Navigation Act, 101n.
New Zealand-Australia Free Trade Agreement:
Article 3:7, 43n.;
consultations under, 23;
industry panels, 23;
preferences under, 38, 39, 131;
Schedule A, 39;
tariff quotas, 24-5, 82
Nitrogenous Fertiliser Subsidy Act, 95; *see also* Subsidies, on production (nitrogenous fertilisers)

Non-tariff barriers:
  four types of, 174;
  negotiation of, 3;
  relationship to non-tariff distortions, 3;
  comparisons with other countries, 7, 133-4;
  of consumer prices, 136;
  definition of, 3, 135;
  of export trade, 5;
  few measurements of, 144;
  general features of, 130-4;
  high cost of, 178;
  instability of, 152;
  interrelatedness of, 137-40;
  lack of appreciation of, 133;
  multilateral negotiations of, 2-3, 7, 166-77;
  of producer prices, 136;
  offsetting distortions, 193-4;
  qualitative measurement of, 7;
  quantitative measurement of, 8-9;
  reasons for, 137;
  and redistribution of incomes, 136-7;
  seven groups, 4-6 *passim*;
  trends in, 152;
  and welfare losses, 3, 135-7, 156;
  see also Non-tariff instruments
Non-tariff instruments:
  appropriate instruments, 205-6;
  classification of, 4, 172-5;
  comparison of, 141-2;
  continual change, 9;
  multiple, 8, 141;
  recommended abolition of, 206-7

OECD:
  export credits, 167;
  government purchasing, 71, 167, 209;
  High Level Study Group, 176
Ottawa Agreement, 204

Patterson, Dr R., 215
Pay-roll Tax Assessment Act 1968, 108, 113n.
Pay-roll tax rebate, *see* Export incentive grants scheme
Phosphate Fertiliser Bounty Act, 95; *see also* Subsidies, on production (phosphatic fertilisers)
Piecemeal policy-making, 178-93
Price stabilisation schemes, 102
Primage duties, 36-7
Processed milk products bounty, 105-7, 129
Production quotas, margarine, 6, 20n.
Prohibited imports:
  aircraft, airframes and aircraft engines, 20;
  margarine, 20, 20n., 131;
  potatoes, 20, 20n., 21;
  for protection of producers, 20-1, 206, 207;
  second-hand goods, 21;
  ships, 20;
  support for quarantine, 79, 81;
  types of prohibitions, 18;
  of undesired goods, 19;
  wheat, 103
Protection Board, *see* Protection Commission
Protection Commission, 209, 222
Purchasing policies, *see* Government purchasing policies

Quantitative restrictions:
  of imports, 2-54 *passim*, 135, *see also* Import licensing; Import quotas; Prohibited imports; Tariff quotas; Voluntary agreements;
  of exports, *see* Export quotas
Quarantine regulations:
  animal quarantine, 81;
  butter, 22;
  dairy products, 81, 82;
  GATT view, 79;
  as non-tariff barrier, 82;
  in other countries, 79;
  plant quarantine, 80;
  potatoes, 21n.;
  in New Zealand, 79, 81-2;
  supported by prohibited imports, 79, 81;
  stringency of, 81;
  uncanned meat, 24;
  wheat, 80, 82
Quotas, *see* Import quotas; Export quotas; Production quotas

Reserve Bank of Australia, 120, 121
Revaluation of Australian dollar, 216-17
Rice, 228
Rules of origin, 6
Rural Industries Board, 209
Rural reconstruction, *see* Adjustment assistance, for rural producers

Sales taxes:
  differential tax rates, 85;
  discriminatory exemptions, 4, 87-9, 130, 206, 207;
  lack of statistics, 89n.;
  as non-tariff barrier, 87-9;
  and resource allocation, 86;
  similarity to non-tariff instruments, 86;
  three ways they affect imports, 86-7

Second-hand goods:
  machinery and equipment, 15, 18;
  ships, 20, 21n.
Shipbuilding, 97, 99, 101, 133, 139, 143-4, 148-9, 215-16, 220, 221; *see also* Subsidies, on production (shipbuilding); Subsidies on shipbuilding, other countries
Small nation assumption, 164
Snape, R. H., vi
Special Advisory Authority, 12-16 *passim*, 67; *see also* Temporary protection
Standards:
  industrial, 83-4, 167;
  health and safety, 82-3
State Governments:
  adjustment assistance to rural producers, 125, 126;
  excluded from study, 6;
  pay-roll taxation, 112, 171;
  purchasing policies, 6, 78n.
State Grants (Rural Reconstruction) Act 1971, 125, 126
Subsidies: as alternative to tariffs, 93-5, 100, 136, 186-7;
  bases, 96-7;
  conflict with adjustment assistance, 129;
  Brigden Committee views, 94-5, 100;
  dates introduced, 96-7;
  on export credit, 120-3, 131;
  on exports, 103-17, 131, 158, 211-12;
  features in common, 98;
  history of, 94, 99-100;
  on inputs used in exports, 117-23;
  to manufacturers, 96-7, 101;
  to mining industries, 97, 101;
  on production (butter and cheese) 92, 96, 102, 129, 151, 152, 226-7, (books) 97, (cellulose acetate flake) 95, 97, 99, (copper) 100, (drilling machines) 97, (gold bullion) 93, 97, 99, (nitrogenous fertilisers) 95, 96, 131, 140, (phosphatic fertilisers) 95, 96, 99, 131, (pyrites) 100, (rayon yarn) 100, (shipbuilding) 6, 95n., 97, 99, 124n., (sulphate of ammonia) 100, (sulphuric acid) 94, 100, (tractors) 96, 99, 100, 131, (urea) 100, (vinyl resin) 100;
  rates of, 96-7, 98-9, 151;
  reasons for preferring subsidies, 94-5;
  restrictions on, 96-9;
  to rural producers, 96, 98, 101, 149-55;
  on shipbuilding, other countries, 141;
  Tariff Board guidelines, 93, 100n.;
  types of, 92
Subsidy equivalent, 142n.
Substitute notices, 54, 180
Substitutes:
  in consumption, 179, 180, 187;
  in production, 179, 180, 187
Sugar, 227
Support value duties, 36, 65-7, 205, 206

Tariff Board:
  adjustment assistance recommended, 124, 196;
  assistance to author, v;
  calculation of effective rates, 41n., 111n.;
  dumping actions, 42;
  'economic and efficient' production, 204-5;
  and externalities, 205;
  guidelines for subsidies, 93-4, 100n.;
  main areas of review, 137-8;
  and quantitative restrictions, 12-18 *passim*;
  review of subsidies, 100;
  Tariff Review, 9, 111, 178, 185, 187-92, 207;
  and temporary protection, 12, 42
Tariff Board Act, 12, 13, 93, 208, 214
Tariff classification, 28, 172
Tariff preferences:
  on by-law imports, 37n.;
  on Commonwealth Government purchases, 37n.;
  to developing countries, 25-7, 131;
  under New Zealand-Australia Free Trade Agreement, 38, 39, 131;
  preferential tariffs, 38
Tariff quotas:
  import-restricting (abolition of) 206, (cheddar cheese) 24, (knitted goods) 17, 27, 130, 173, (pork meat) 24, 172, (small-pitch chain) 27, 130, 172;
  import expanding (under New Zealand-Australia Free Trade Agreement) 24-5, 172, (preferences to developing countries) 25-7, 172
Tariffs: *ad valorem*, 30;
  alternative, 39;
  composite, 39;
  effective rates, *see* Effective protection;
  equivalent tariffs, 159-61;
  implicit tariffs, *see* Implicit tariffs;

Tariffs (continued):
   on knitted shirts, 17;
   on by-law imports, *see* Customs by-laws;
   on government imports, 36;
   on normal imports, 36;
   prohibitive, 145, 161, 162, 207;
   types of rates, 39
Tariff simplification, 28, 35
Tariff fixing by administration, 5
Temporary protection, 16, 54, 131, 172, 208; *see also* Special Advisory Authority
Textile industry:
   adjustment assistance, 124n.;
   composite tariff rates, 39;
   and dumping, 59;
   and import licensing, 14-15, 131;
   import watch, 222;
   and importance of non-tariff instruments, 133;
   in other countries, 141;
   rationalisation of, 16-17;
   Tariff Board review of, 138-9;
   tariff quotas, 17;
   temporary protection, 16, 52;
   Textile and Apparel Industry Advisory Panel, 221
Tobacco industry:
   data, 228;
   excise taxes, 90-1;
   price stabilisation, 91, 103
Trade Marks Act, 82
Trade Policy Research Centre, v
Two Airlines Policy, 20
Two-price schemes, 102-3, 125, 158, 218; *see also* Dairy industry, two-price scheme; Wheat industry, two-price scheme

UK:
   in London Program, 2n.;
   and value for duty, 34;
   see also EEC, UK accession to
United Kingdom-Australia Trade Agreement, 38, 44
UNCTAD, 26, 220
US, 2

Value for duty:
   actual value 31;
   current domestic value, 29, 30n., 31-2;
   fair market value, 30n.;
   f.o.b. basis, 30, 32-4 *passim*;
   as non-tariff instrument, 172;
   normal price, 31;
   and trade diversion, 33-4
Vernon Committee Report:
   composite tariff rates, 39n.;
   little attention to non-tariff instruments, 132, 132n.;
   margins of tariff preferences, 38n.;
   non-tariff instruments, v;
   tariff on inputs, 155;
   temporary protection, 54n.;
   uniform tariff proposal, 189-90;
   view of balance of payments, 104n.;
   view of by-laws; 50n.;
   view of dumping, 64;
   views on bounties, 94n., 99n.
Voluntary agreements:
   abolition of, 206;
   ignorance of, 133;
   intention of, 172;
   with Japan, 23-4;
   with New Zealand (butter) 22, (lamb) 21-2, (peas and beans) 23
Voluntary restraints, 23

Welfare loss, *see* Non-tariff distortions, and welfare losses
Wheat industry:
   data, 227;
   devaluation compensation, 114, 116;
   prohibited imports, 81, 103;
   quarantine restrictions, *see* Quarantine regulations;
   stabilisation scheme, 103, 151, 218;
   two-piece scheme, 103
Whitlam, Rt Hon. E. G., 213n., 215, 219
Wool industry:
   emergency assistance, 102;
   few subsidies to, 155;
   price stabilisation, 102
Wreidt, Senator K., 215

Peter Lloyd is a graduate and M.A. of the Victoria University, Wellington and a Ph.D. of Duke University, North Carolina. He is now a senior fellow in the Department of Economics, Research School of Pacific Studies, Australian National University. His main interests are international trade and micro-economic theory.

Dr Lloyd is the author of *International Trade Problems of Small Nations* (1968) and *New Zealand Manufacturing Production and Trade with Australia* (1971).

Text set in 10 pt Times New Roman two point leaded and
printed on 85 gsm Semi Matt at
The Griffin Press, Adelaide,
South Australia